0500000243659 5

GRAPHI
Wai
Dar

D1177660

AUG 2 7 2013

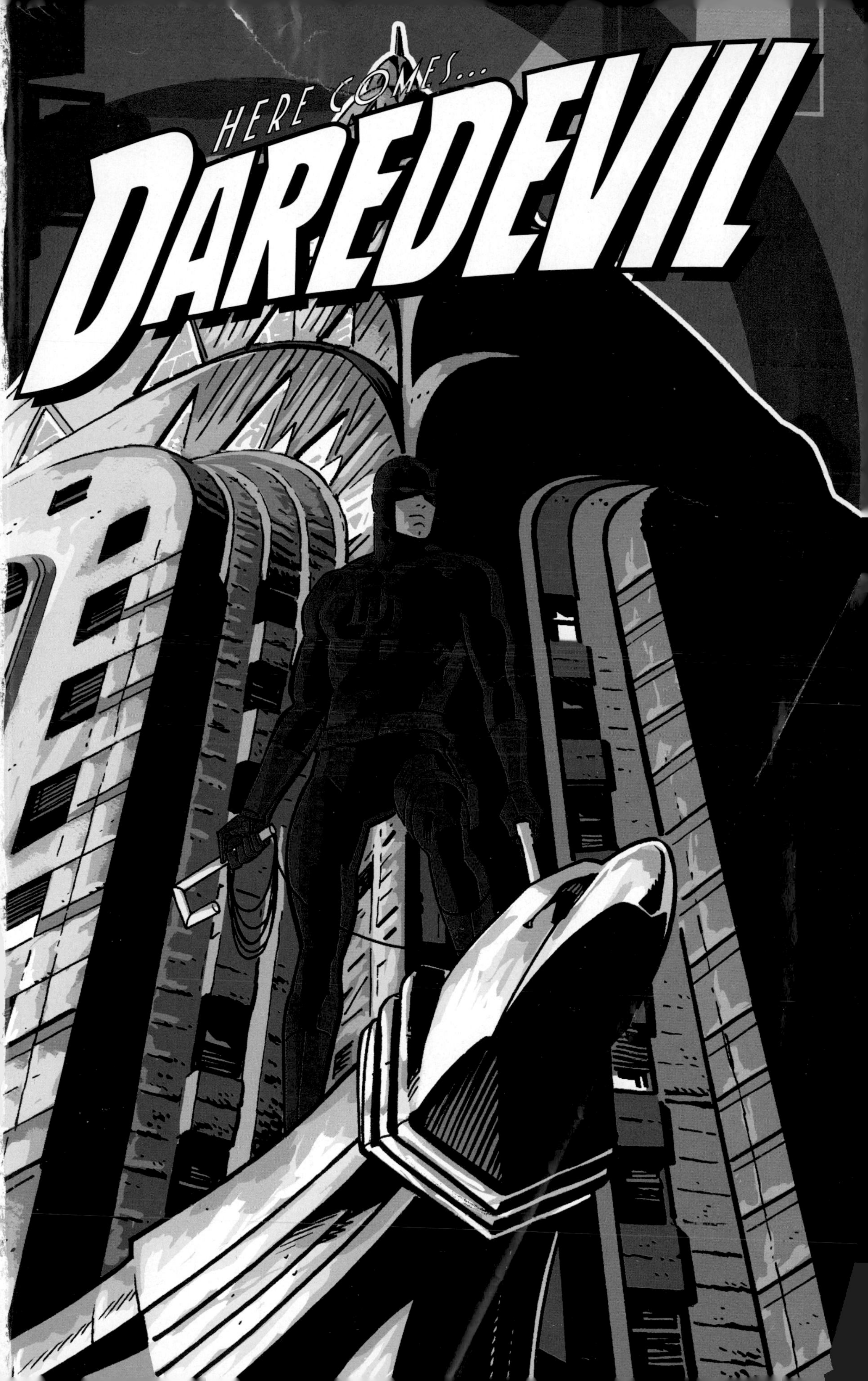
HERE COMES...
DAREDEVIL

WRITER
MARK WAID

ARTIST
CHRIS SAMNEE

COLOR ARTIST
JAVIER RODRIGUEZ

LETTERER
VC'S JOE CARAMAGNA

COVER ARTISTS
PAOLO RIVERA (#22)
CHRIS SAMNEE
& JAVIER RODRIGUEZ (#23-27)

ASSISTANT EDITOR
ELLIE PYLE

EDITOR
STEPHEN WACKER

COLLECTION EDITOR & DESIGN **CORY LEVINE**
ASSISTANT EDITORS **ALEX STARBUCK** & **NELSON RIBEIRO**
EDITORS, SPECIAL PROJECTS **JENNIFER GRÜNWALD** & **MARK D. BEAZLEY**
SENIOR EDITOR, SPECIAL PROJECTS **JEFF YOUNGQUIST**
SVP OF DIGITAL & PRINT PUBLISHING SALES **DAVID GABRIEL**

EDITOR IN CHIEF **AXEL ALONSO**
CHIEF CREATIVE OFFICER **JOE QUESADA**
PUBLISHER **DAN BUCKLEY**
EXECUTIVE PRODUCER **ALAN FINE**

DAREDEVIL BY MARK WAID VOL. 5. Contains material originally published in magazine form as DAREDEVIL #22-27. First printing 2013. ISBN# 978-0-7851-6104-2. Published by MARVEL WORLDWIDE, INC., a subsidiary of MARVEL ENTERTAINMENT, LLC. OFFICE OF PUBLICATION: 135 West 50th Street, New York, NY 10020. **Printed in the U.S.A.** ALAN FINE, EVP - Office of the President, Marvel Worldwide, Inc. and EVP & CMO Marvel Characters B.V.; DAN BUCKLEY, Publisher & President - Print, Animation & Digital Divisions; JOE QUESADA, Chief Creative Officer; TOM BREVOORT, SVP of Publishing; DAVID BOGART, SVP of Operations & Procurement, Publishing; C.B. CEBULSKI, SVP of Creator & Content Development; DAVID GABRIEL, SVP of Print & Digital Publishing Sales; JIM O'KEEFE, VP of Operations & Logistics; DAN CARR, Executive Director of Publishing Technology; SUSAN CRESPI, Editorial Operations Manager; ALEX MORALES, Publishing Operations Manager; STAN LEE, Chairman Emeritus. For information regarding advertising in Marvel Comics or on Marvel.com, please contact Niza Disla, Director of Marvel Partnerships, at ndisla@marvel.com. For Marvel subscription inquiries, please call 800-217-9158. **Manufactured between 6/14/2013 and 7/22/2013 by R.R. DONNELLEY, INC., SALEM, VA, USA.**

10 9 8 7 6 5 4 3 2 1

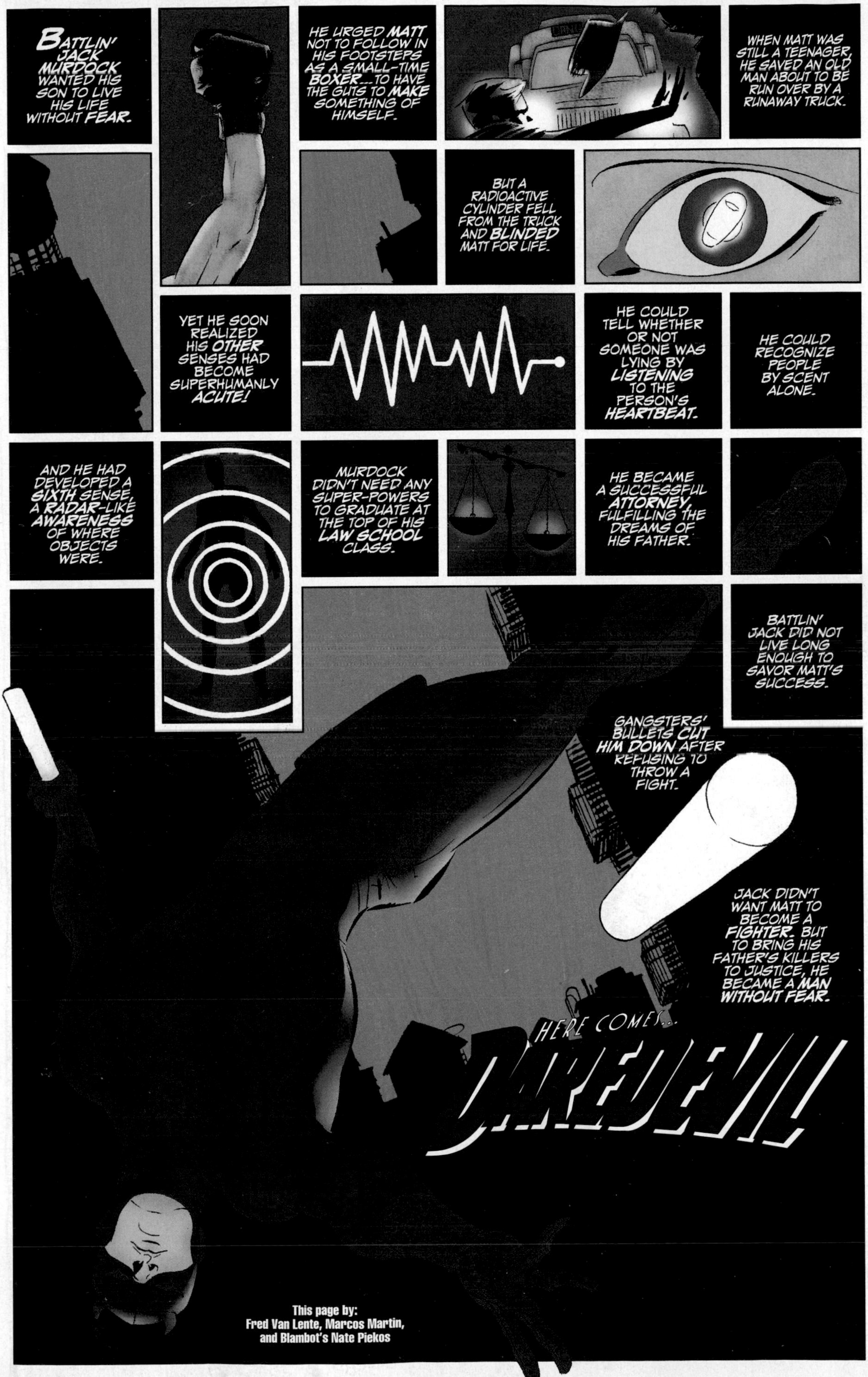

BATTLIN' JACK MURDOCK WANTED HIS SON TO LIVE HIS LIFE WITHOUT FEAR.

HE URGED MATT NOT TO FOLLOW IN HIS FOOTSTEPS AS A SMALL-TIME BOXER...TO HAVE THE GUTS TO MAKE SOMETHING OF HIMSELF.

WHEN MATT WAS STILL A TEENAGER, HE SAVED AN OLD MAN ABOUT TO BE RUN OVER BY A RUNAWAY TRUCK.

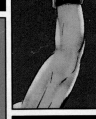

BUT A RADIOACTIVE CYLINDER FELL FROM THE TRUCK AND BLINDED MATT FOR LIFE.

YET HE SOON REALIZED HIS OTHER SENSES HAD BECOME SUPERHUMANLY ACUTE!

HE COULD TELL WHETHER OR NOT SOMEONE WAS LYING BY LISTENING TO THE PERSON'S HEARTBEAT.

HE COULD RECOGNIZE PEOPLE BY SCENT ALONE.

AND HE HAD DEVELOPED A SIXTH SENSE, A RADAR-LIKE AWARENESS OF WHERE OBJECTS WERE.

MURDOCK DIDN'T NEED ANY SUPER-POWERS TO GRADUATE AT THE TOP OF HIS LAW SCHOOL CLASS.

HE BECAME A SUCCESSFUL ATTORNEY, FULFILLING THE DREAMS OF HIS FATHER.

BATTLIN' JACK DID NOT LIVE LONG ENOUGH TO SAVOR MATT'S SUCCESS.

GANGSTERS' BULLETS CUT HIM DOWN AFTER REFUSING TO THROW A FIGHT.

JACK DIDN'T WANT MATT TO BECOME A FIGHTER. BUT TO BRING HIS FATHER'S KILLERS TO JUSTICE, HE BECAME A MAN WITHOUT FEAR.

HERE COMES...

DAREDEVIL!

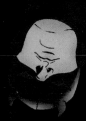

This page by:
Fred Van Lente, Marcos Martin,
and Blambot's Nate Piekos

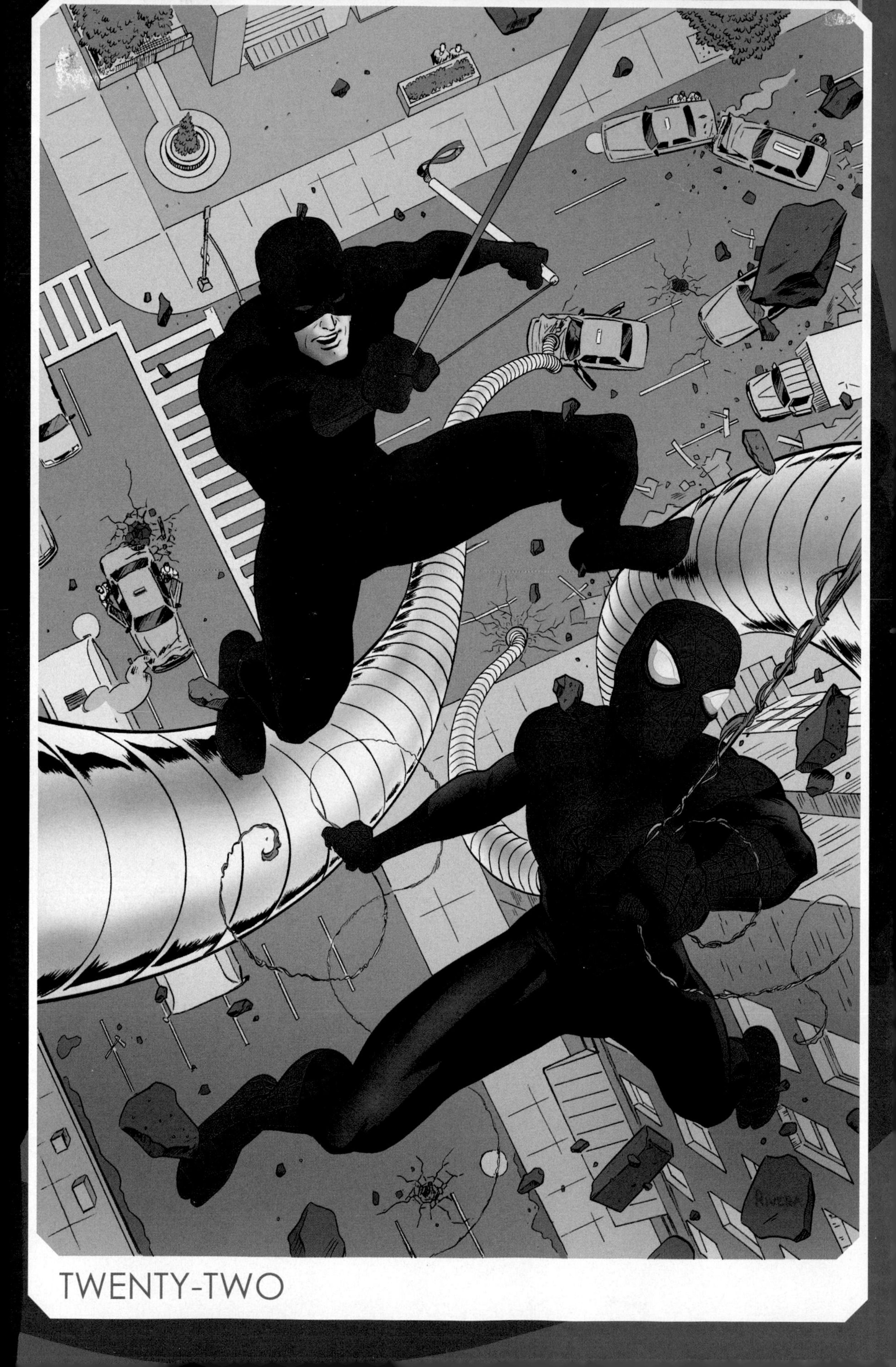

TWENTY-TWO

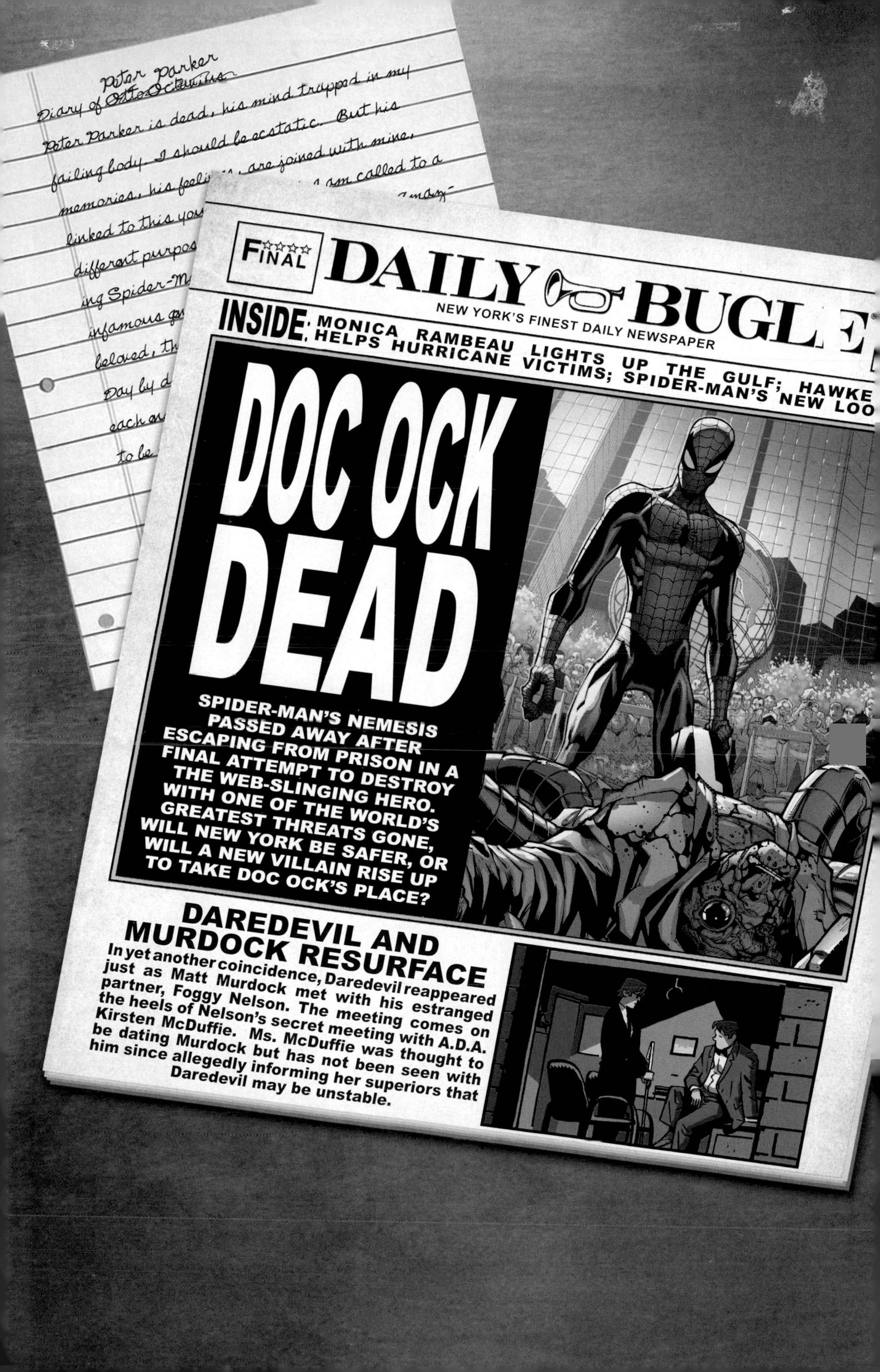
Peter Parker
Diary of Otto Octavius
Peter Parker is dead, his mind trapped in my
failing body. I should be ecstatic. But his
memories, his feelings, are joined with mine,
linked to this you... I am called to a
different purpos...
ing Spider-M...
infamous go...
beloved, th...
Day by d...
each on...
to be...
FINAL
DAILY BUGLE
NEW YORK'S FINEST DAILY NEWSPAPER
INSIDE: MONICA RAMBEAU LIGHTS UP THE GULF; HAWKE
HELPS HURRICANE VICTIMS; SPIDER-MAN'S NEW LOO
DOC OCK DEAD
SPIDER-MAN'S NEMESIS PASSED AWAY AFTER ESCAPING FROM PRISON IN A FINAL ATTEMPT TO DESTROY THE WEB-SLINGING HERO. WITH ONE OF THE WORLD'S GREATEST THREATS GONE, WILL NEW YORK BE SAFER, OR WILL A NEW VILLAIN RISE UP TO TAKE DOC OCK'S PLACE?
DAREDEVIL AND MURDOCK RESURFACE
In yet another coincidence, Daredevil reappeared just as Matt Murdock met with his estranged partner, Foggy Nelson. The meeting comes on the heels of Nelson's secret meeting with A.D.A. Kirsten McDuffie. Ms. McDuffie was thought to be dating Murdock but has not been seen with him since allegedly informing her superiors that Daredevil may be unstable.

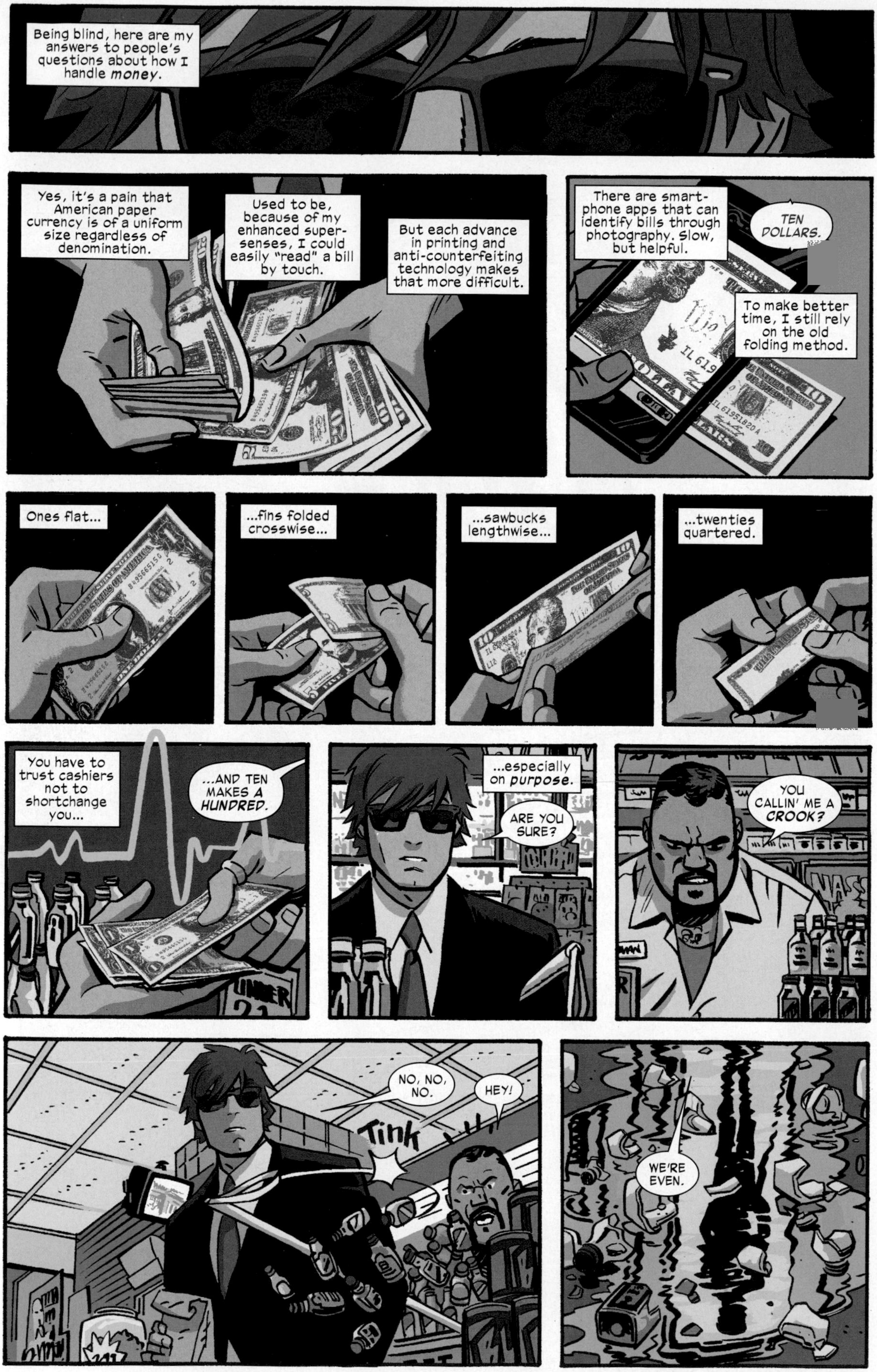
Being blind, here are my answers to people's questions about how I handle *money*.
Yes, it's a pain that American paper currency is of a uniform size regardless of denomination.
Used to be, because of my enhanced super-senses, I could easily "read" a bill by touch.
But each advance in printing and anti-counterfeiting technology makes that more difficult.
There are smart-phone apps that can identify bills through photography. Slow, but helpful.
TEN DOLLARS.
To make better time, I still rely on the old folding method.
Ones flat...
...fins folded crosswise...
...sawbucks lengthwise...
...twenties quartered.
You have to trust cashiers not to shortchange you...
...AND TEN MAKES A *HUNDRED*.
...especially on *purpose*.
ARE YOU SURE?
YOU CALLIN' ME A *CROOK?*
NO, NO, NO.
HEY!
Tink
WE'RE EVEN.

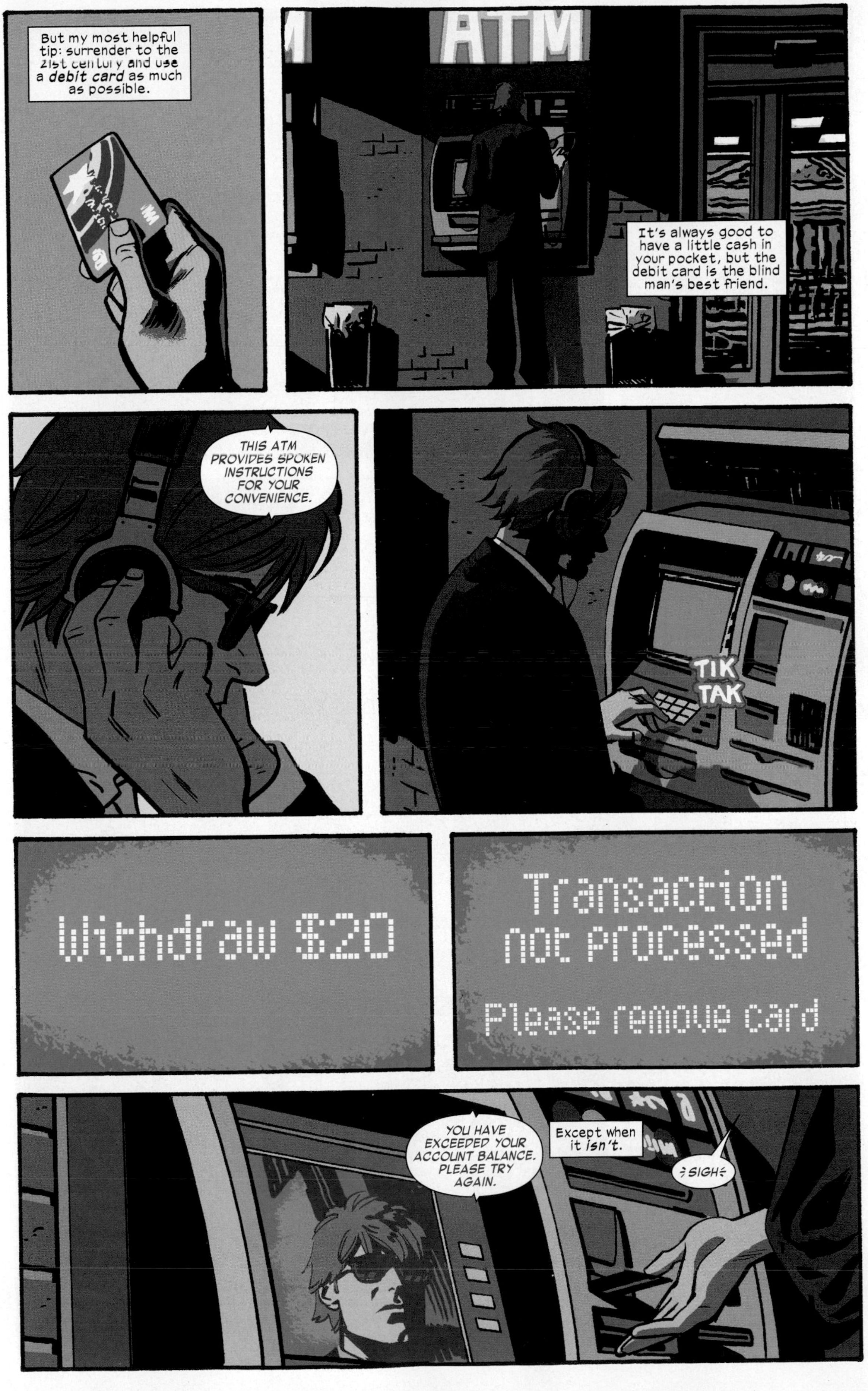

But my most helpful tip: surrender to the 21st century and use a *debit card* as much as possible.
It's always good to have a little cash in your pocket, but the debit card is the blind man's best friend.
THIS ATM PROVIDES SPOKEN INSTRUCTIONS FOR YOUR CONVENIENCE.
TIK
TAK
Withdraw $20
Transaction not processed
Please remove card
YOU HAVE EXCEEDED YOUR ACCOUNT BALANCE. PLEASE TRY AGAIN.
Except when it *isn't*.
SIGH

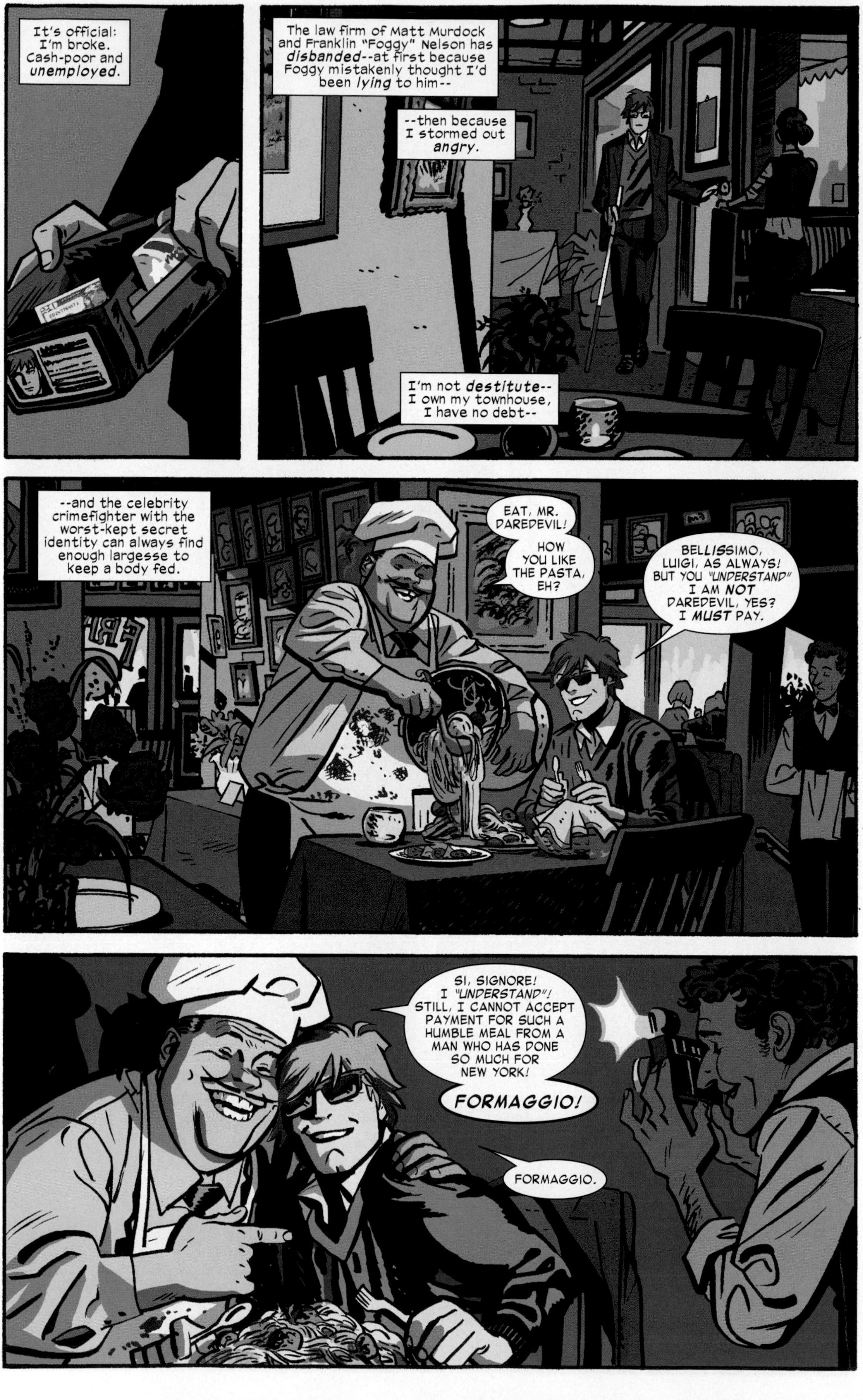
It's official: I'm broke. Cash-poor and *unemployed*.
The law firm of Matt Murdock and Franklin "Foggy" Nelson has *disbanded*--at first because Foggy mistakenly thought I'd been *lying* to him--
--then because I stormed out *angry*.
I'm not *destitute*-- I own my townhouse, I have no debt--
--and the celebrity crimefighter with the worst-kept secret identity can always find enough largesse to keep a body fed.
EAT, MR. DAREDEVIL!
HOW YOU LIKE THE PASTA, EH?
BELL*ISS*IMO, LUIGI, AS ALWAYS! BUT YOU *"UNDERSTAND"* I AM **NOT** DAREDEVIL, YES? I **MUST** PAY.
SI, SIGNORE! I *"UNDERSTAND"*! STILL, I CANNOT ACCEPT PAYMENT FOR SUCH A HUMBLE MEAL FROM A MAN WHO HAS DONE SO MUCH FOR NEW YORK!
FORMAGGIO!
FORMAGGIO.

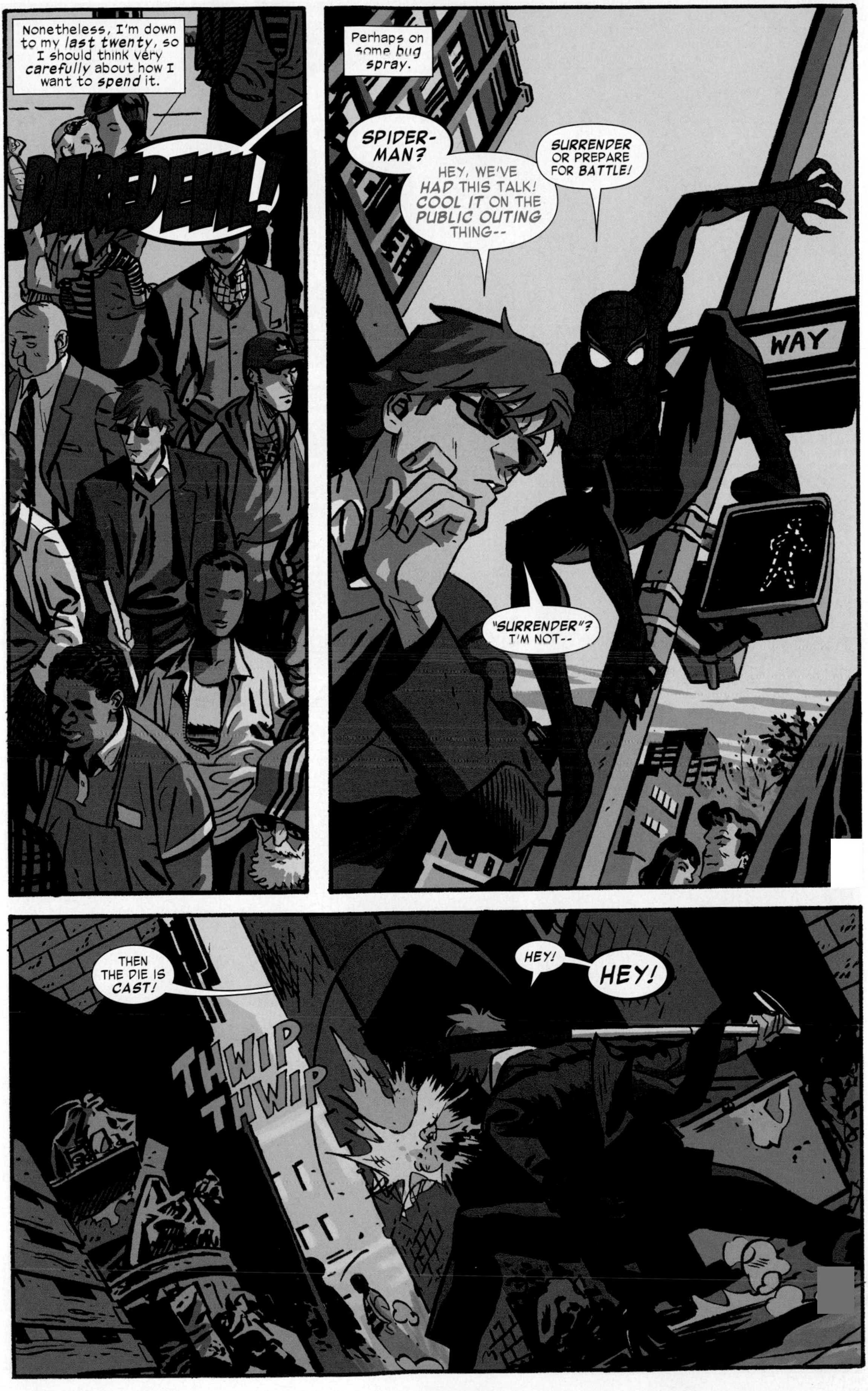
Nonetheless, I'm down to my *last twenty*, so I should think very *carefully* about how I want to *spend* it.
DAREDEVIL!
Perhaps on some *bug spray*.
SPIDER-MAN?
HEY, WE'VE HAD THIS TALK! COOL IT ON THE PUBLIC OUTING THING--
SURRENDER OR PREPARE FOR BATTLE!
WAY
"SURRENDER"? I'M NOT--
THEN THE DIE IS CAST!
HEY!
HEY!
THWIP THWIP

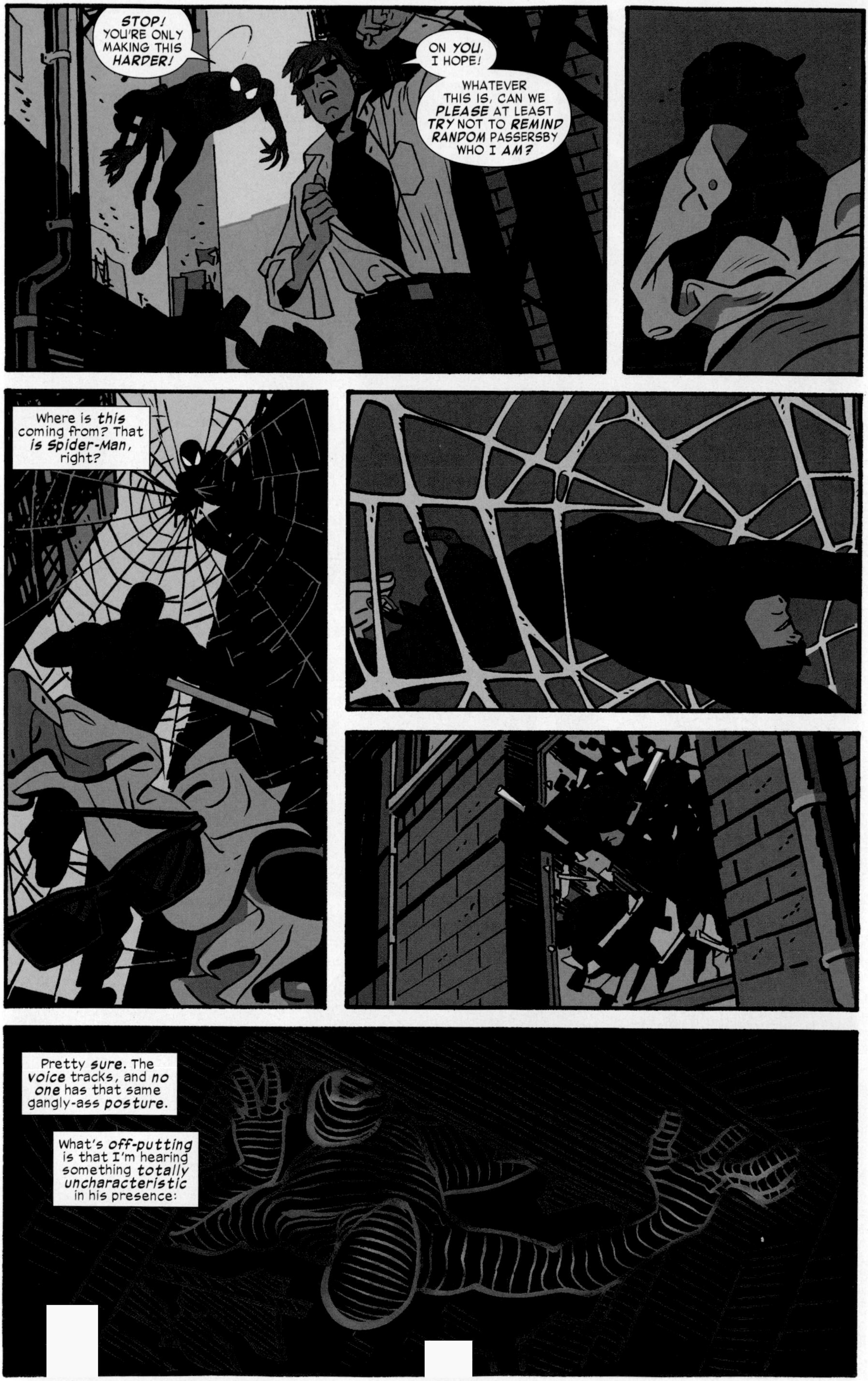

STOP! YOU'RE ONLY MAKING THIS HARDER!
ON YOU, I HOPE!
WHATEVER THIS IS, CAN WE PLEASE AT LEAST TRY NOT TO REMIND RANDOM PASSERSBY WHO I AM?
Where is this coming from? That is Spider-Man, right?
Pretty sure. The voice tracks, and no one has that same gangly-ass posture.
What's off-putting is that I'm hearing something totally uncharacteristic in his presence:

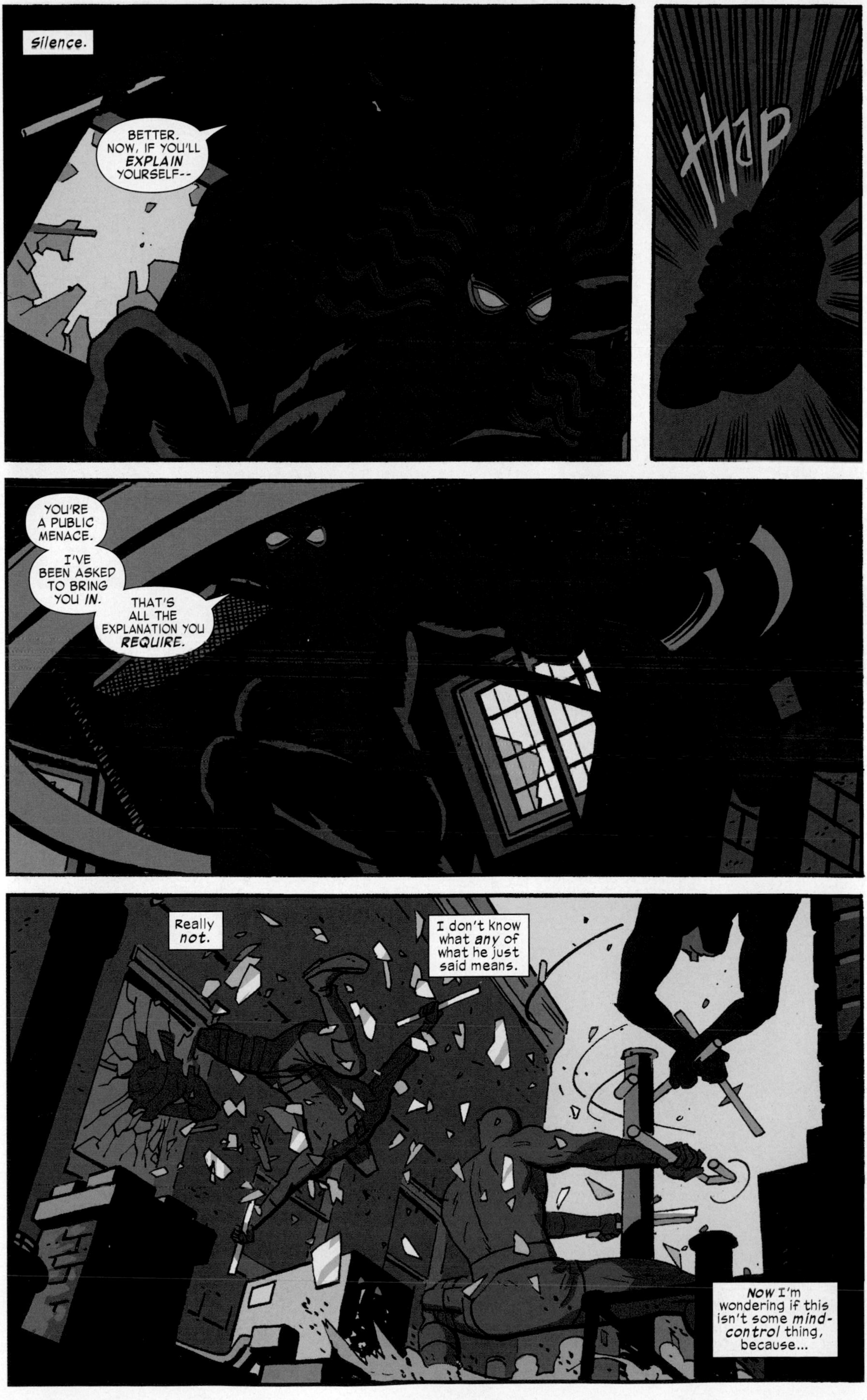
Silence.
BETTER. NOW, IF YOU'LL EXPLAIN YOURSELF--
thap
YOU'RE A PUBLIC MENACE.
I'VE BEEN ASKED TO BRING YOU IN.
THAT'S ALL THE EXPLANATION YOU REQUIRE.
Really not.
I don't know what any of what he just said means.
NOW I'm wondering if this isn't some mind-control thing, because...

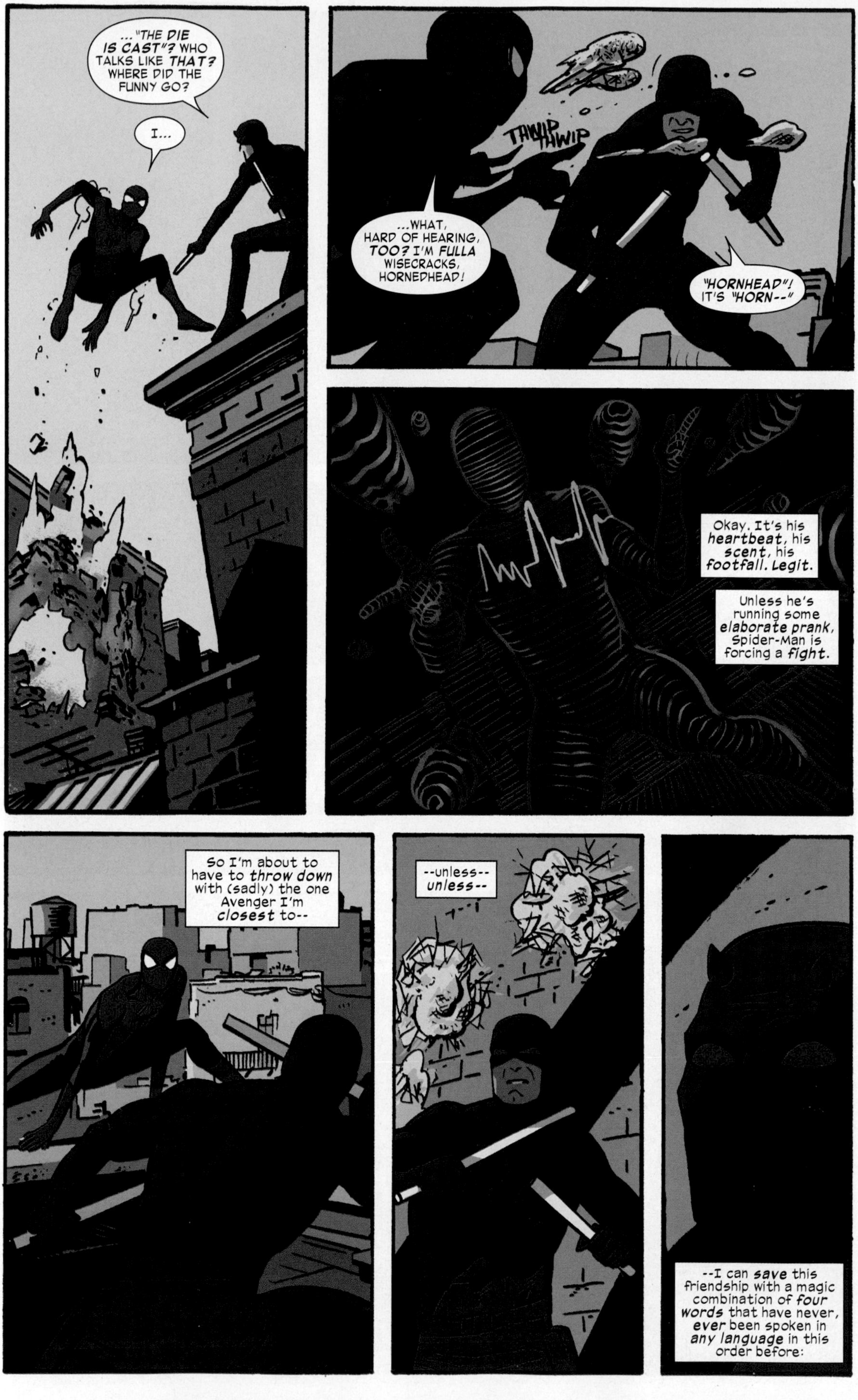
..."THE DIE IS CAST"? WHO TALKS LIKE THAT? WHERE DID THE FUNNY GO?
I...
THWIP THWIP
...WHAT, HARD OF HEARING, TOO? I'M FULLA WISECRACKS, HORNEDHEAD!
"HORNHEAD"! IT'S "HORN--"
Okay. It's his heartbeat, his scent, his footfall. Legit.
Unless he's running some elaborate prank, Spider-Man is forcing a fight.
So I'm about to have to throw down with (sadly) the one Avenger I'm closest to--
--unless-- unless--
--I can save this friendship with a magic combination of four words that have never, ever been spoken in any language in this order before:

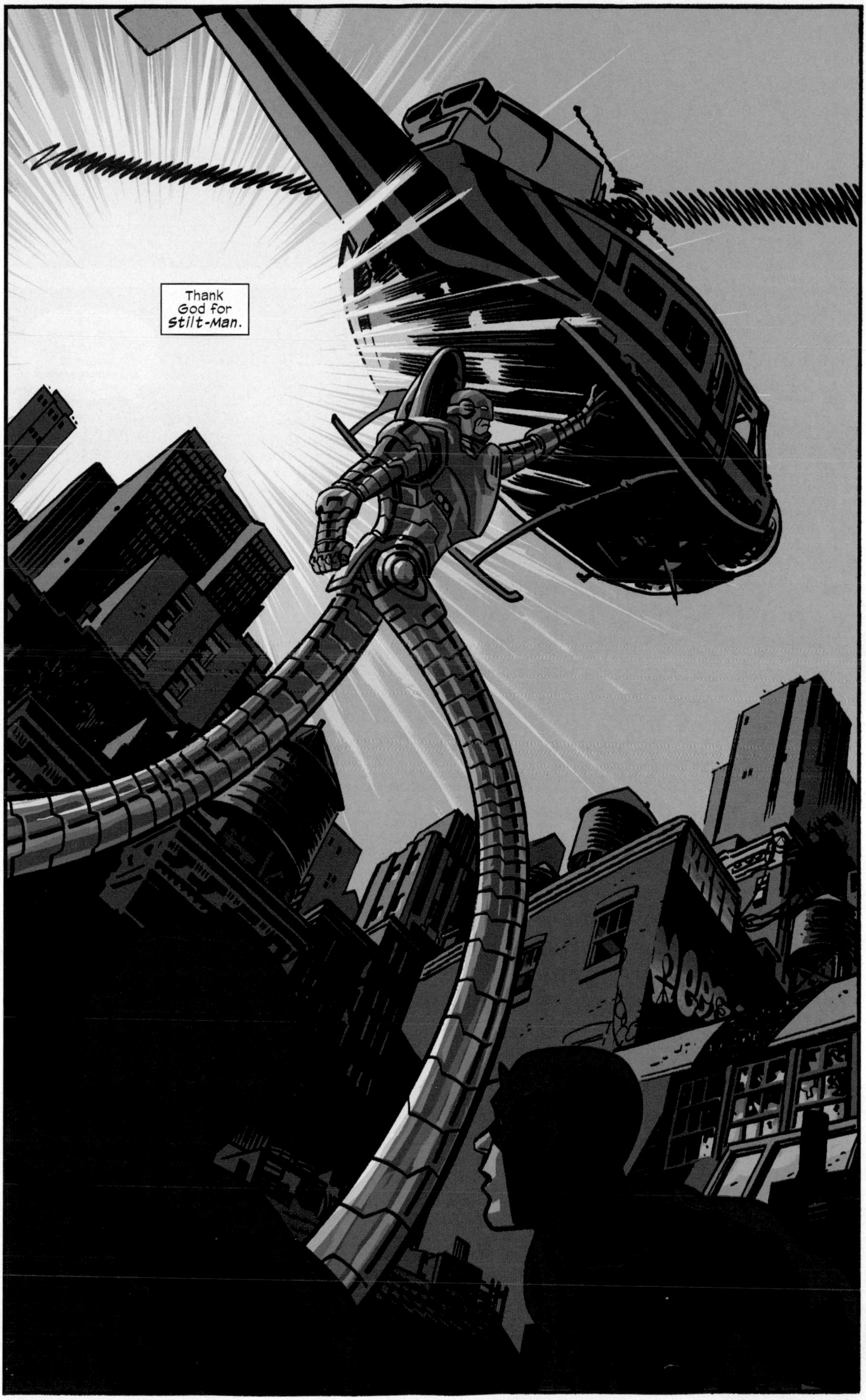
Thank God for Stilt-Man.

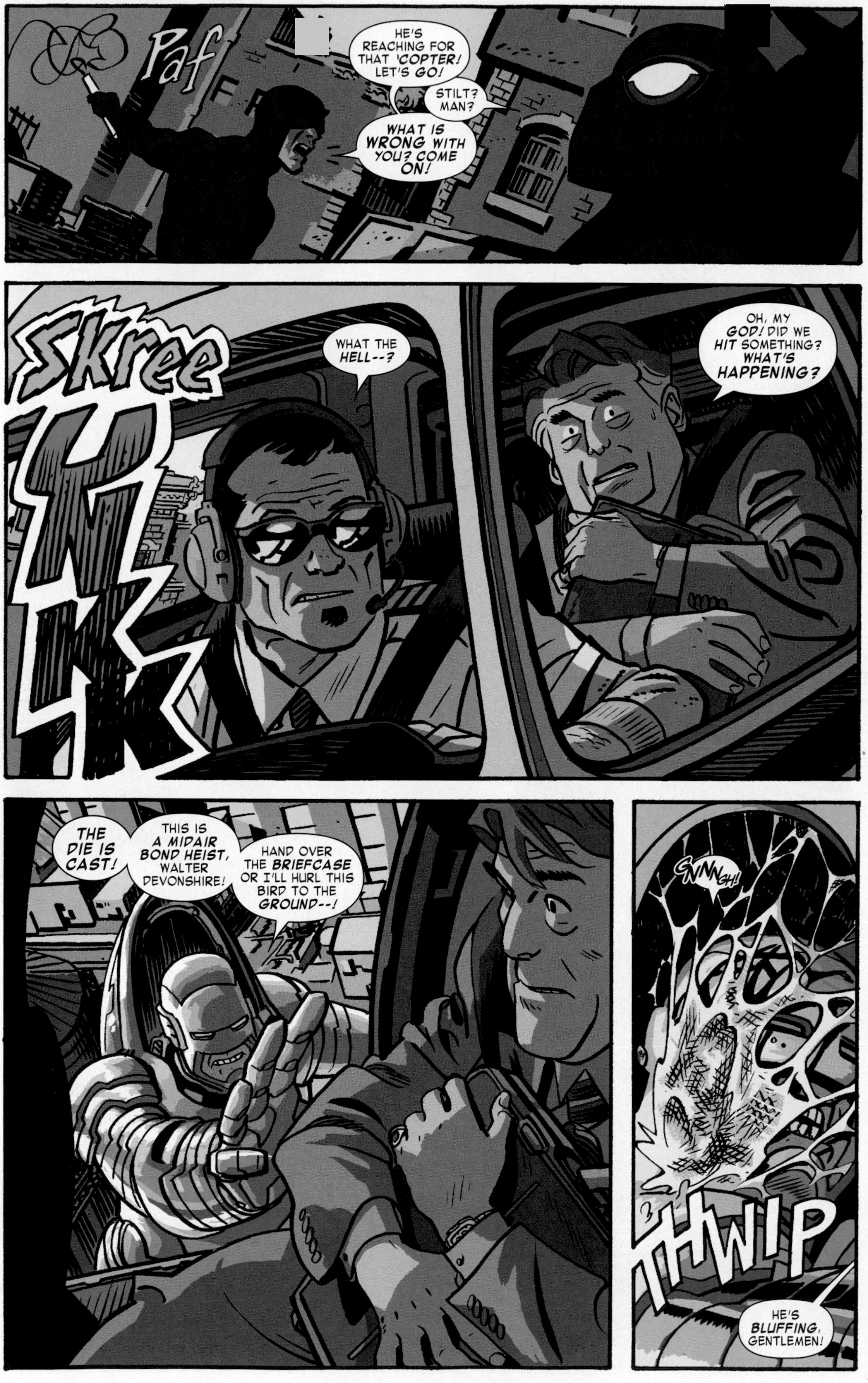
Paf
HE'S REACHING FOR THAT 'COPTER! LET'S GO!
STILT? MAN?
WHAT IS WRONG WITH YOU? COME ON!
Skree
WHAT THE HELL--?
OH, MY GOD! DID WE HIT SOMETHING? WHAT'S HAPPENING?
THE DIE IS CAST!
THIS IS A MIDAIR BOND HEIST, WALTER DEVONSHIRE!
HAND OVER THE BRIEFCASE OR I'LL HURL THIS BIRD TO THE GROUND--!
GNNNGH!
THWIP
HE'S BLUFFING, GENTLEMEN!

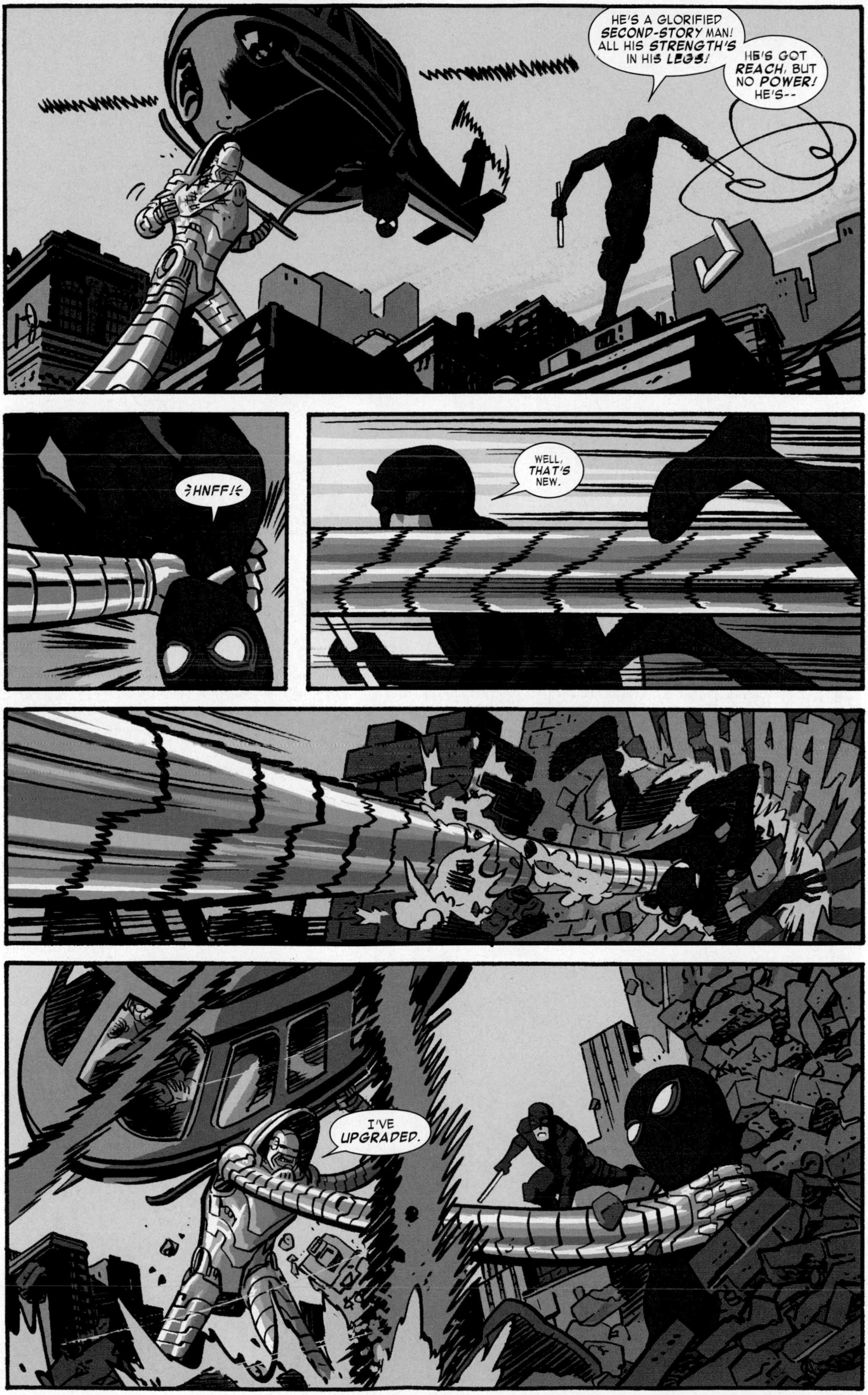
HE'S A GLORIFIED SECOND-STORY MAN! ALL HIS STRENGTH'S IN HIS LEGS!
HE'S GOT REACH, BUT NO POWER! HE'S--
HNFF!
WELL, THAT'S NEW.
I'VE UPGRADED.

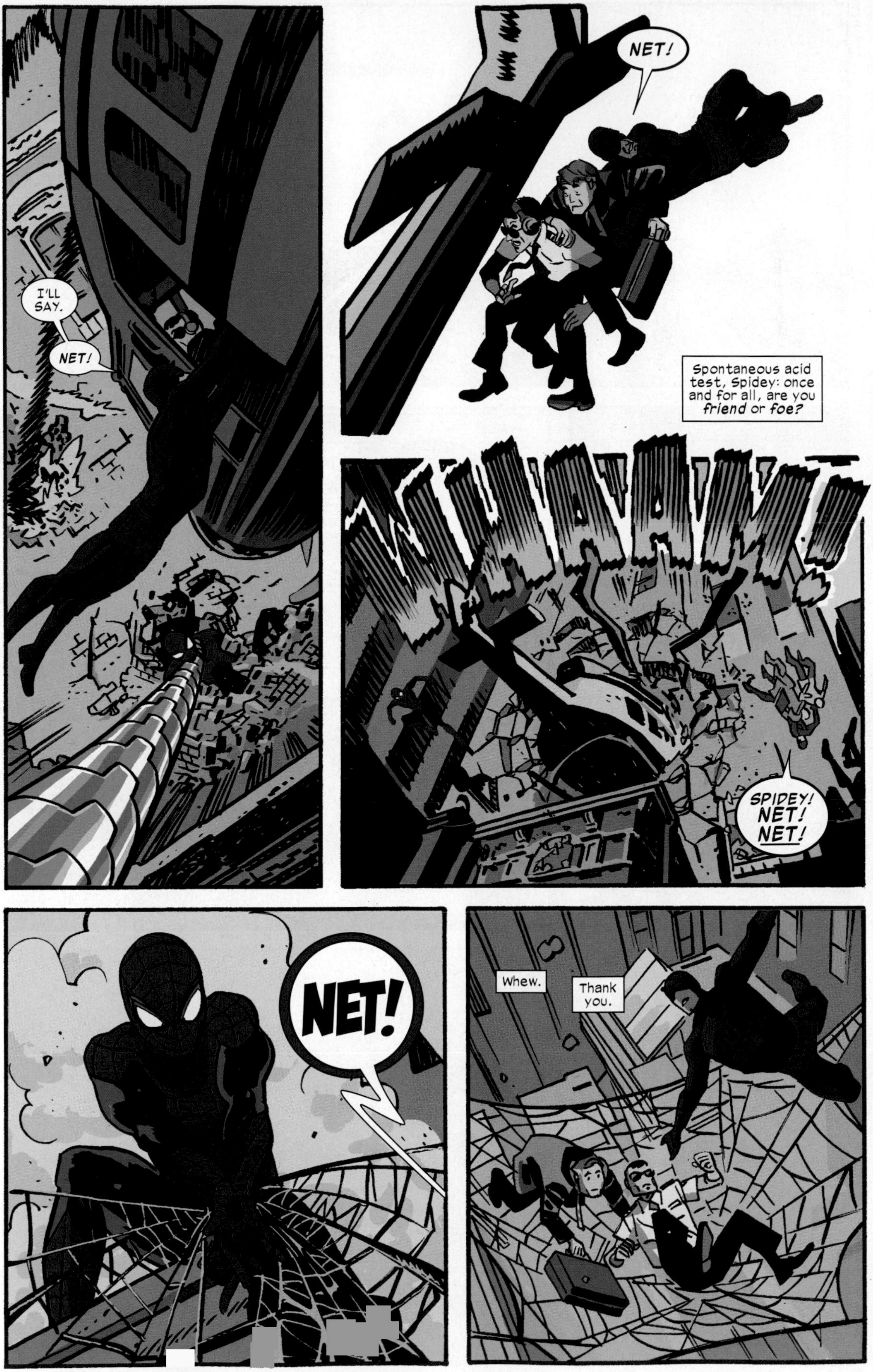

I'LL SAY.
NET!
NET!
Spontaneous acid test, Spidey: once and for all, are you *friend* or *foe?*
WHAAAM!
SPIDEY! NET! NET!
NET!
Whew.
Thank you.

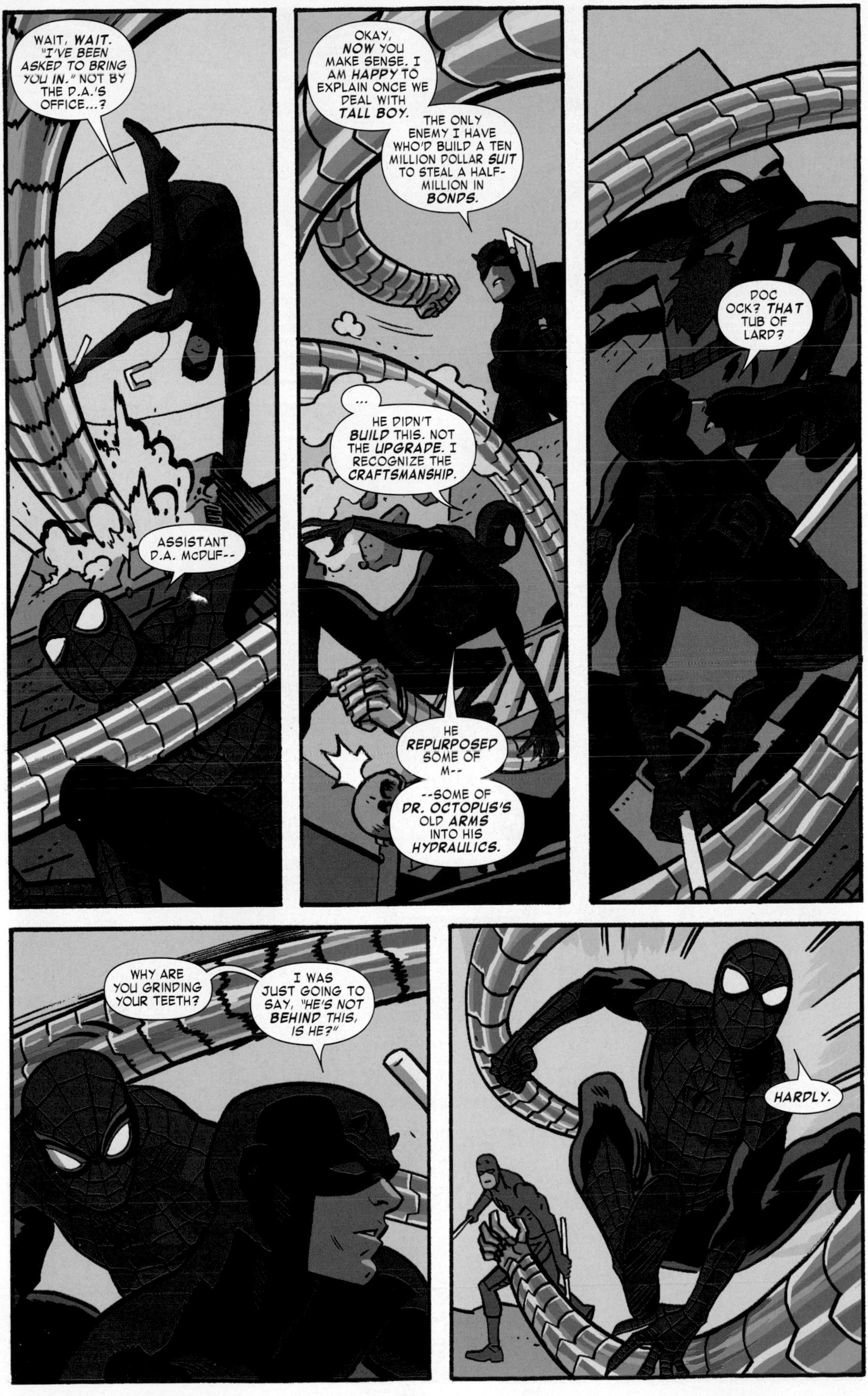
WAIT, WAIT. "I'VE BEEN ASKED TO BRING YOU IN." NOT BY THE D.A.'S OFFICE...?
ASSISTANT D.A. McDUF--
OKAY, NOW YOU MAKE SENSE. I AM HAPPY TO EXPLAIN ONCE WE DEAL WITH TALL BOY.
THE ONLY ENEMY I HAVE WHO'D BUILD A TEN MILLION DOLLAR SUIT TO STEAL A HALF-MILLION IN BONDS.
...
HE DIDN'T BUILD THIS. NOT THE UPGRADE. I RECOGNIZE THE CRAFTSMANSHIP.
HE REPURPOSED SOME OF M--
--SOME OF DR. OCTOPUS'S OLD ARMS INTO HIS HYDRAULICS.
DOC OCK? THAT TUB OF LARD?
WHY ARE YOU GRINDING YOUR TEETH?
I WAS JUST GOING TO SAY, "HE'S NOT BEHIND THIS, IS HE?"
HARDLY.

WHO ARE *YOU* TO CO-OPT ANOTHER MAN'S *CREATIONS*, YOU *CHARLATAN?* YOU *BABOON?* YOU'RE NOTHING BUT A *MENIAL THIEF*--

--HNNGH!

SO? YOU COME *WINDMILLING* YOUR ARMS AT *ME*, I'LL RETURN THE *FAVOR!* I KNOW YOU'RE *STRONG*, BUT *NOW*--

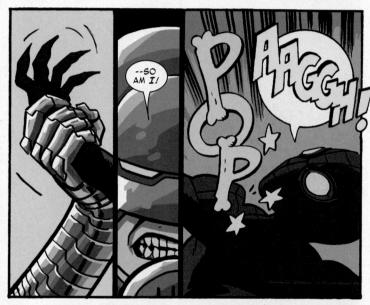

--SO AM *I!*

P-P-P-P AAGGH!

Headstrong as *ever*. And coming from *me*--

How do I shut this *down?* Even if I can get him to drop *spidey*, how can I stop him from popping *my* limbs, *too?*

By picking the perfect *strike zone.*

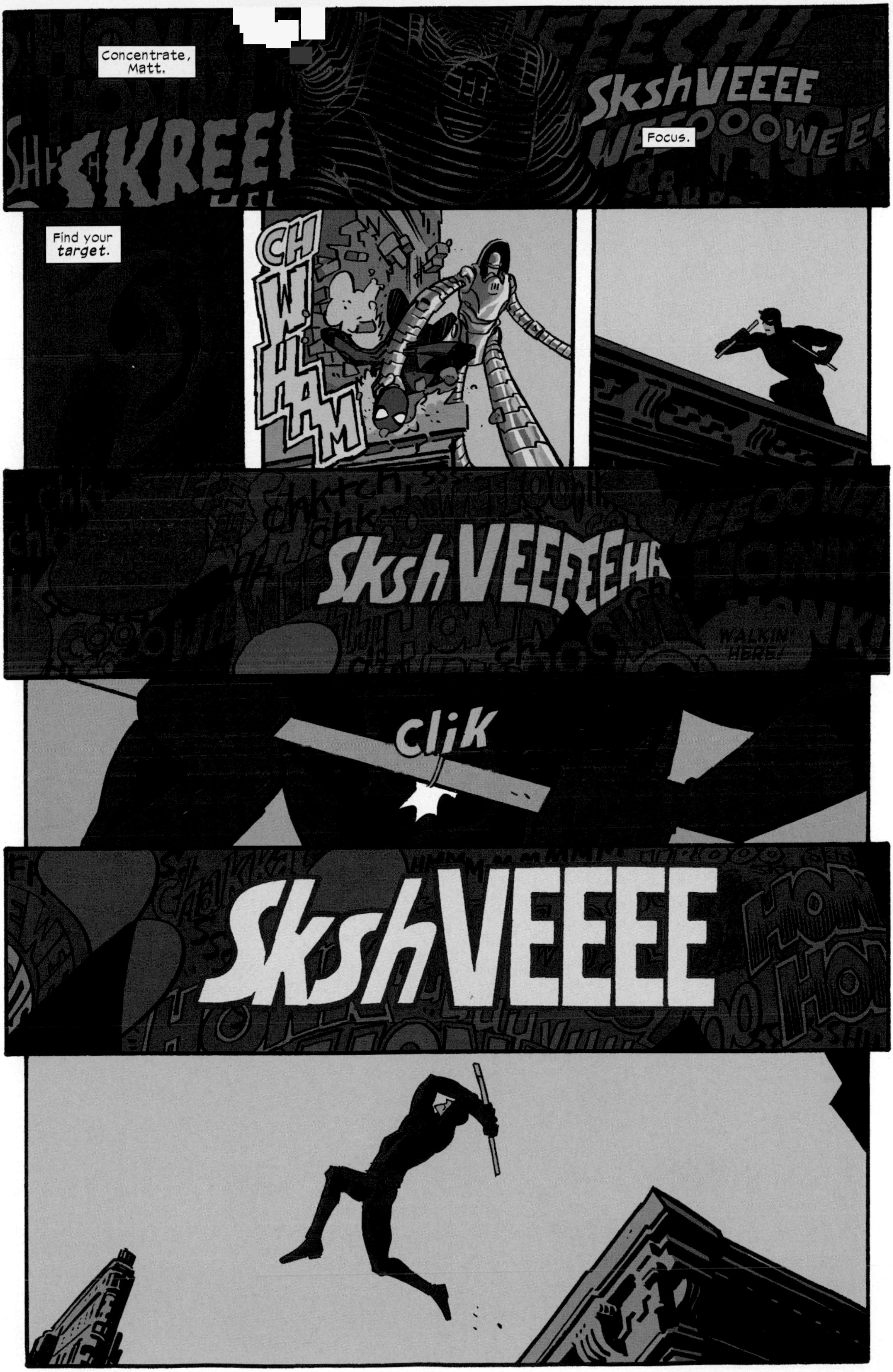
Concentrate, Matt.
SKREE!
SkshVEEEE
Focus.
Find your target.
CH W. W. HAM
SkshVEEEEHH
WALKIN' HERE!
clik
SkshVEEEE

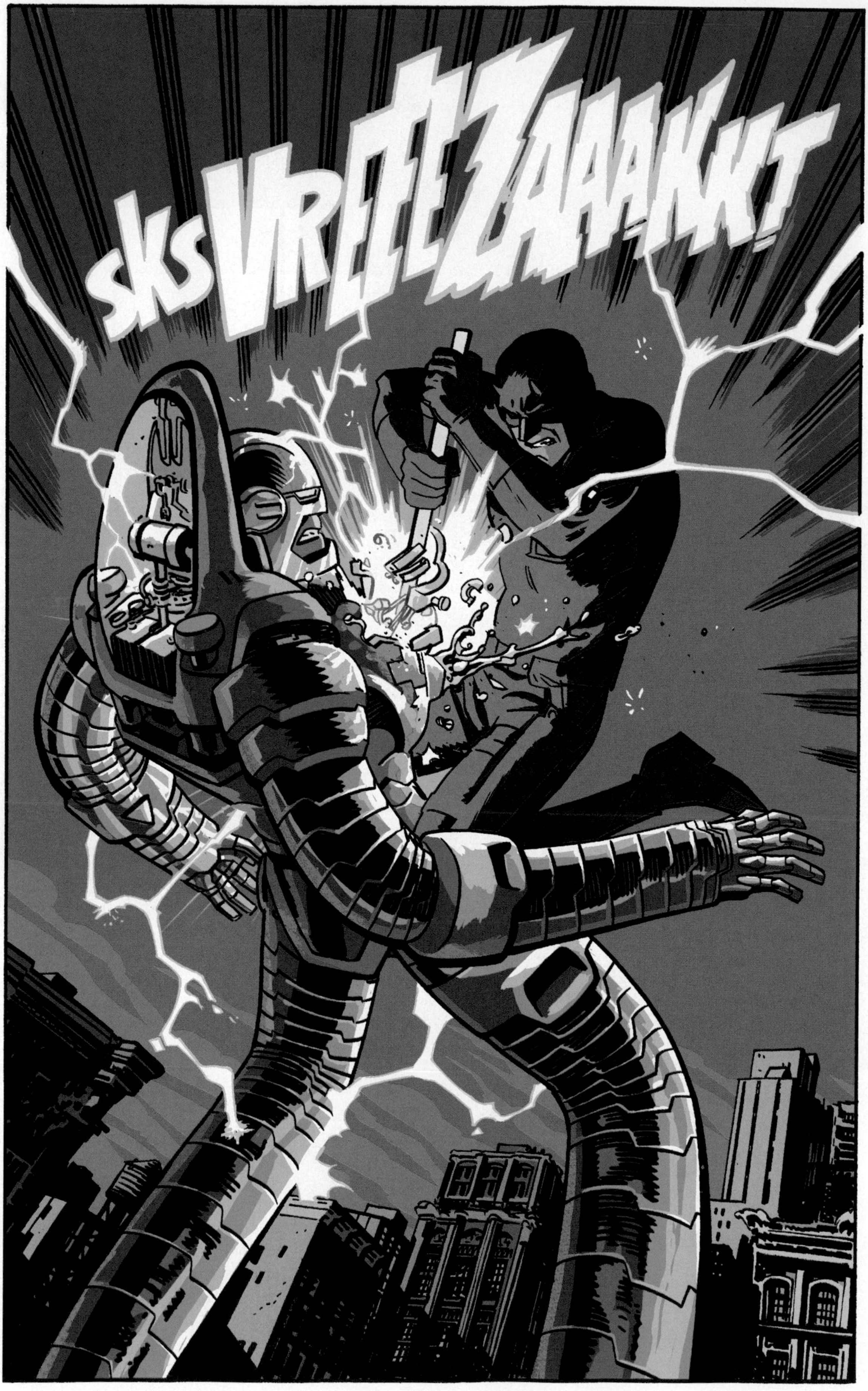
sksVREEEZAAAKK!

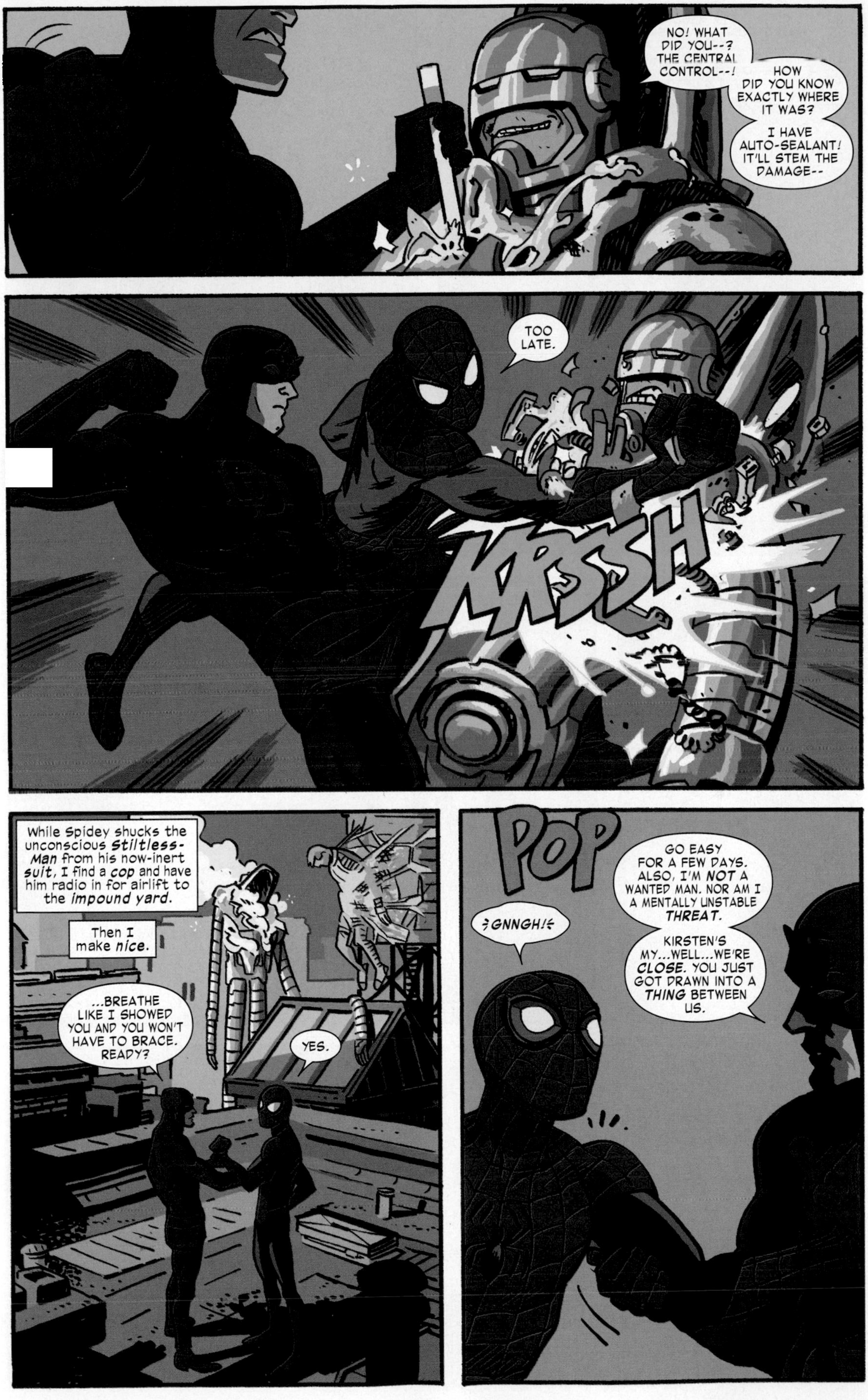
NO! WHAT DID YOU--? THE CENTRAL CONTROL--!
HOW DID YOU KNOW EXACTLY WHERE IT WAS?
I HAVE AUTO-SEALANT! IT'LL STEM THE DAMAGE--
TOO LATE.
KRSSH
While Spidey shucks the unconscious Stiltless-Man from his now-inert suit, I find a cop and have him radio in for airlift to the impound yard.
Then I make nice.
...BREATHE LIKE I SHOWED YOU AND YOU WON'T HAVE TO BRACE. READY?
YES.
POP
GNNGH!
GO EASY FOR A FEW DAYS. ALSO, I'M NOT A WANTED MAN. NOR AM I A MENTALLY UNSTABLE THREAT.
KIRSTEN'S MY...WELL...WE'RE CLOSE. YOU JUST GOT DRAWN INTO A THING BETWEEN US.

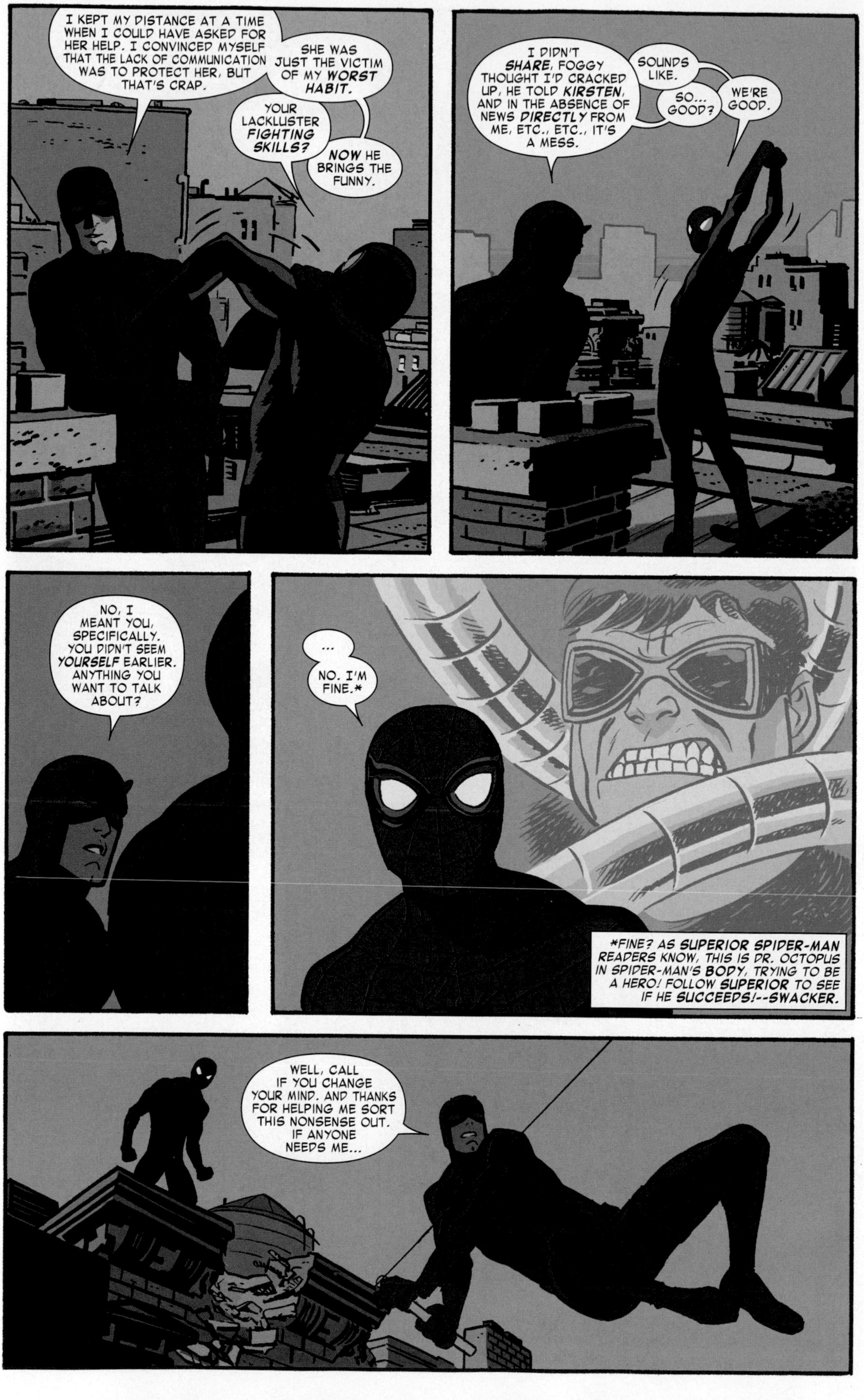
I KEPT MY DISTANCE AT A TIME WHEN I COULD HAVE ASKED FOR HER HELP. I CONVINCED MYSELF THAT THE LACK OF COMMUNICATION WAS TO PROTECT HER, BUT THAT'S CRAP.
SHE WAS JUST THE VICTIM OF MY WORST HABIT.
YOUR LACKLUSTER FIGHTING SKILLS?
NOW HE BRINGS THE FUNNY.
I DIDN'T SHARE, FOGGY THOUGHT I'D CRACKED UP, HE TOLD KIRSTEN, AND IN THE ABSENCE OF NEWS DIRECTLY FROM ME, ETC., ETC., IT'S A MESS.
SOUNDS LIKE.
SO... GOOD?
WE'RE GOOD.
NO, I MEANT YOU, SPECIFICALLY. YOU DIDN'T SEEM YOURSELF EARLIER. ANYTHING YOU WANT TO TALK ABOUT?
...
NO. I'M FINE.*
*FINE? AS SUPERIOR SPIDER-MAN READERS KNOW, THIS IS DR. OCTOPUS IN SPIDER-MAN'S BODY, TRYING TO BE A HERO! FOLLOW SUPERIOR TO SEE IF HE SUCCEEDS!--SWACKER.
WELL, CALL IF YOU CHANGE YOUR MIND. AND THANKS FOR HELPING ME SORT THIS NONSENSE OUT. IF ANYONE NEEDS ME...

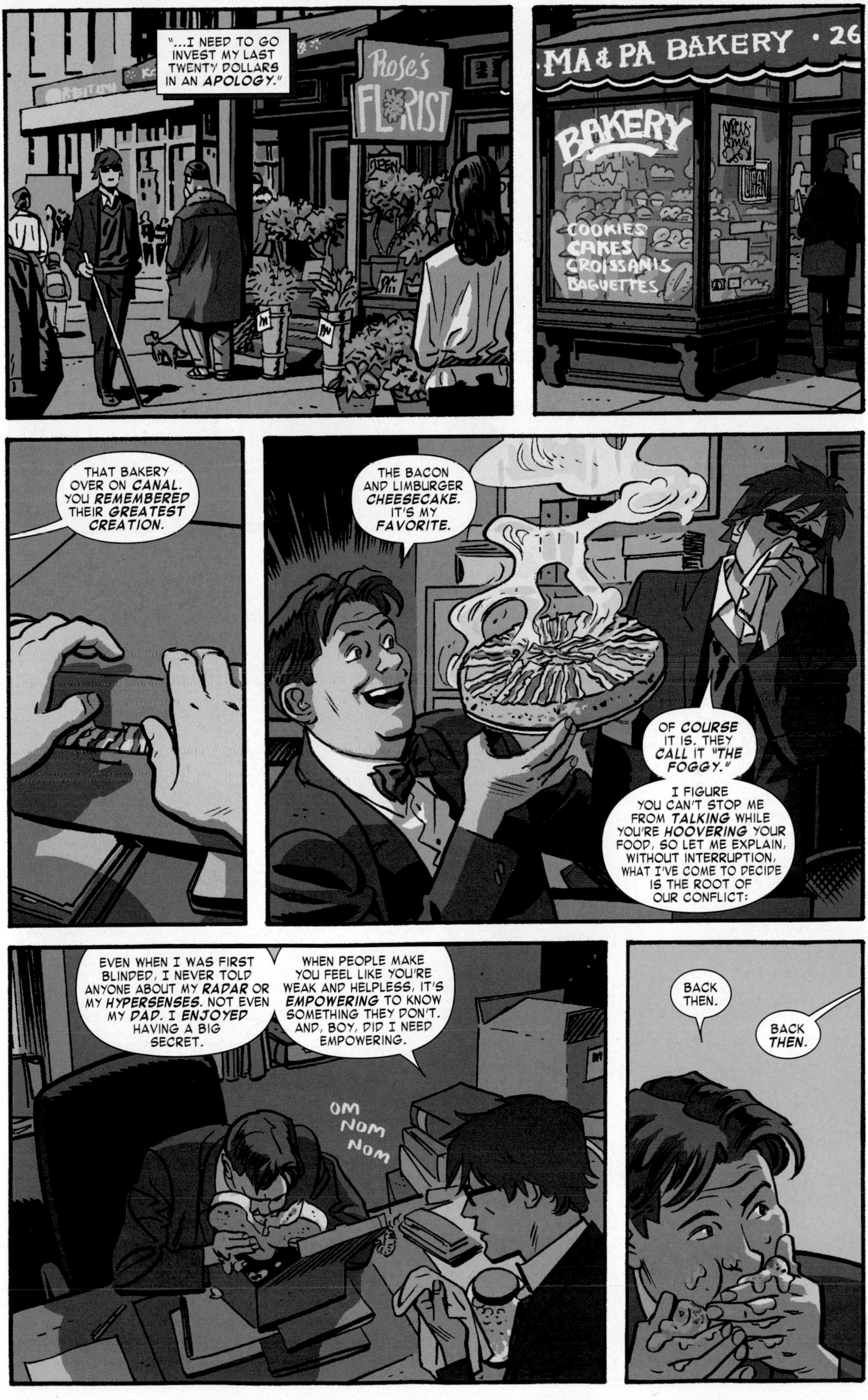
"...I NEED TO GO INVEST MY LAST TWENTY DOLLARS IN AN APOLOGY."
Rose's FLORIST
MA & PA BAKERY • 26
BAKERY
COOKIES
CAKES
CROISSANTS
BAGUETTES
THAT BAKERY OVER ON CANAL. YOU REMEMBERED THEIR GREATEST CREATION.
THE BACON AND LIMBURGER CHEESECAKE. IT'S MY FAVORITE.
OF COURSE IT IS. THEY CALL IT "THE FOGGY."
I FIGURE YOU CAN'T STOP ME FROM TALKING WHILE YOU'RE HOOVERING YOUR FOOD, SO LET ME EXPLAIN, WITHOUT INTERRUPTION, WHAT I'VE COME TO DECIDE IS THE ROOT OF OUR CONFLICT:
EVEN WHEN I WAS FIRST BLINDED, I NEVER TOLD ANYONE ABOUT MY RADAR OR MY HYPERSENSES. NOT EVEN MY DAD. I ENJOYED HAVING A BIG SECRET.
WHEN PEOPLE MAKE YOU FEEL LIKE YOU'RE WEAK AND HELPLESS, IT'S EMPOWERING TO KNOW SOMETHING THEY DON'T. AND, BOY, DID I NEED EMPOWERING.
OM NOM NOM
BACK THEN.
BACK THEN.

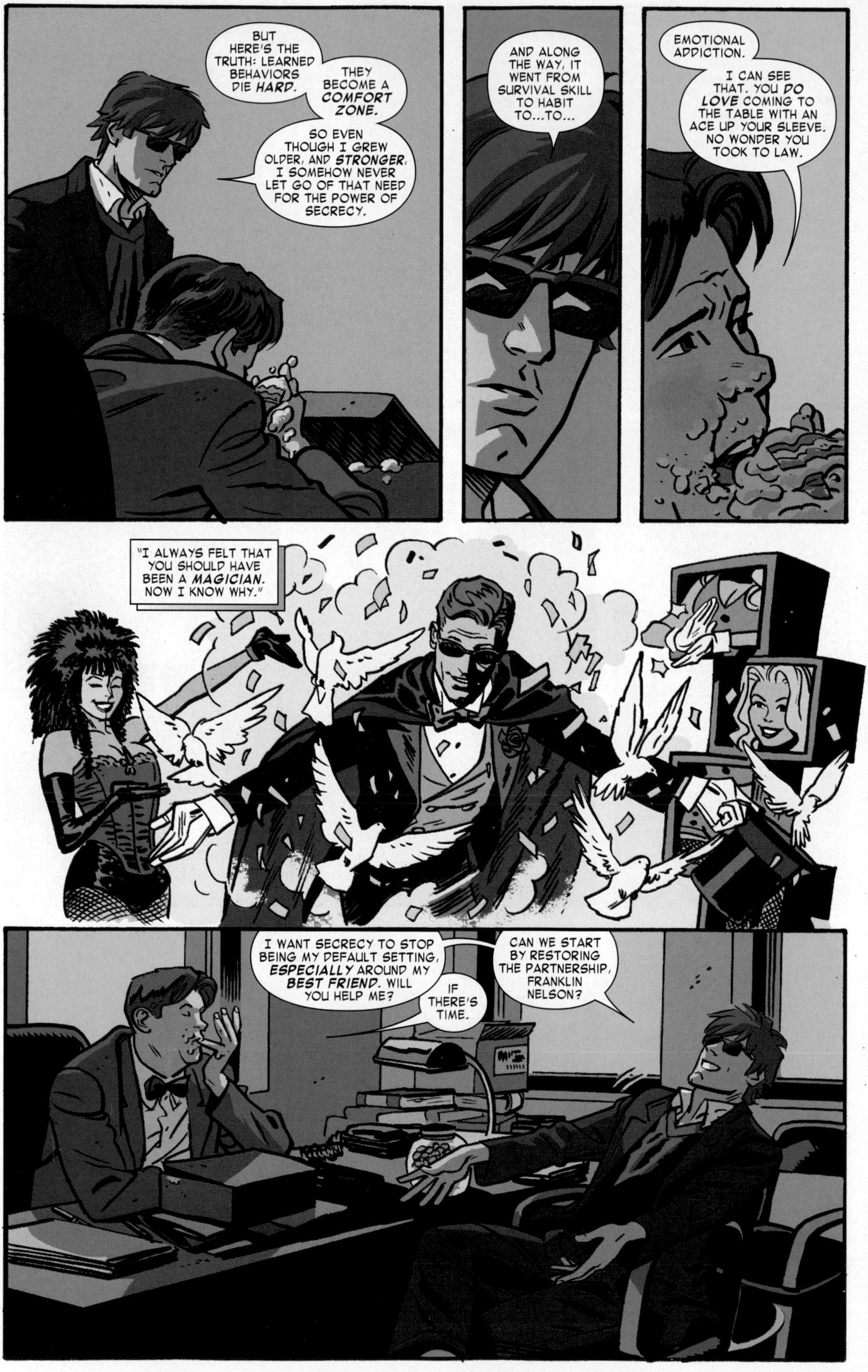
BUT HERE'S THE TRUTH: LEARNED BEHAVIORS DIE HARD.
THEY BECOME A COMFORT ZONE.
SO EVEN THOUGH I GREW OLDER, AND STRONGER, I SOMEHOW NEVER LET GO OF THAT NEED FOR THE POWER OF SECRECY.
AND ALONG THE WAY, IT WENT FROM SURVIVAL SKILL TO HABIT TO...TO...
EMOTIONAL ADDICTION.
I CAN SEE THAT. YOU DO LOVE COMING TO THE TABLE WITH AN ACE UP YOUR SLEEVE. NO WONDER YOU TOOK TO LAW.
"I ALWAYS FELT THAT YOU SHOULD HAVE BEEN A MAGICIAN. NOW I KNOW WHY."
I WANT SECRECY TO STOP BEING MY DEFAULT SETTING, ESPECIALLY AROUND MY BEST FRIEND. WILL YOU HELP ME?
IF THERE'S TIME.
CAN WE START BY RESTORING THE PARTNERSHIP, FRANKLIN NELSON?

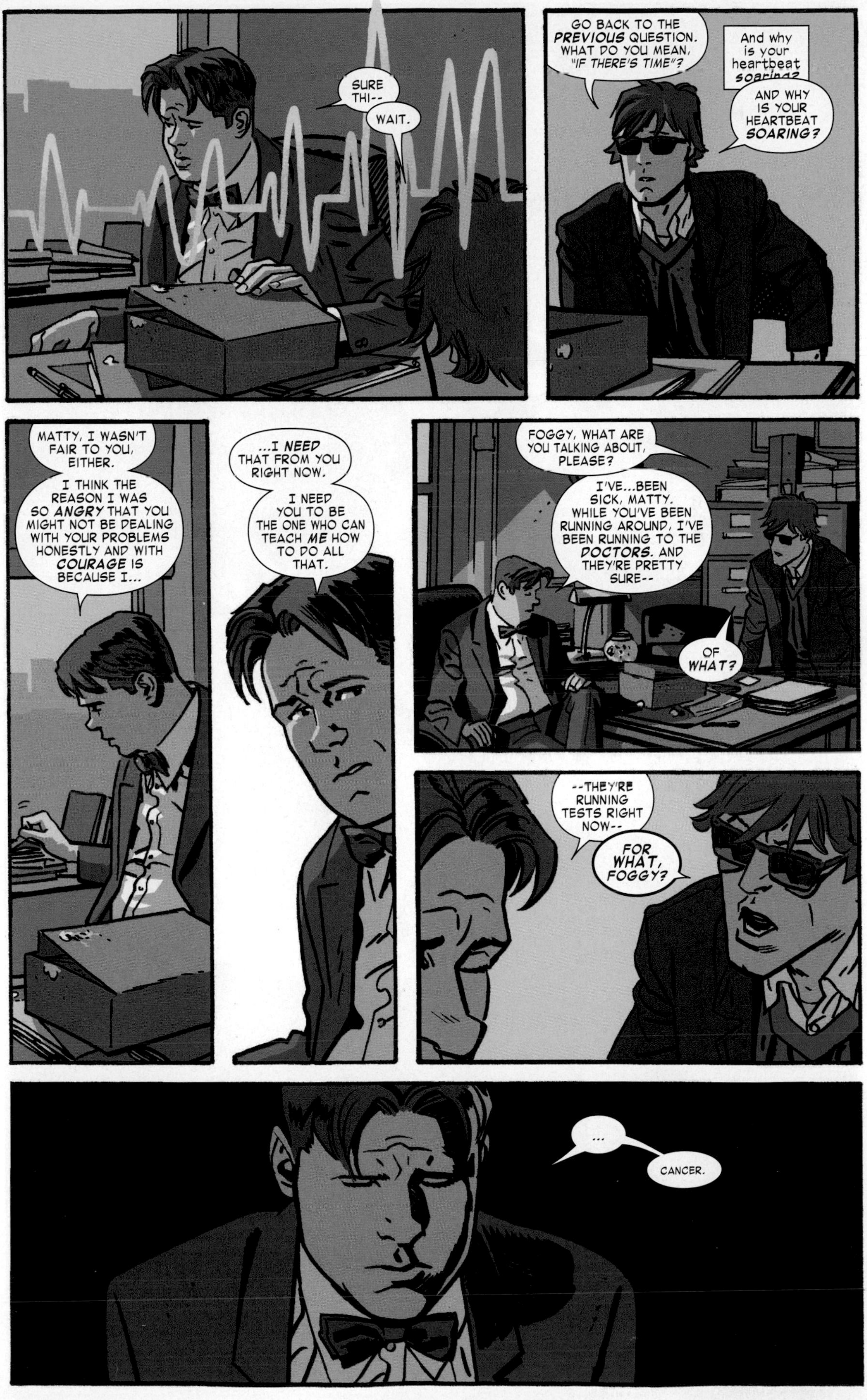
SURE THI--
WAIT.
GO BACK TO THE PREVIOUS QUESTION. WHAT DO YOU MEAN, "IF THERE'S TIME"?
And why is your heartbeat soaring?
AND WHY IS YOUR HEARTBEAT SOARING?
MATTY, I WASN'T FAIR TO YOU, EITHER.
I THINK THE REASON I WAS SO ANGRY THAT YOU MIGHT NOT BE DEALING WITH YOUR PROBLEMS HONESTLY AND WITH COURAGE IS BECAUSE I...
...I NEED THAT FROM YOU RIGHT NOW.
I NEED YOU TO BE THE ONE WHO CAN TEACH ME HOW TO DO ALL THAT.
FOGGY, WHAT ARE YOU TALKING ABOUT, PLEASE?
I'VE...BEEN SICK, MATTY. WHILE YOU'VE BEEN RUNNING AROUND, I'VE BEEN RUNNING TO THE DOCTORS. AND THEY'RE PRETTY SURE--
OF WHAT?
--THEY'RE RUNNING TESTS RIGHT NOW--
FOR WHAT, FOGGY?
...
CANCER.

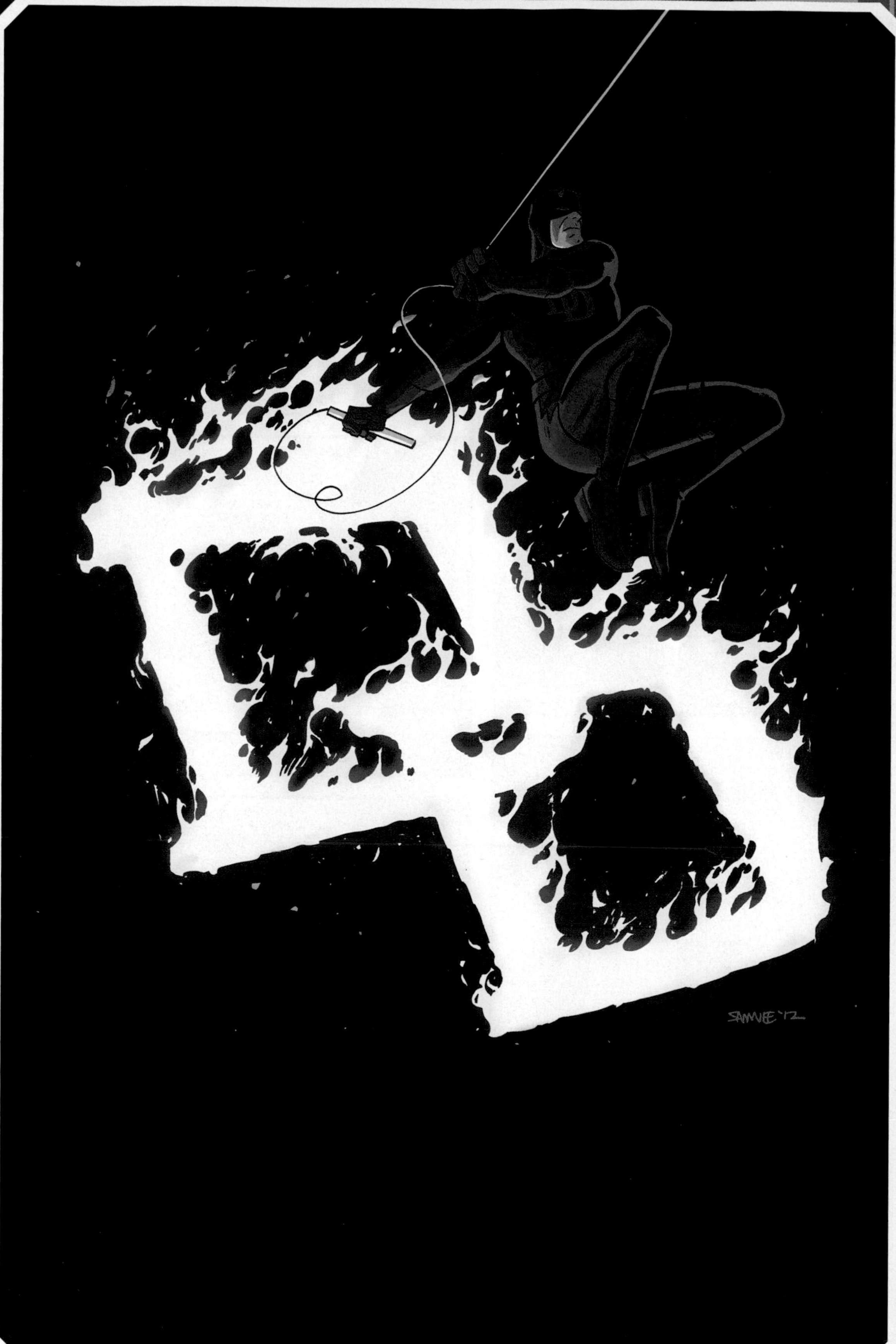
SAMNEE '12

TWENTY-THREE

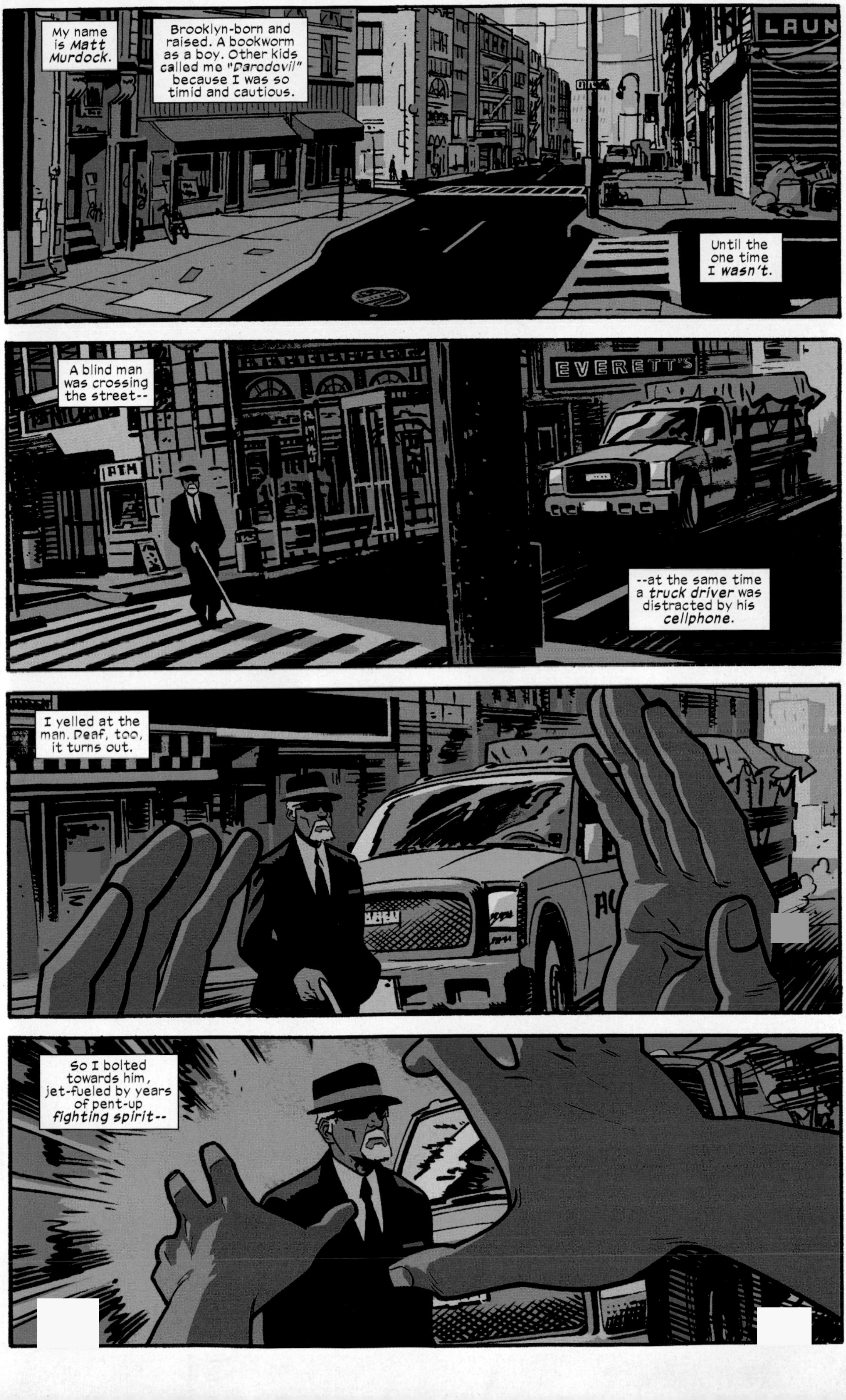
My name is *Matt Murdock*.
Brooklyn-born and raised. A bookworm as a boy. Other kids called me *"Daredevil"* because I was so timid and cautious.
LAUN
Until the one time I *wasn't*.
A blind man was crossing the street--
ATM
EVERETT'S
--at the same time a *truck driver* was distracted by his *cellphone*.
I yelled at the man. Deaf, too, it turns out.
So I bolted towards him, jet-fueled by years of pent-up *fighting spirit*--

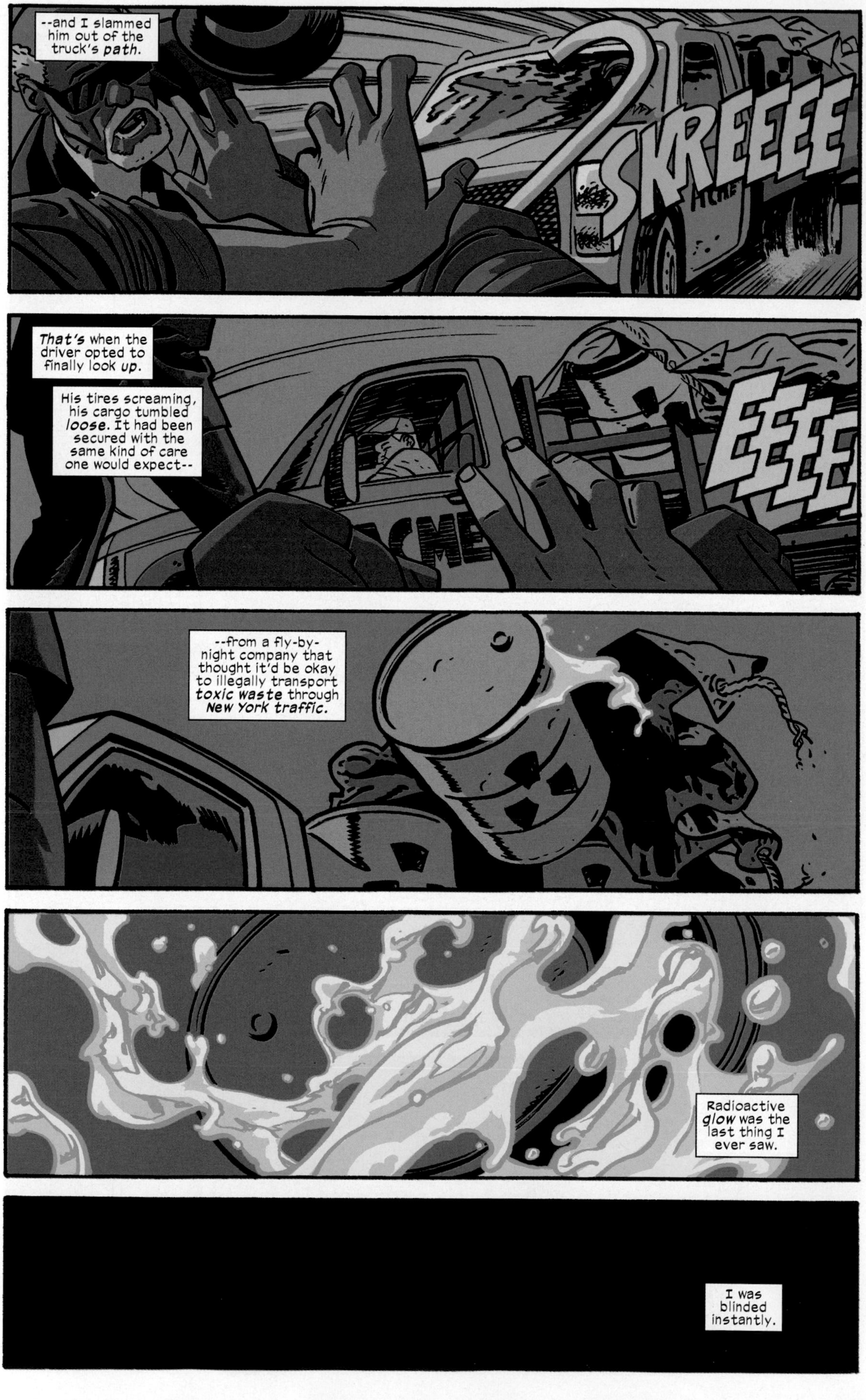
--and I slammed him out of the truck's *path*.
SKREEEE
That's when the driver opted to finally look *up*.
His tires screaming, his cargo tumbled *loose*. It had been secured with the same kind of care one would expect--
EEEE
ACME
--from a fly-by-night company that thought it'd be okay to illegally transport *toxic waste* through *New York traffic*.
Radioactive *glow* was the last thing I ever saw.
I was blinded instantly.

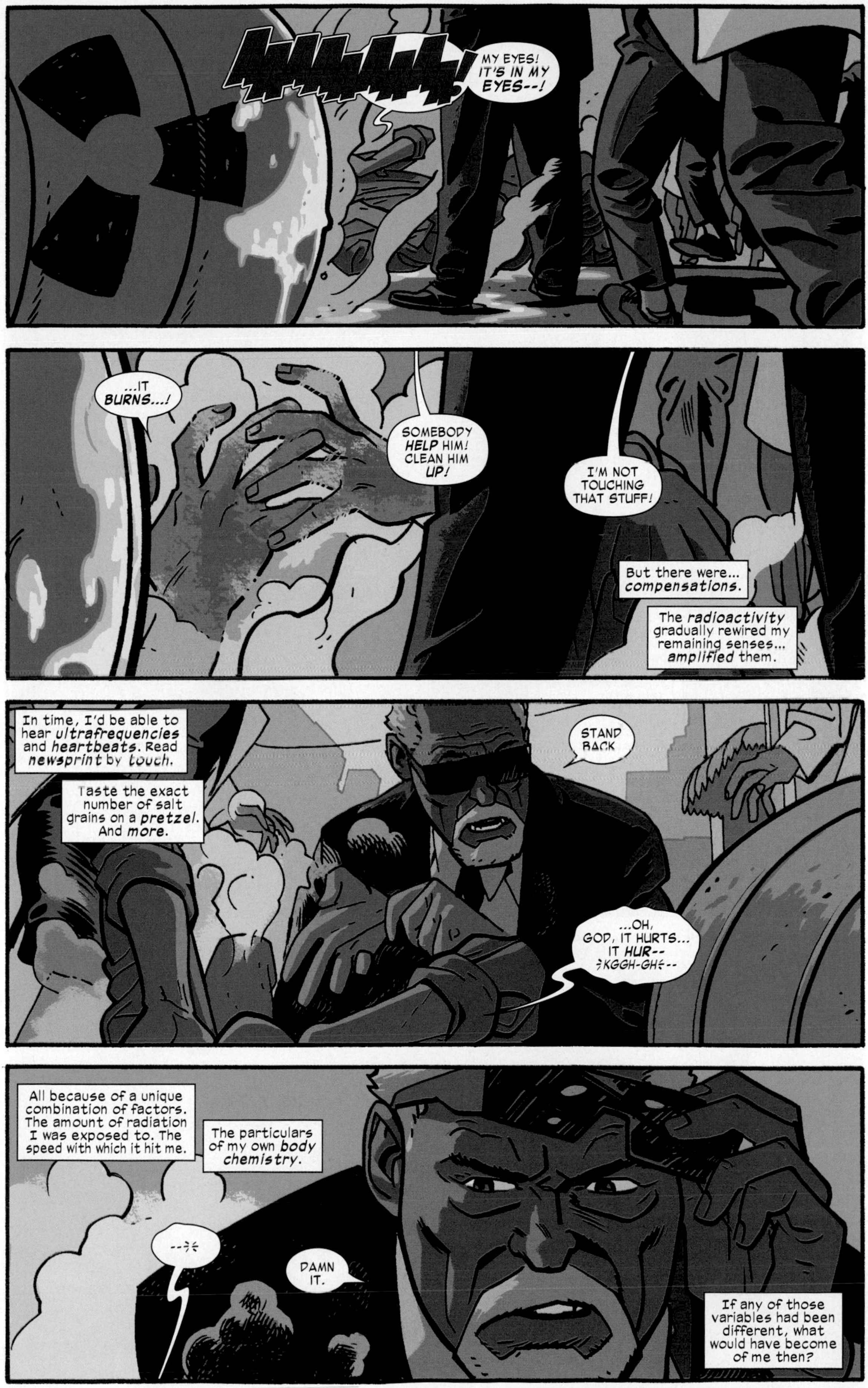
MY EYES! IT'S IN MY EYES--!
...IT BURNS...!
SOMEBODY HELP HIM! CLEAN HIM UP!
I'M NOT TOUCHING THAT STUFF!
But there were... compensations.
The radioactivity gradually rewired my remaining senses... amplified them.
In time, I'd be able to hear ultrafrequencies and heartbeats. Read newsprint by touch.
Taste the exact number of salt grains on a pretzel. And more.
STAND BACK
...OH, GOD, IT HURTS... IT HUR-- KGGH-GH--
All because of a unique combination of factors. The amount of radiation I was exposed to. The speed with which it hit me.
The particulars of my own body chemistry.
DAMN IT.
If any of those variables had been different, what would have become of me then?

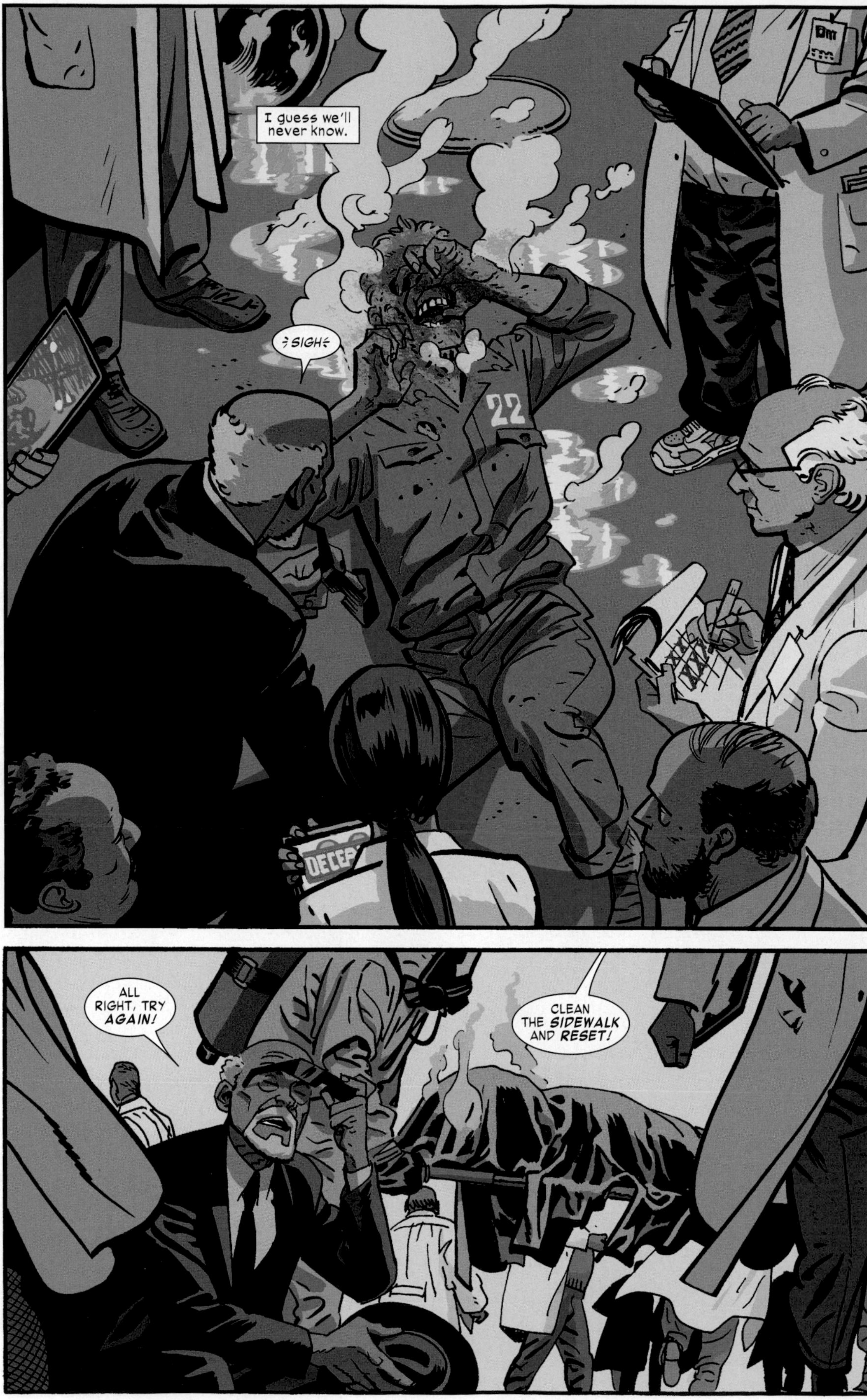
I guess we'll never know.
SIGH
ALL RIGHT, TRY AGAIN!
CLEAN THE SIDEWALK AND RESET!

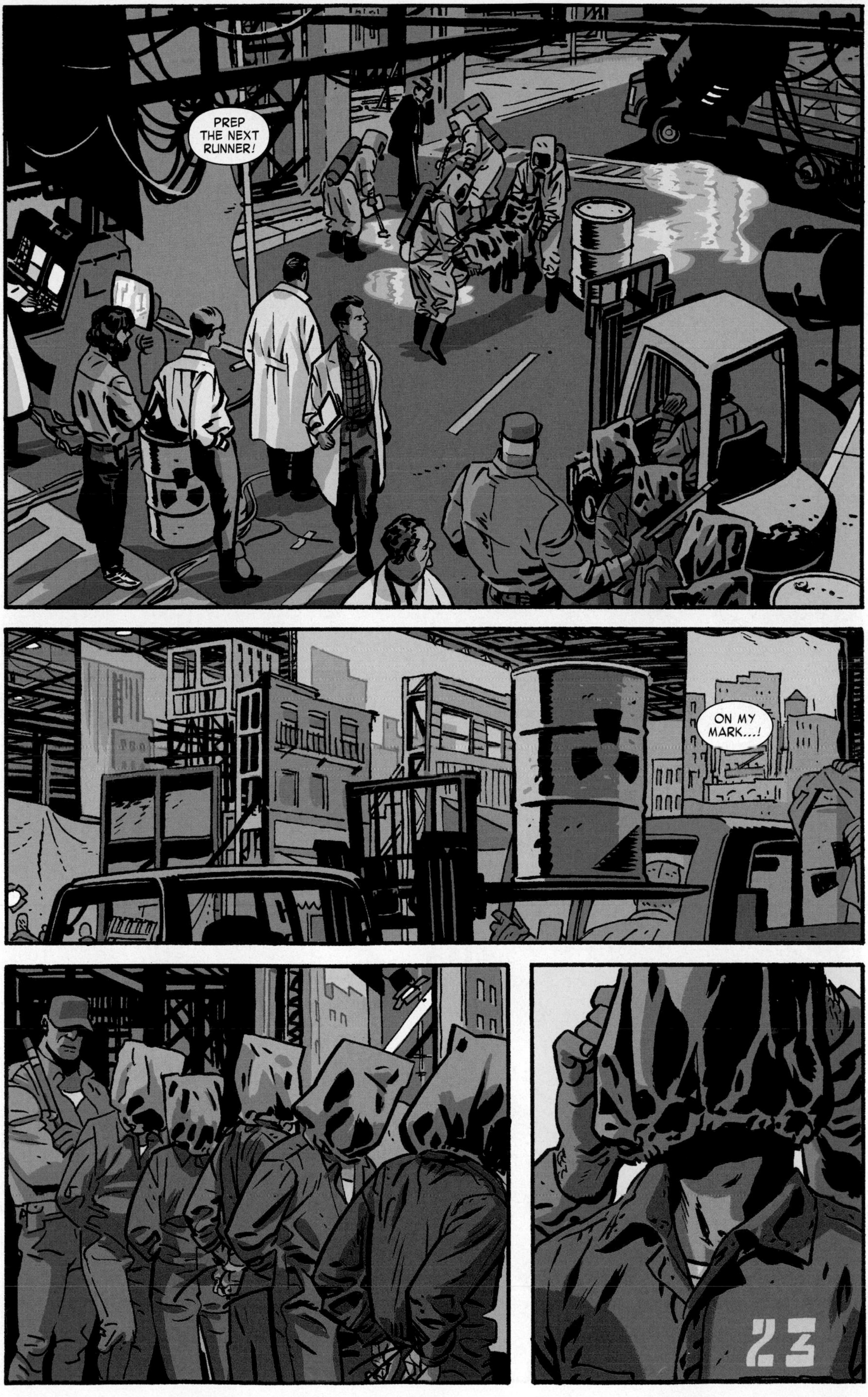
PREP THE NEXT RUNNER!
ON MY MARK...!
23

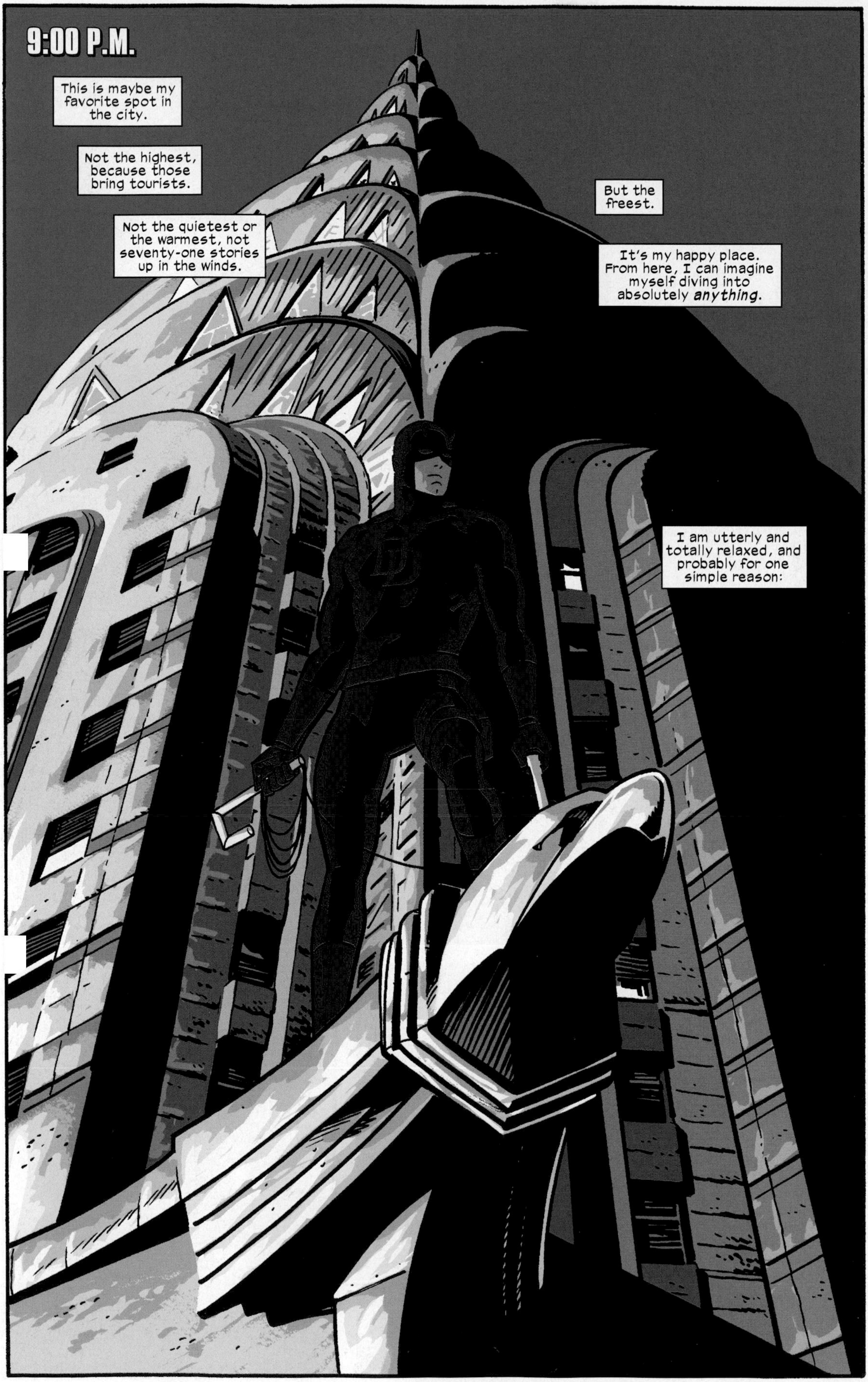
9:00 P.M.
This is maybe my favorite spot in the city.
Not the highest, because those bring tourists.
Not the quietest or the warmest, not seventy-one stories up in the winds.
But the freest.
It's my happy place. From here, I can imagine myself diving into absolutely *anything*.
I am utterly and totally relaxed, and probably for one simple reason:

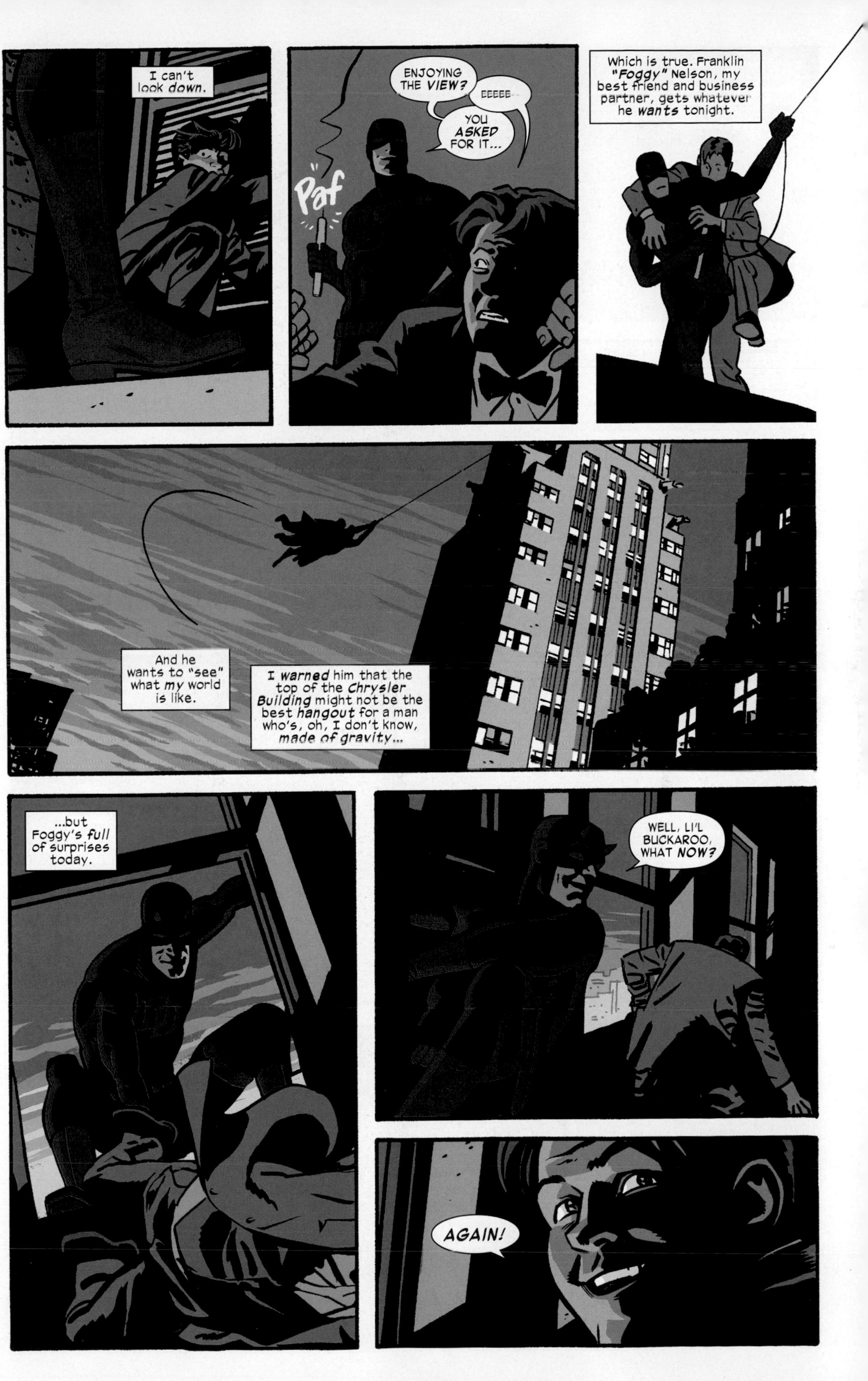
I can't look *down*.
ENJOYING THE *VIEW?*
EEEEE
YOU *ASKED* FOR IT...
Paf
Which is true. Franklin *"Foggy"* Nelson, my best friend and business partner, gets whatever he *wants* tonight.
And he wants to "see" what *my* world is like.
I *warned* him that the top of the *Chrysler Building* might not be the best *hangout* for a man who's, oh, I don't know, *made of gravity...*
...but Foggy's *full* of surprises today.
WELL, LI'L BUCKAROO, WHAT *NOW?*
AGAIN!

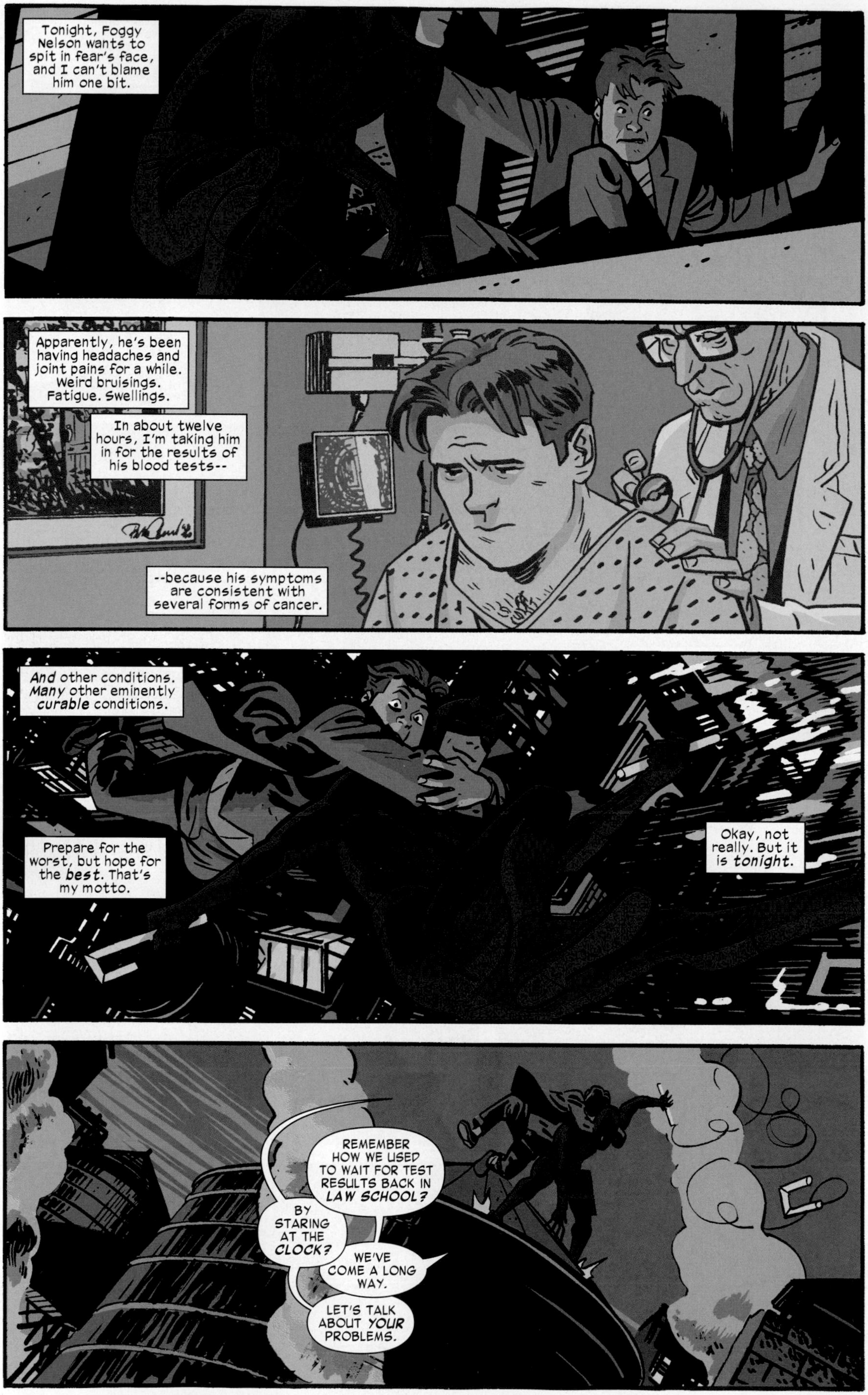

Tonight, Foggy Nelson wants to spit in fear's face, and I can't blame him one bit.
Apparently, he's been having headaches and joint pains for a while. Weird bruisings. Fatigue. Swellings.
In about twelve hours, I'm taking him in for the results of his blood tests--
--because his symptoms are consistent with several forms of cancer.
And other conditions. *Many* other eminently *curable* conditions.
Prepare for the worst, but hope for the *best*. That's my motto.
Okay, not really. But it is *tonight*.
REMEMBER HOW WE USED TO WAIT FOR TEST RESULTS BACK IN *LAW SCHOOL?*
BY STARING AT THE *CLOCK?*
WE'VE COME A LONG WAY.
LET'S TALK ABOUT *YOUR* PROBLEMS.

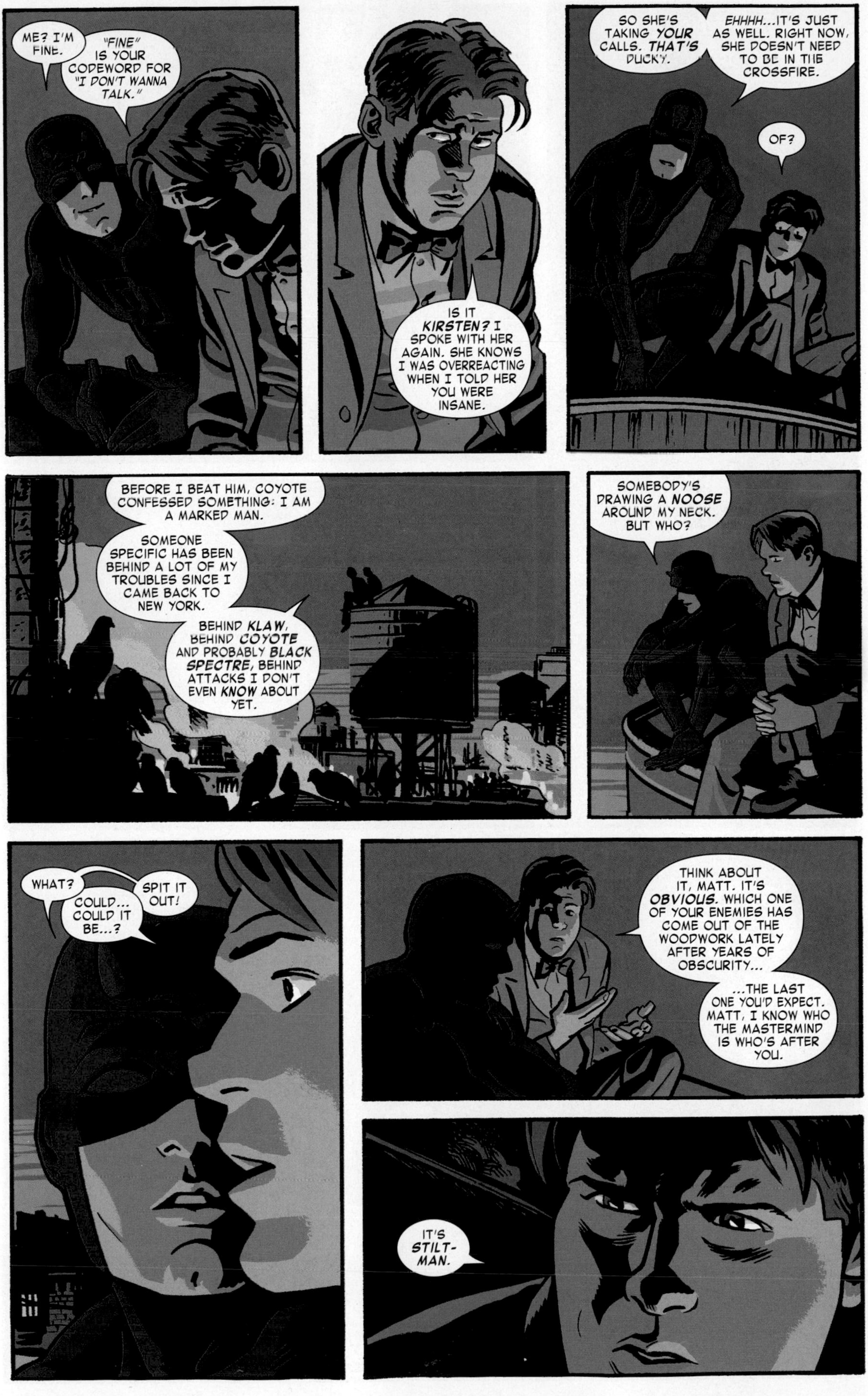
ME? I'M FINE.
"FINE" IS YOUR CODEWORD FOR "I DON'T WANNA TALK."
IS IT KIRSTEN? I SPOKE WITH HER AGAIN. SHE KNOWS I WAS OVERREACTING WHEN I TOLD HER YOU WERE INSANE.
SO SHE'S TAKING YOUR CALLS. THAT'S DUCKY.
EHHHH...IT'S JUST AS WELL. RIGHT NOW, SHE DOESN'T NEED TO BE IN THE CROSSFIRE.
OF?
BEFORE I BEAT HIM, COYOTE CONFESSED SOMETHING: I AM A MARKED MAN.
SOMEONE SPECIFIC HAS BEEN BEHIND A LOT OF MY TROUBLES SINCE I CAME BACK TO NEW YORK.
BEHIND KLAW, BEHIND COYOTE AND PROBABLY BLACK SPECTRE, BEHIND ATTACKS I DON'T EVEN KNOW ABOUT YET.
SOMEBODY'S DRAWING A NOOSE AROUND MY NECK. BUT WHO?
WHAT?
COULD... COULD IT BE...?
SPIT IT OUT!
THINK ABOUT IT, MATT. IT'S OBVIOUS. WHICH ONE OF YOUR ENEMIES HAS COME OUT OF THE WOODWORK LATELY AFTER YEARS OF OBSCURITY...
...THE LAST ONE YOU'D EXPECT. MATT, I KNOW WHO THE MASTERMIND IS WHO'S AFTER YOU.
IT'S STILT-MAN.

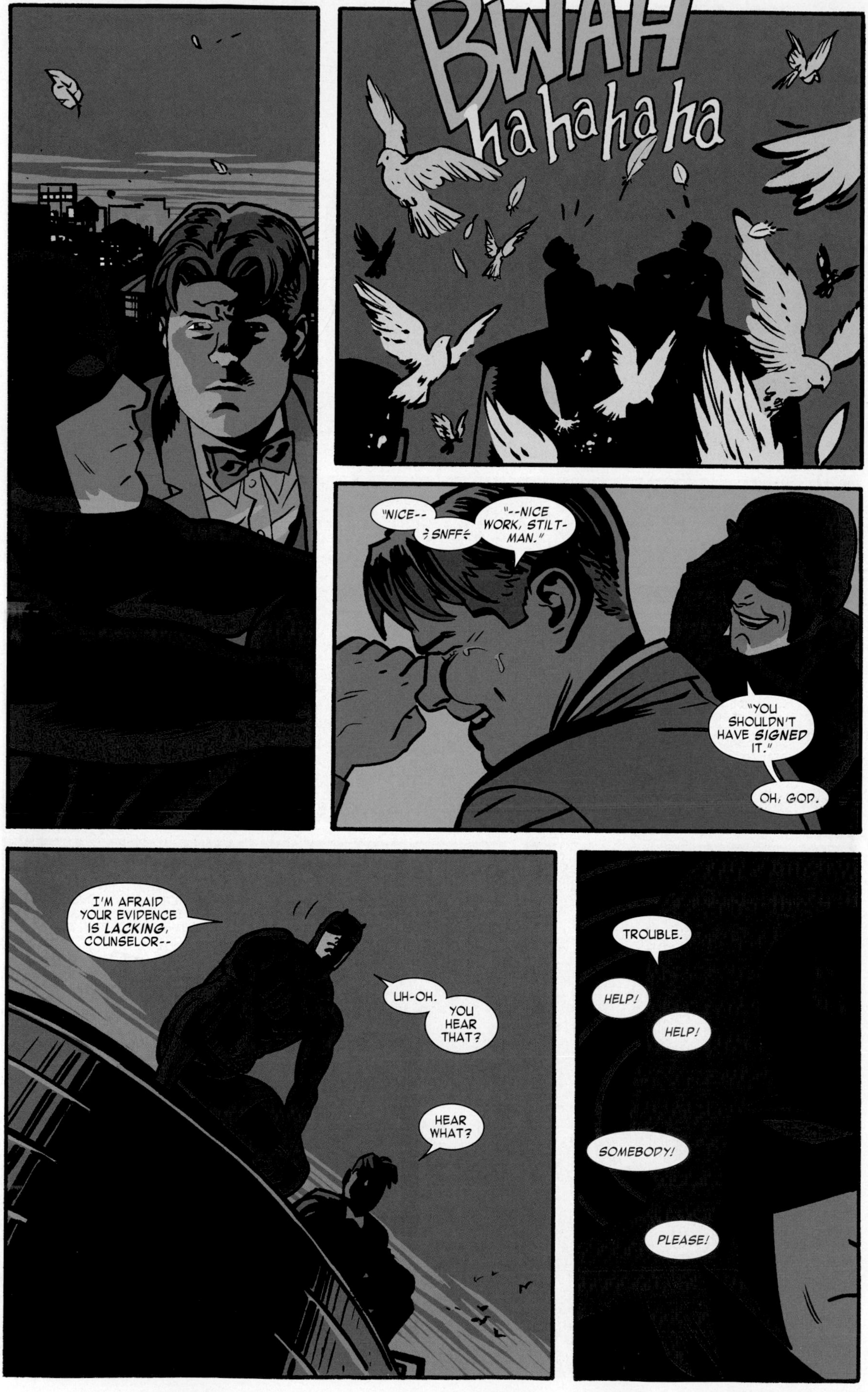
BWAH ha ha ha ha ha
"NICE--
SNFF
"--NICE WORK, STILT-MAN."
"YOU SHOULDN'T HAVE SIGNED IT."
OH, GOD.
I'M AFRAID YOUR EVIDENCE IS LACKING, COUNSELOR--
UH-OH. YOU HEAR THAT?
HEAR WHAT?
TROUBLE.
HELP!
HELP!
SOMEBODY!
PLEASE!

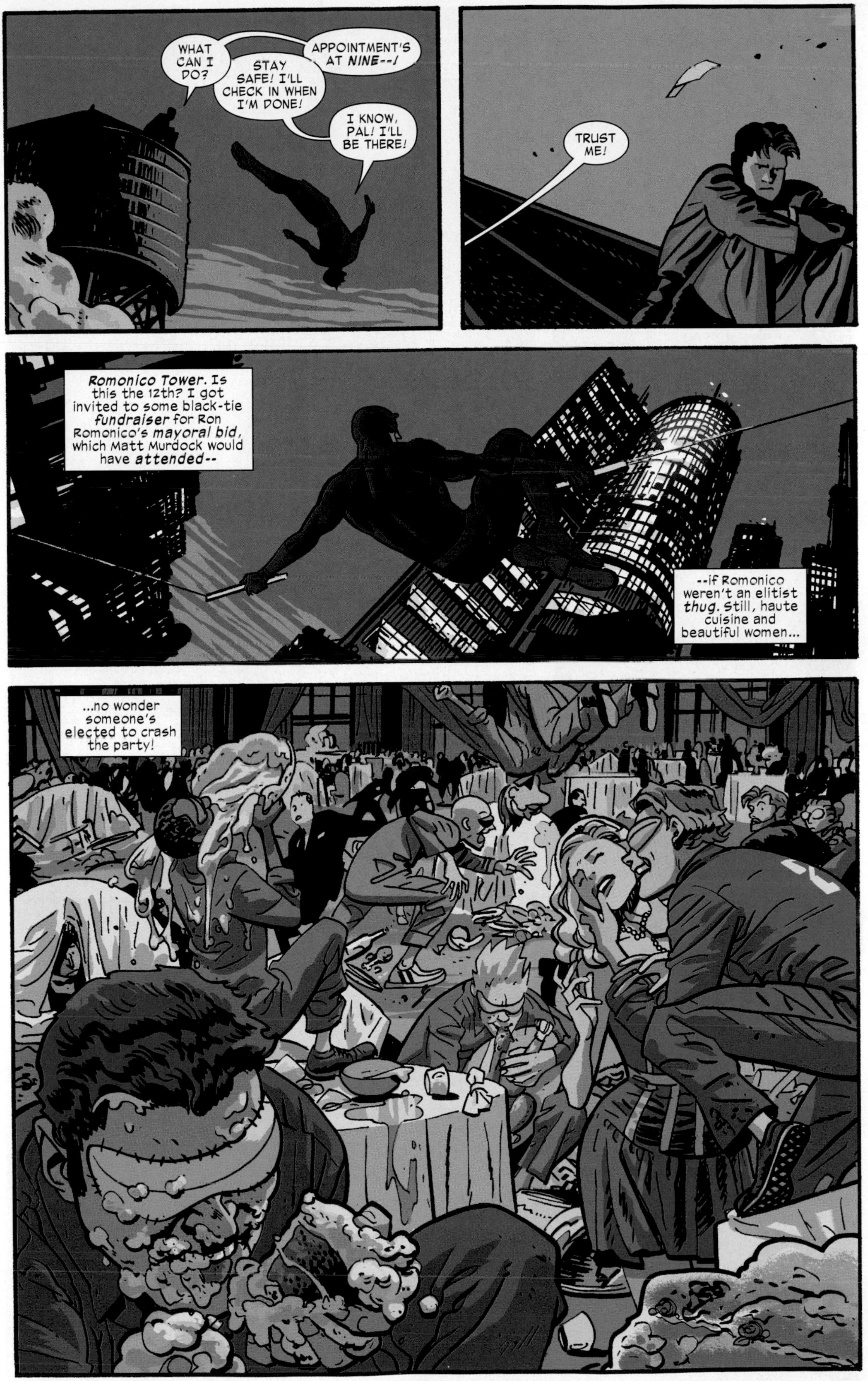
WHAT CAN I DO?
APPOINTMENT'S AT NINE--!
STAY SAFE! I'LL CHECK IN WHEN I'M DONE!
I KNOW, PAL! I'LL BE THERE!
TRUST ME!
Romonico Tower. Is this the 12th? I got invited to some black-tie fundraiser for Ron Romonico's mayoral bid, which Matt Murdock would have attended--
--if Romonico weren't an elitist thug. Still, haute cuisine and beautiful women...
...no wonder someone's elected to crash the party!

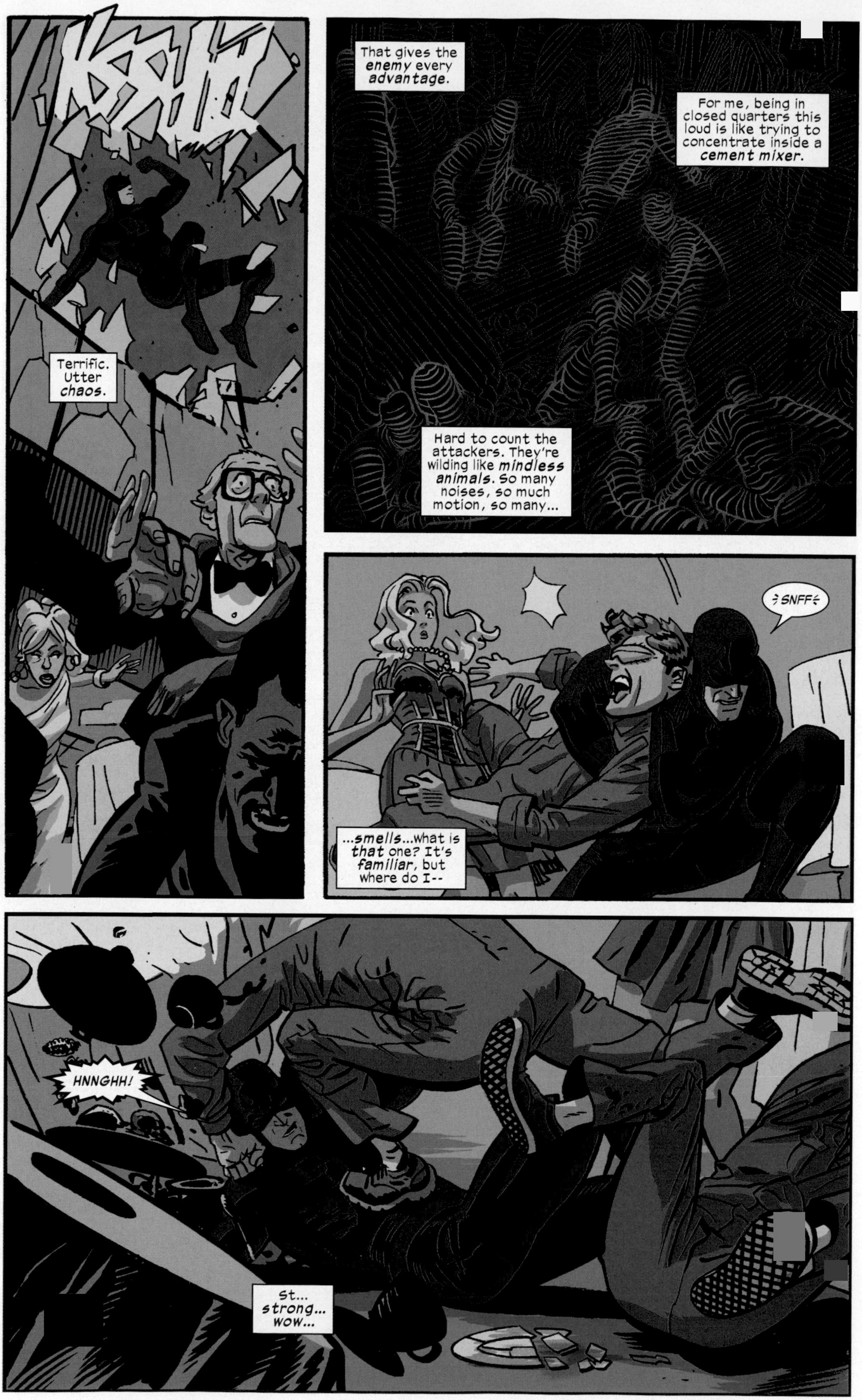
Terrific. Utter *chaos.*
That gives the *enemy* every *advantage.*
For me, being in closed quarters this loud is like trying to concentrate inside a ***cement mixer.***
Hard to count the attackers. They're wilding like ***mindless animals.*** So many noises, so much motion, so many...
SNFF
...*smells*...what is *that* one? It's *familiar,* but where do I--
HNNGHH!
St... *strong...* wow...

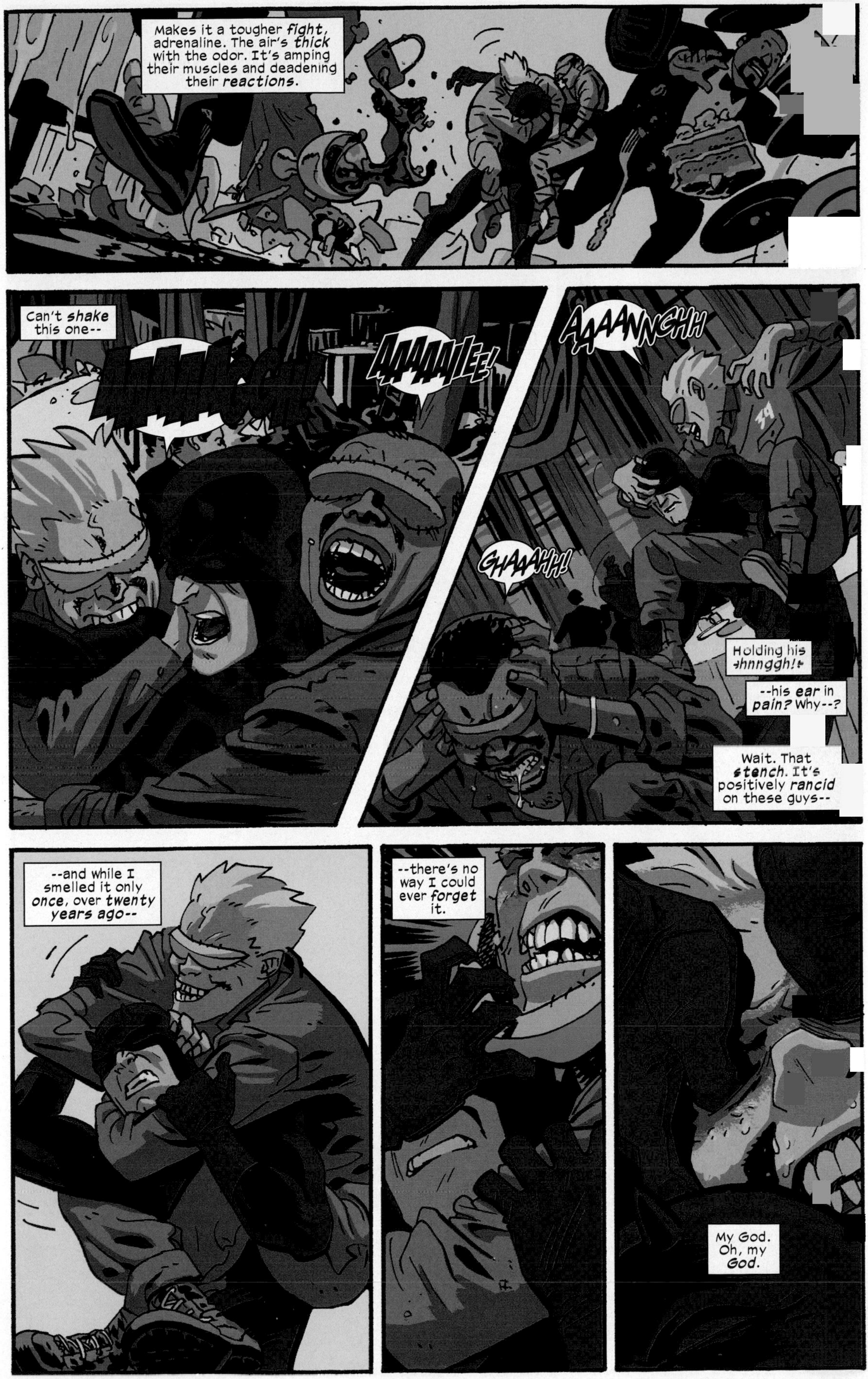
Makes it a tougher *fight*, adrenaline. The air's *thick* with the odor. It's amping their muscles and deadening their *reactions*.
Can't *shake* this one--
AAAAAIIEE!
AAAANNGHH
GHAAAHH!
Holding his ~~*hnnggh!*~~
--his *ear* in *pain?* Why--?
Wait. That *stench*. It's positively *rancid* on these guys--
--and while I smelled it only *once*, over *twenty years ago*--
--there's no way I could ever *forget* it.
My God. Oh, my *God*.

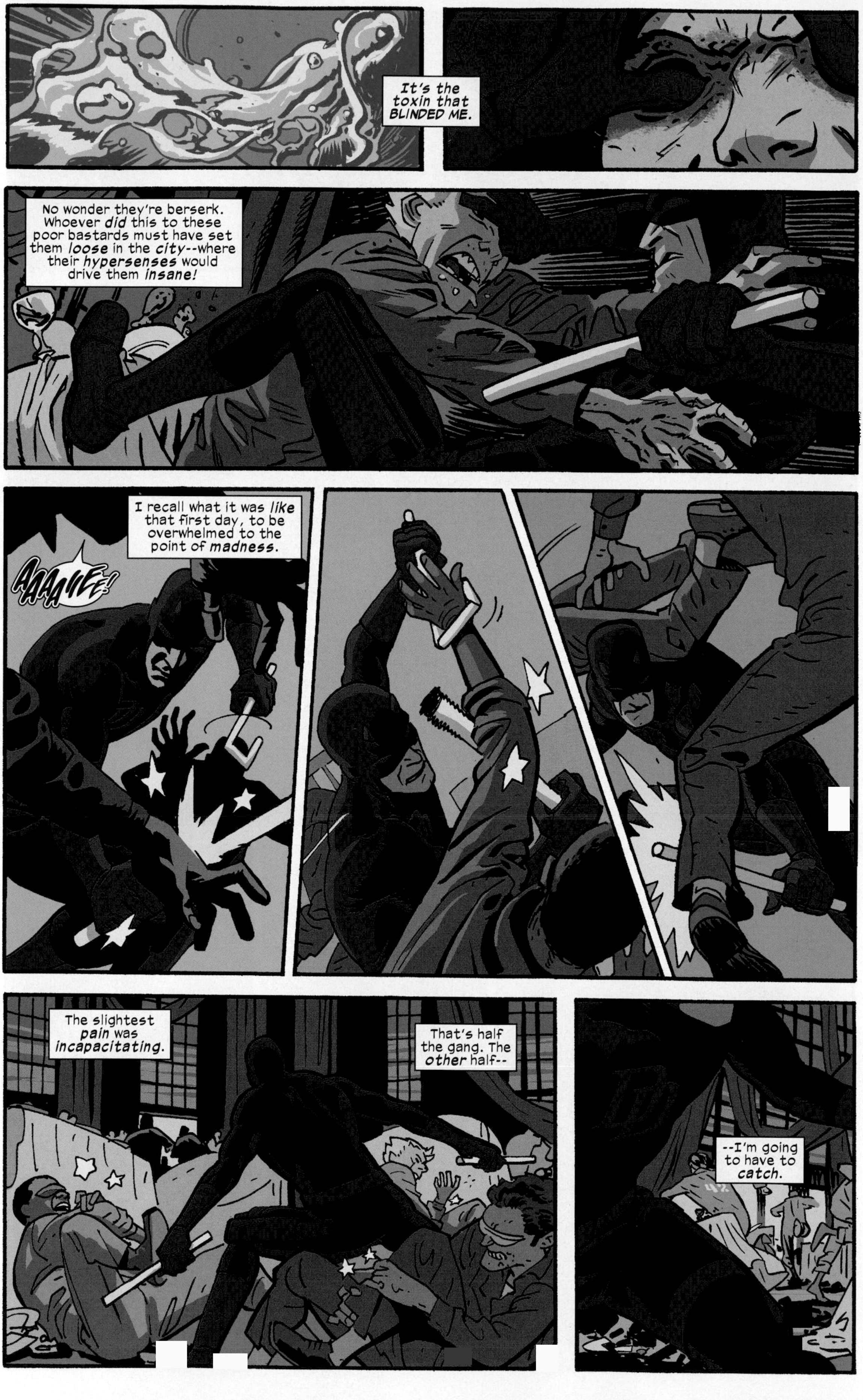

It's the toxin that BLINDED ME.
No wonder they're berserk. Whoever did this to these poor bastards must have set them loose in the city--where their hypersenses would drive them insane!
I recall what it was like that first day, to be overwhelmed to the point of madness.
AAAAUEE!
The slightest pain was incapacitating.
That's half the gang. The other half--
--I'm going to have to catch.

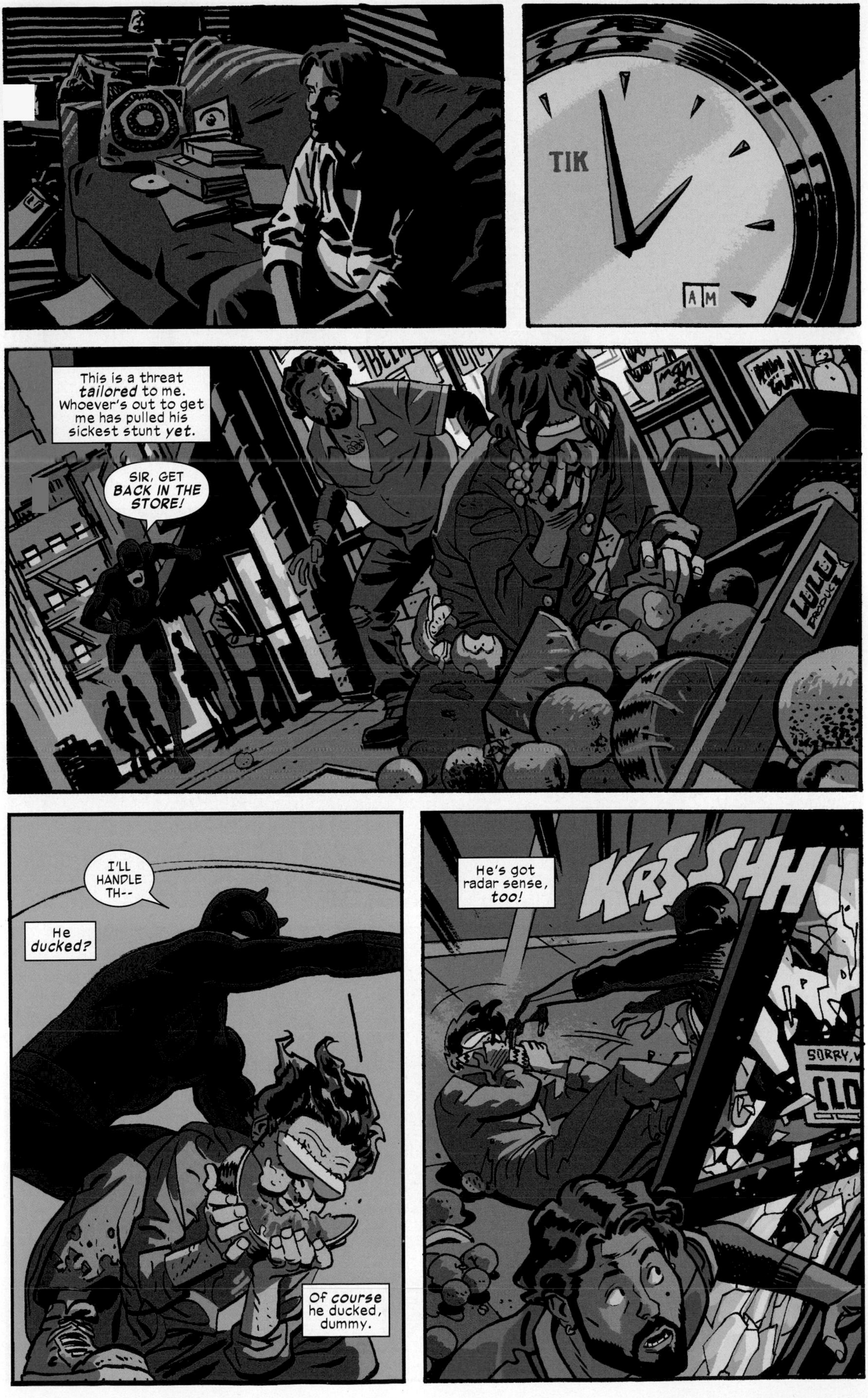
TIK
AM
This is a threat tailored to me. Whoever's out to get me has pulled his sickest stunt yet.
SIR, GET BACK IN THE STORE!
I'LL HANDLE TH--
He ducked?
Of course he ducked, dummy.
He's got radar sense, too!
KRSSHH
SORRY, W
CLO

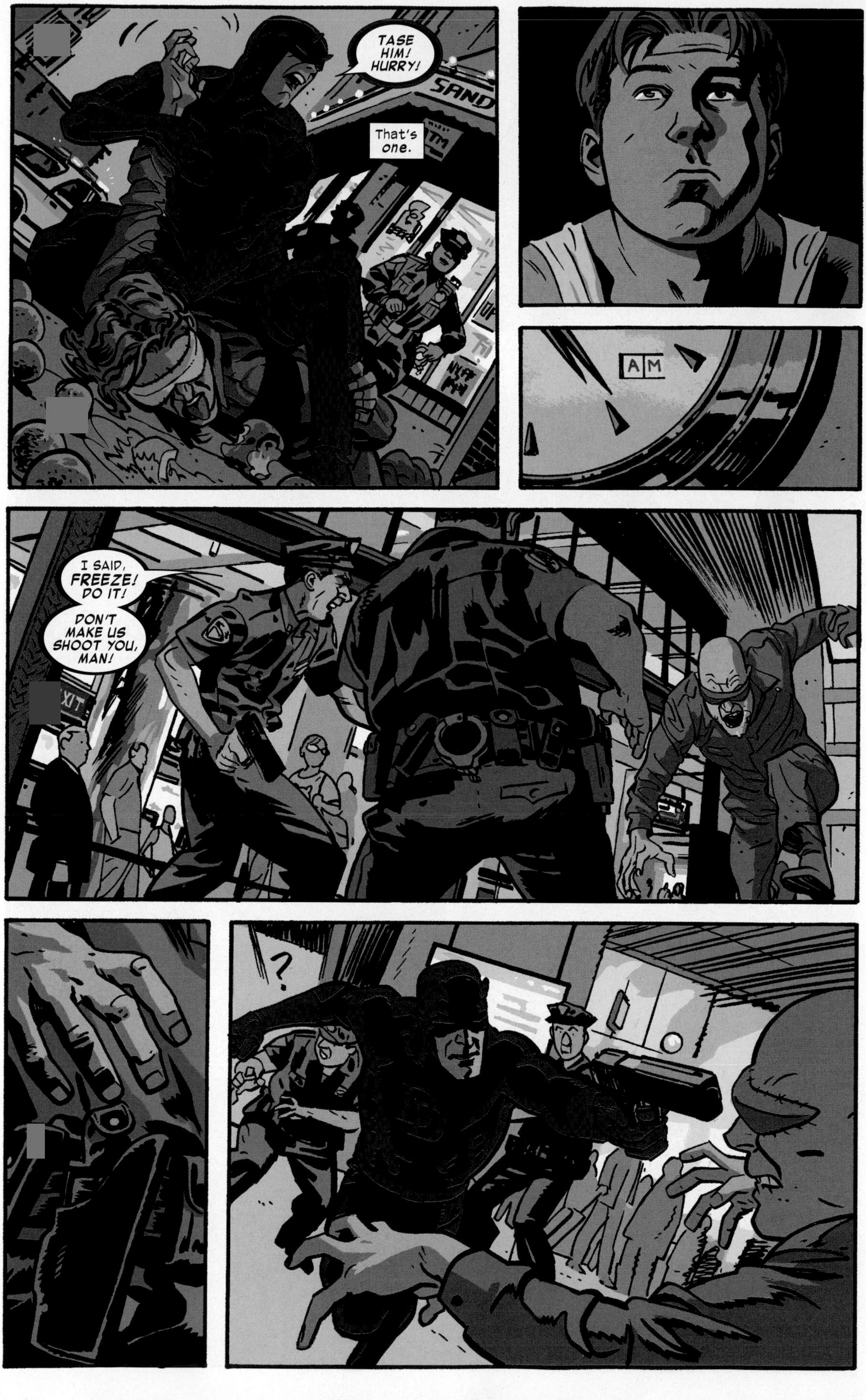
SAND
TASE HIM! HURRY!
That's one.
AM
I SAID, FREEZE! DO IT!
DON'T MAKE US SHOOT YOU, MAN!
EXIT
?

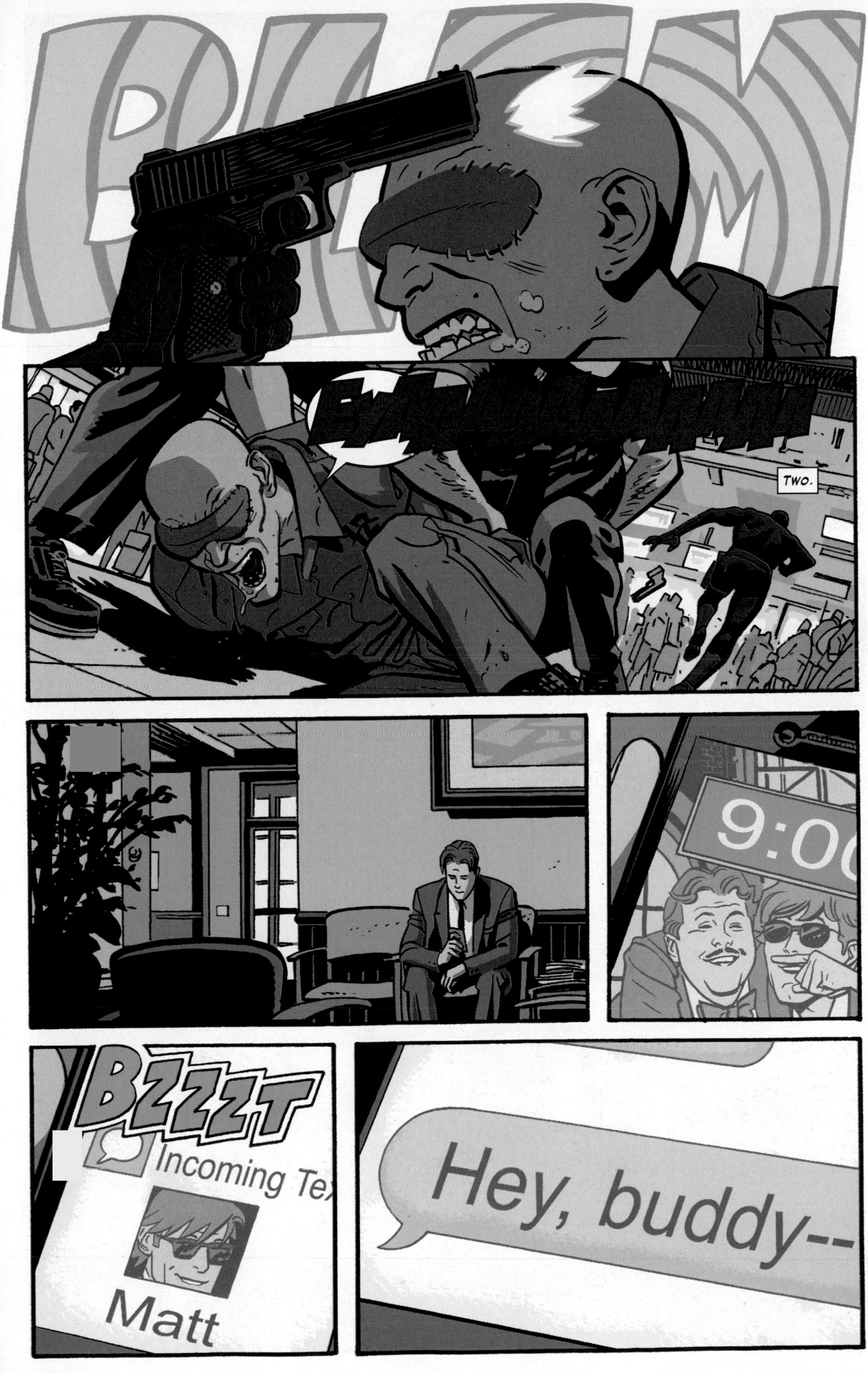
TWO.
9:0
BZZZT
Incoming Tex
Matt
Hey, buddy--

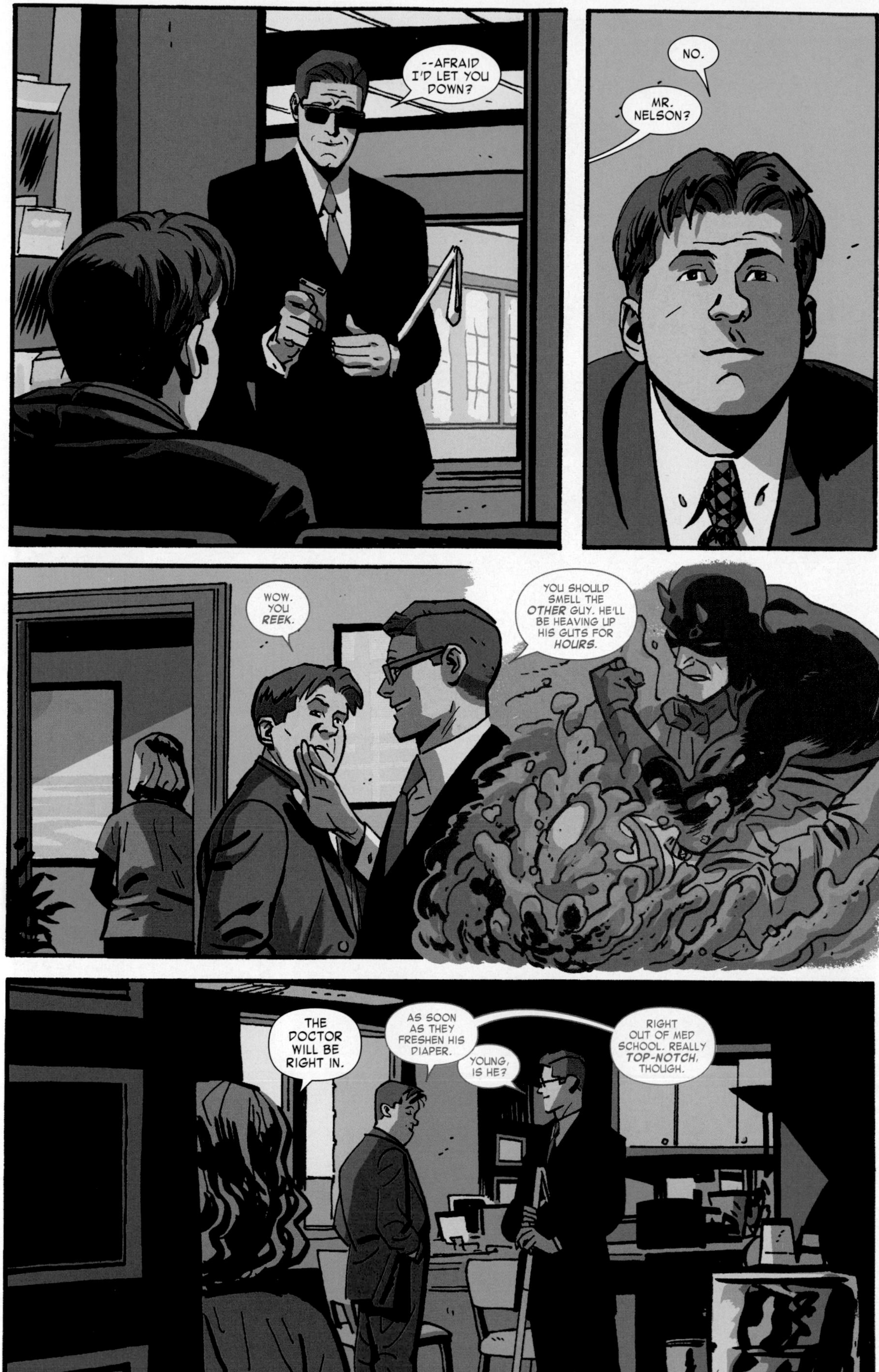
--AFRAID I'D LET YOU DOWN?
NO.
MR. NELSON?
WOW. YOU REEK.
YOU SHOULD SMELL THE OTHER GUY. HE'LL BE HEAVING UP HIS GUTS FOR HOURS.
THE DOCTOR WILL BE RIGHT IN.
AS SOON AS THEY FRESHEN HIS DIAPER.
YOUNG, IS HE?
RIGHT OUT OF MED SCHOOL. REALLY TOP-NOTCH, THOUGH.

HI, MR. NELSON. I SEE YOU BROUGHT A FRIEND.

WELL, HE HAS A THING FOR NURSES.

AH. ONE SECOND. LET ME JUST CHECK THE LAST OF THESE RESULTS...

It's gonna be okay.

It's gonna be fine. I can read the doctor. I can feel it.

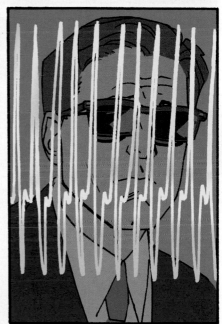

Poor Foggy, though. He's trying to play it cool, but his heartbeat's so loud, I don't even *recognize* it. It's--

It's not Foggy's.

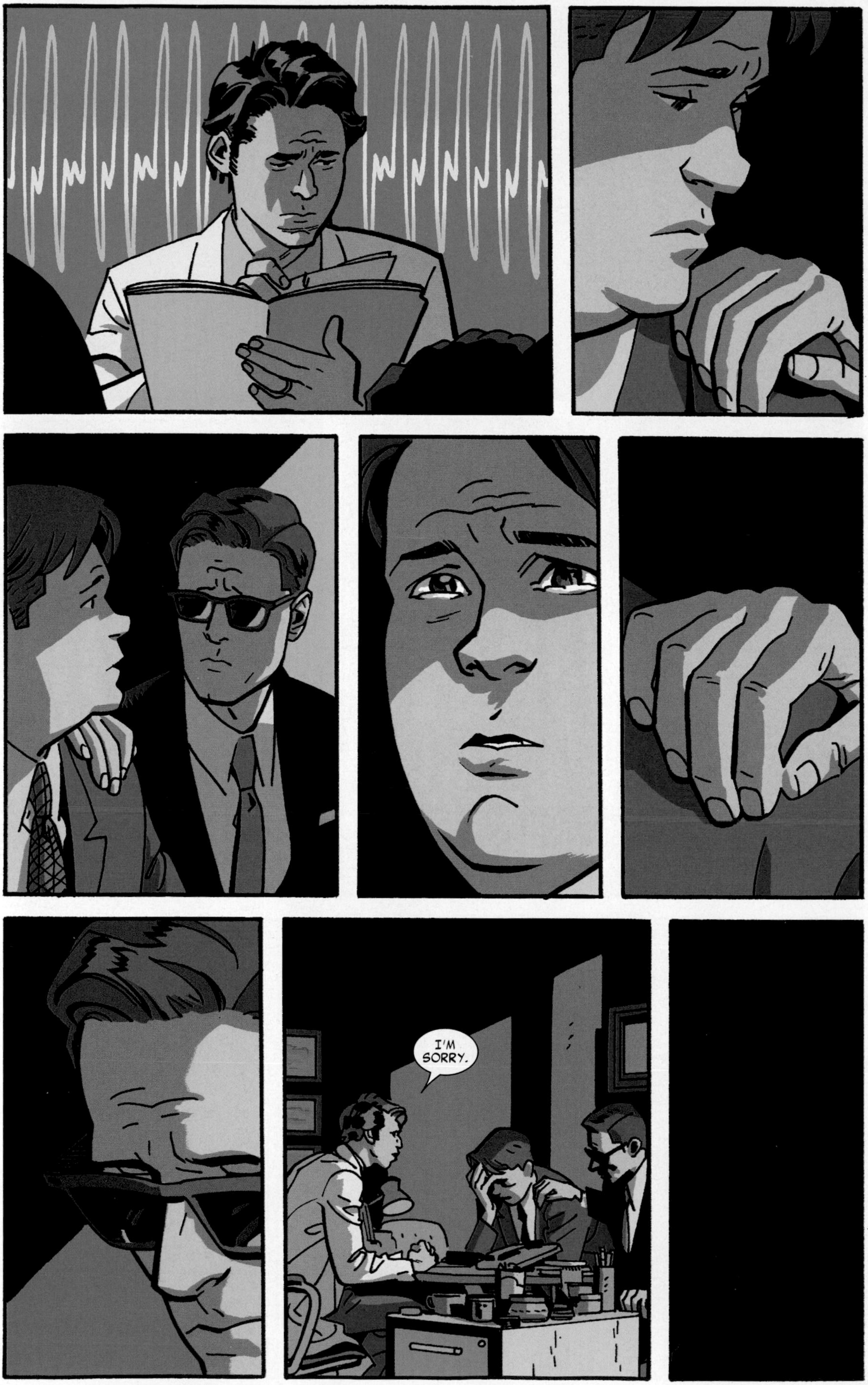
I'M SORRY.

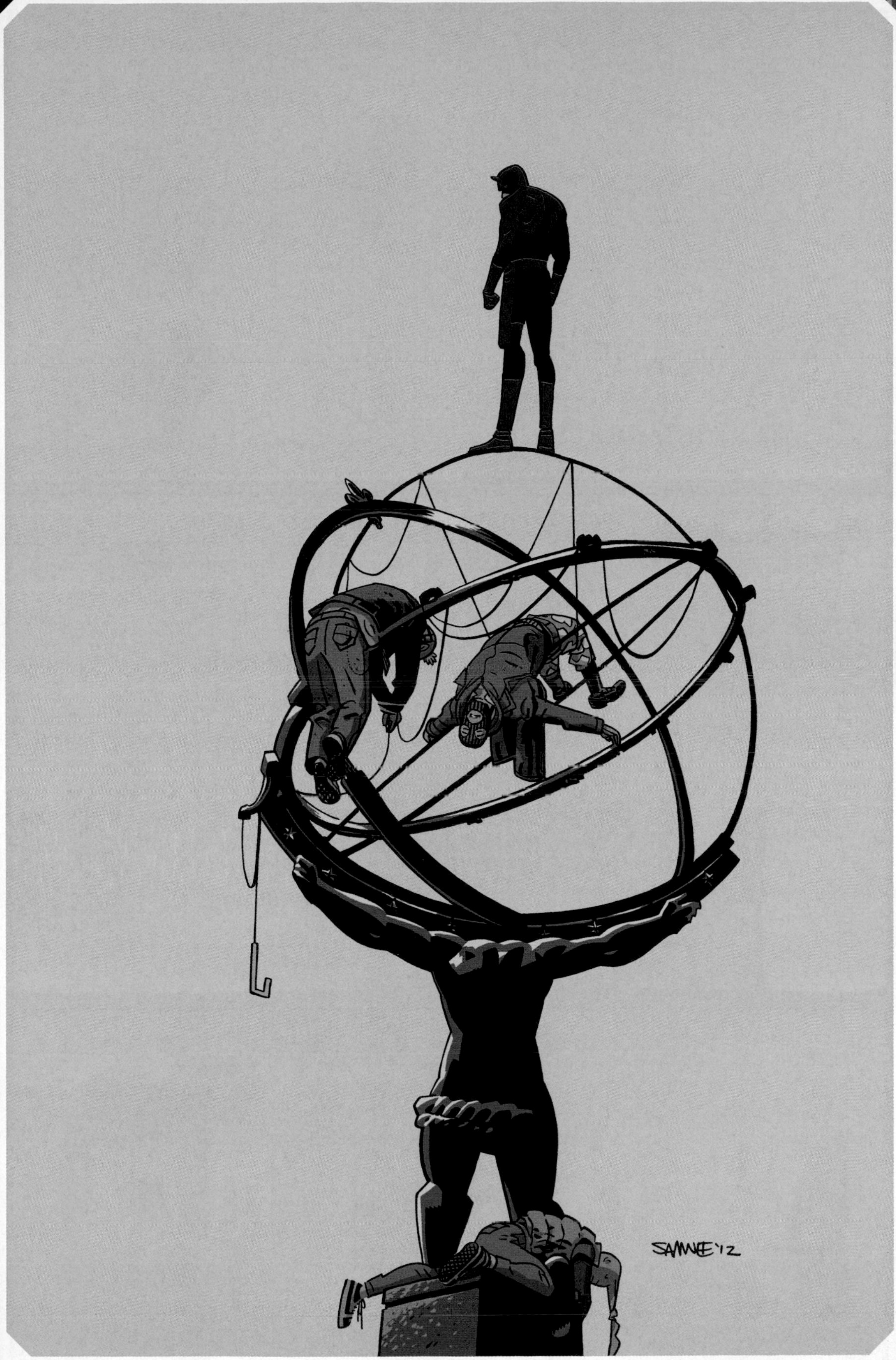
SAMNEE '12

TWENTY-FOUR

WELL, I THINK IT'S ALL COMING TOGETHER NICELY.

SURELY--HE--SUSPECTS...

WHICH--CREATES--ITS--OWN--MYSTERY...

EXCLUSIVE
Milla Donovan
wife of
DAREDEVIL

24 TIPS TO TAME YOUR MANE

Is your ma leading a double life

I DON'T FOLLOW.

The REVEALER

SAVAGE WILDERS ATTACK CITY

VILLAIN SPO KIDNAPP FROM CUSTO

YOU SENT KLAW. COYOTE. THE WILDERS.

MORE THAT HE'S LIKELY UNAWARE OF.

LOCAL INTEREST

DAILY BUGLE
KLAW CREATUR ON THE LOOSE

COYOTE'S SCHEM UNEARTHE

The REVEALER
MEGACRIME
ES EXPOSED

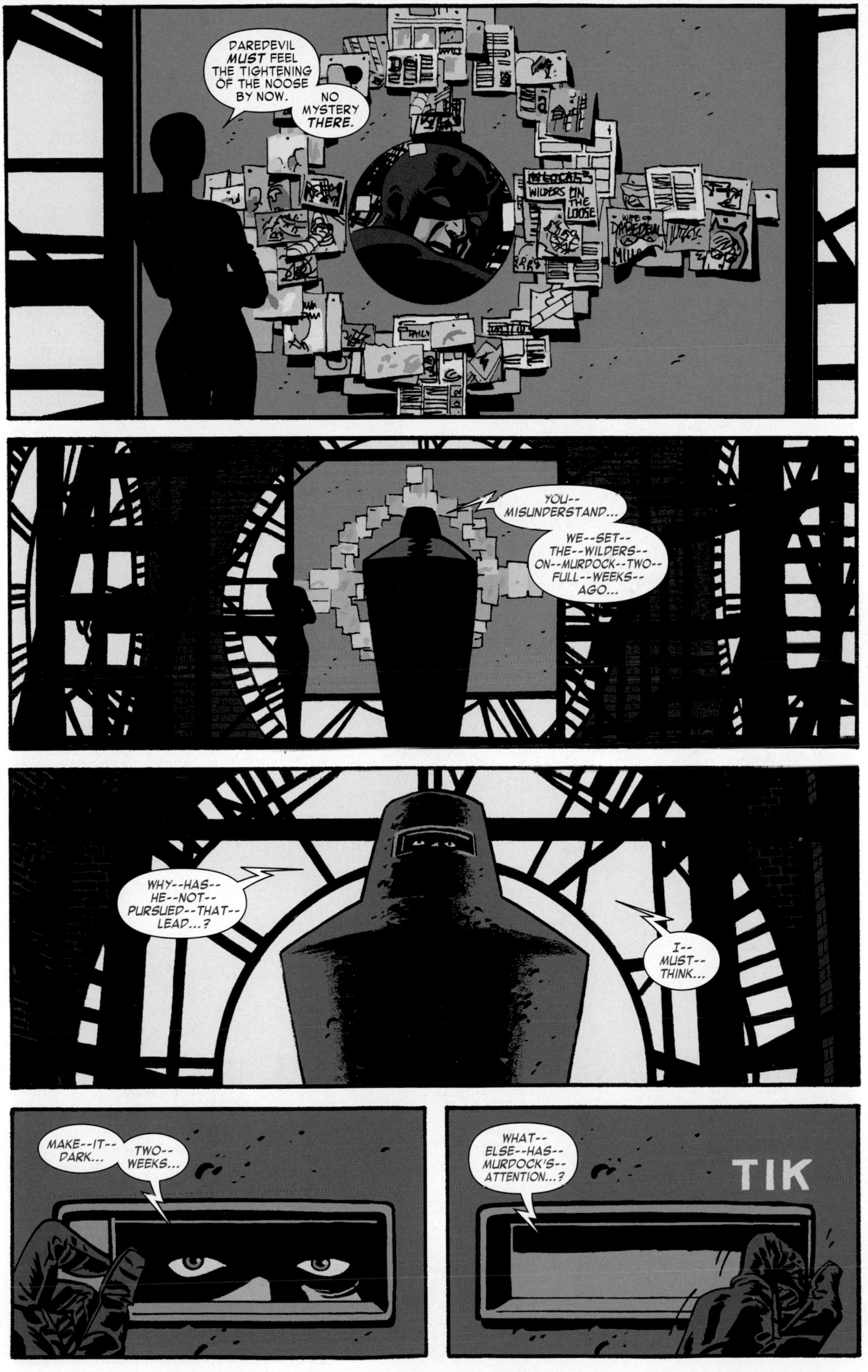
DAREDEVIL MUST FEEL THE TIGHTENING OF THE NOOSE BY NOW.
NO MYSTERY THERE.
WILDERS ON THE LOOSE
YOU-- MISUNDERSTAND...
WE--SET-- THE--WILDERS-- ON--MURDOCK--TWO-- FULL--WEEKS-- AGO...
WHY--HAS-- HE--NOT-- PURSUED--THAT-- LEAD...?
I-- MUST-- THINK...
MAKE--IT-- DARK...
TWO-- WEEKS...
WHAT-- ELSE--HAS-- MURDOCK'S-- ATTENTION...?
TIK

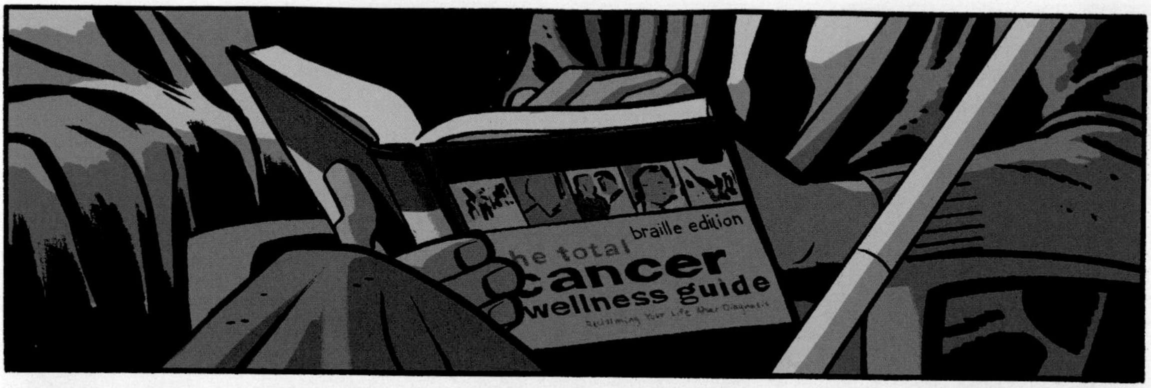
braille edition
he total
ancer
wellness guide

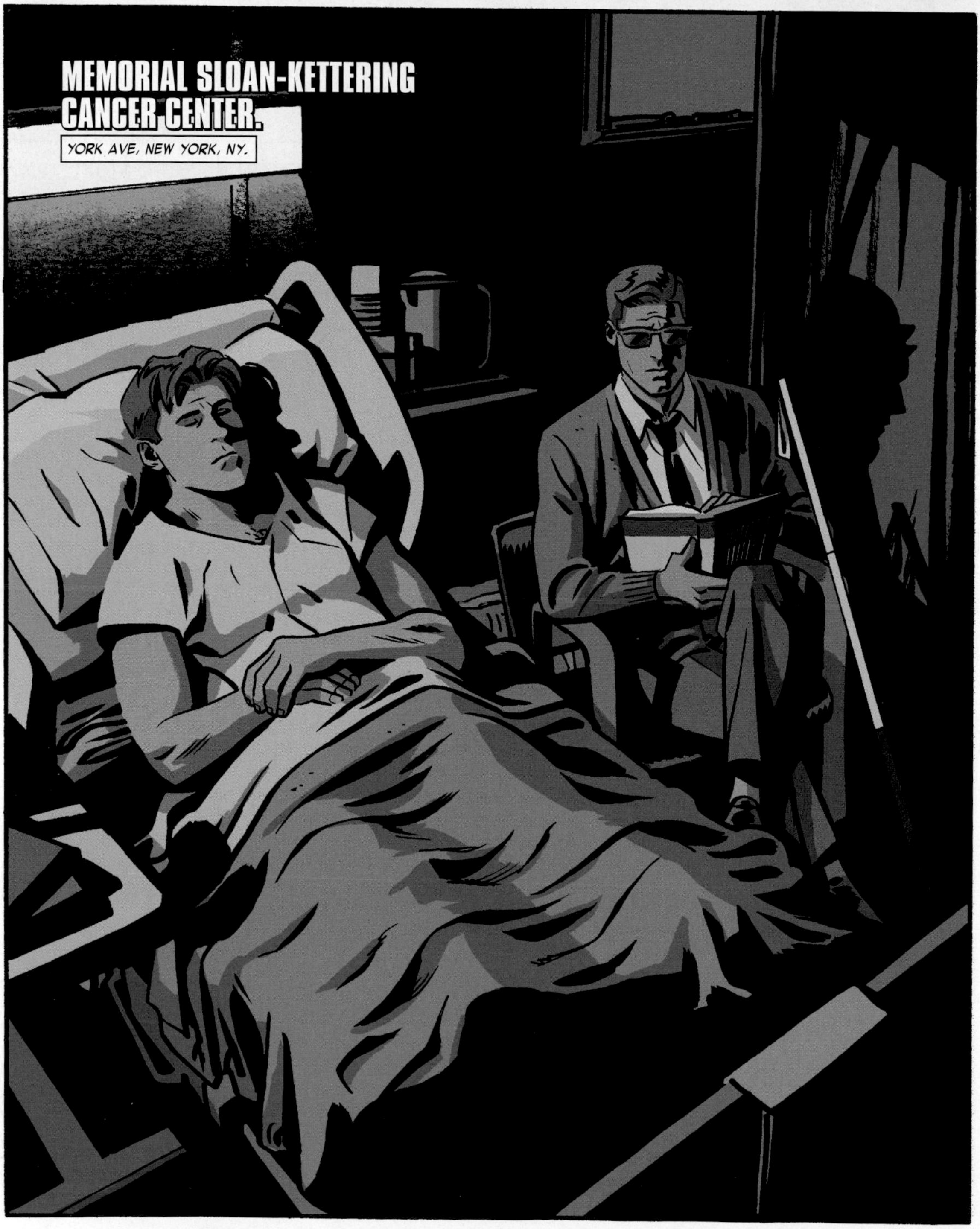
MEMORIAL SLOAN-KETTERING
CANCER CENTER.
YORK AVE, NEW YORK, NY.

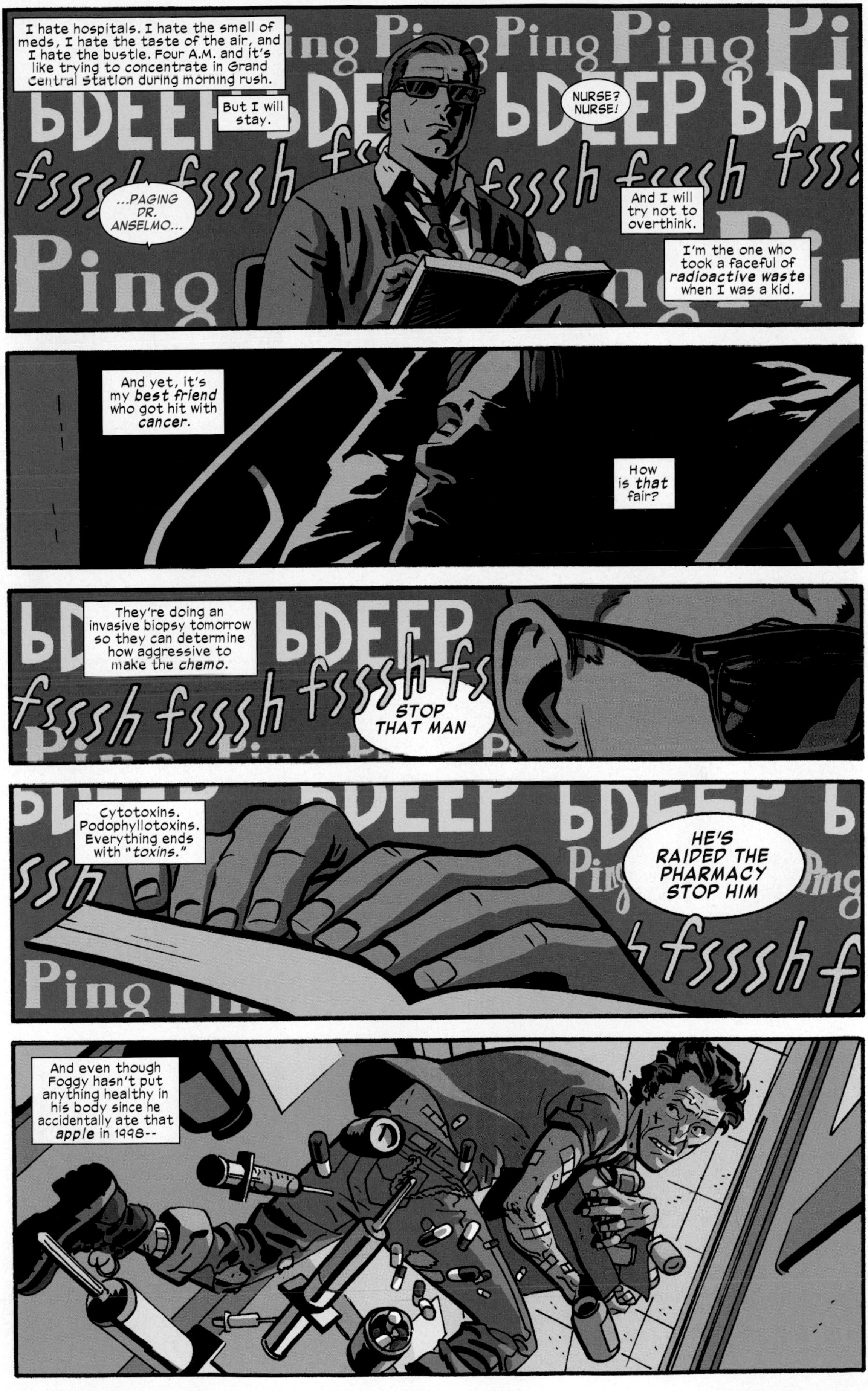

I hate hospitals. I hate the smell of meds, I hate the taste of the air, and I hate the bustle. Four A.M. and it's like trying to concentrate in Grand Central Station during morning rush.
Ping Ping Ping Ping
BDEEP BDEEP BDEEP BDE
But I will stay.
NURSE? NURSE!
fsssh fsssh fsssh fsssh fsss
...PAGING DR. ANSELMO...
And I will try not to overthink.
I'm the one who took a faceful of *radioactive waste* when I was a kid.
Ping
And yet, it's my *best friend* who got hit with *cancer*.
How is *that* fair?
BDEEP
They're doing an invasive biopsy tomorrow so they can determine how aggressive to make the *chemo*.
fsssh fsssh fsssh fs
STOP THAT MAN
BDEEP BDEEP
Cytotoxins. Podophyllotoxins. Everything ends with "*toxins.*"
HE'S RAIDED THE PHARMACY STOP HIM
fsssh
Ping
And even though Foggy hasn't put anything healthy in his body since he accidentally ate that *apple* in 1998--

--that's still going to be *rough* on him.

TOK

HNNNNH!

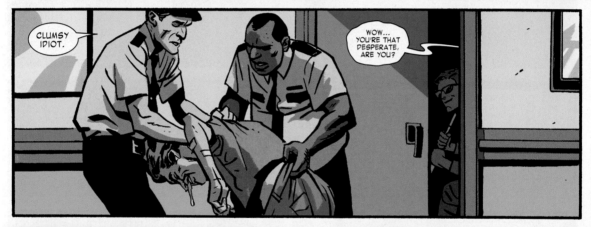

CLUMSY IDIOT.

WOW... YOU'RE THAT DESPERATE, ARE YOU?

I'M FINE.

STOP. SITTING STILL IS *KILLING* YOU. YOU'RE *DYING* FOR ACTION.

STOP *HOVERING.* I'M *GOOD.* GO FIGHT *ELECTRO* OR SOMETHING.

CITY CAN DO WITHOUT DAREDEVIL A LITTLE LONGER.

THEN GO TALK TO KIRSTEN.

I'D RATHER FIGHT *ELECTRO.*

GO.

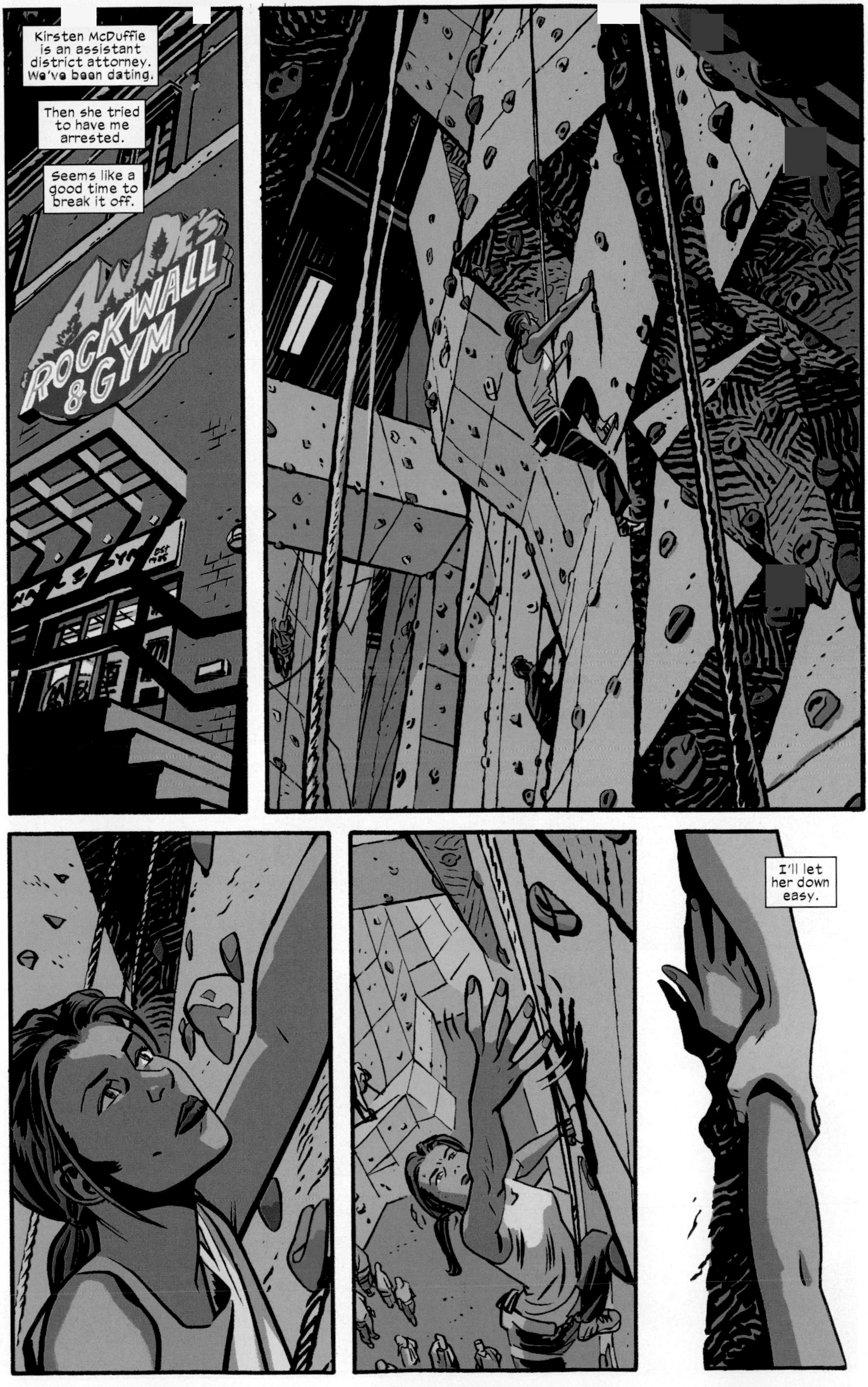
Kirsten McDuffie is an assistant district attorney. We've been dating.
Then she tried to have me arrested.
Seems like a good time to break it off.
ROCKWALL & GYM
I'll let her down easy.

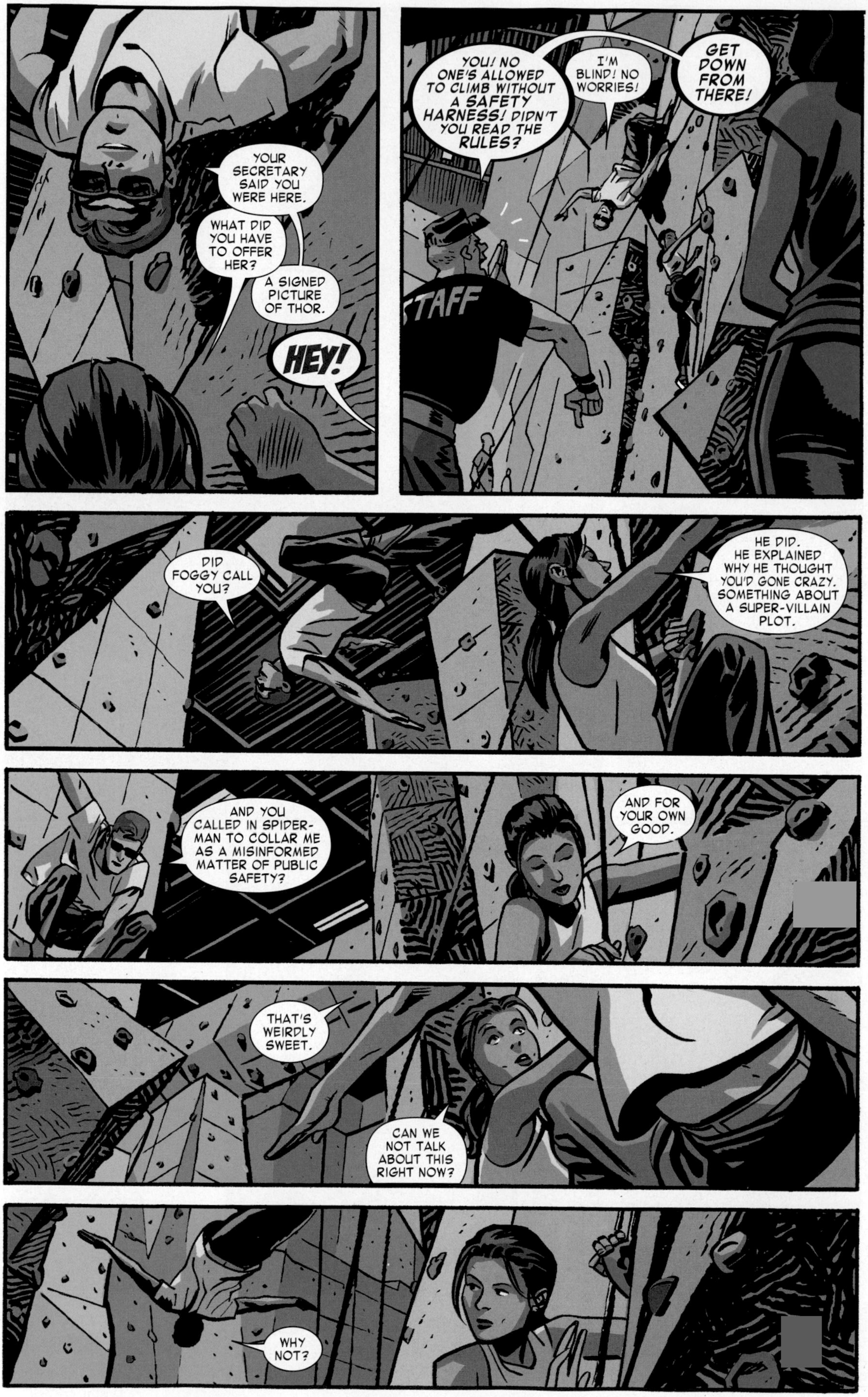
YOUR SECRETARY SAID YOU WERE HERE.
WHAT DID YOU HAVE TO OFFER HER?
A SIGNED PICTURE OF THOR.
HEY!
YOU! NO ONE'S ALLOWED TO CLIMB WITHOUT A SAFETY HARNESS! DIDN'T YOU READ THE RULES?
I'M BLIND! NO WORRIES!
GET DOWN FROM THERE!
STAFF
DID FOGGY CALL YOU?
HE DID. HE EXPLAINED WHY HE THOUGHT YOU'D GONE CRAZY. SOMETHING ABOUT A SUPER-VILLAIN PLOT.
AND YOU CALLED IN SPIDER-MAN TO COLLAR ME AS A MISINFORMED MATTER OF PUBLIC SAFETY?
AND FOR YOUR OWN GOOD.
THAT'S WEIRDLY SWEET.
CAN WE NOT TALK ABOUT THIS RIGHT NOW?
WHY NOT?

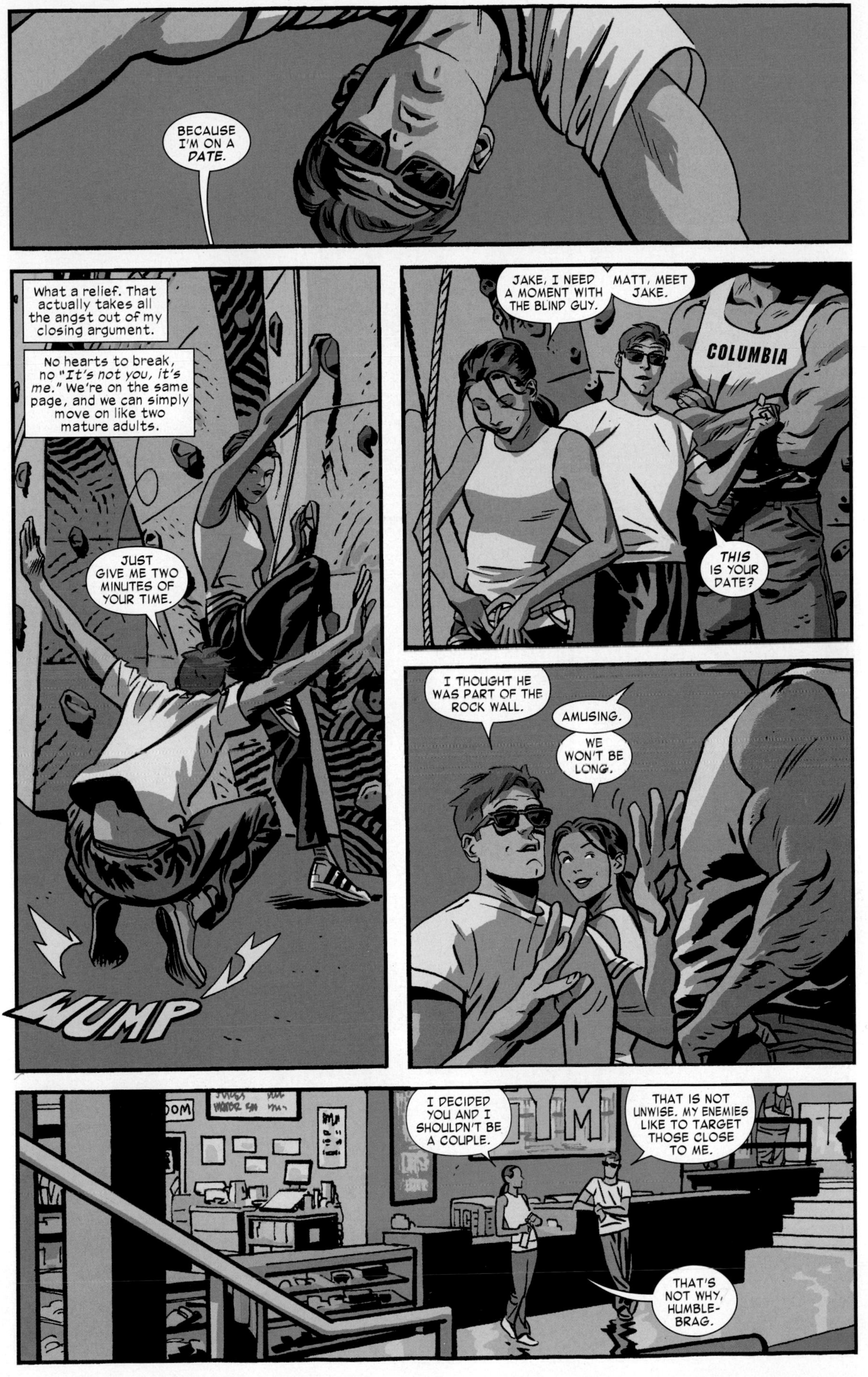
BECAUSE I'M ON A *DATE.*
What a relief. That actually takes all the angst out of my closing argument.
No hearts to break, no "*It's not you, it's me.*" We're on the same page, and we can simply move on like two mature adults.
JUST GIVE ME TWO MINUTES OF YOUR TIME.
WUMP
JAKE, I NEED A MOMENT WITH THE BLIND GUY.
MATT, MEET JAKE.
COLUMBIA
THIS IS YOUR DATE?
I THOUGHT HE WAS PART OF THE ROCK WALL.
AMUSING.
WE WON'T BE LONG.
I DECIDED YOU AND I SHOULDN'T BE A COUPLE.
THAT IS NOT UNWISE. MY ENEMIES LIKE TO TARGET THOSE CLOSE TO ME.
THAT'S NOT WHY, HUMBLE-BRAG.

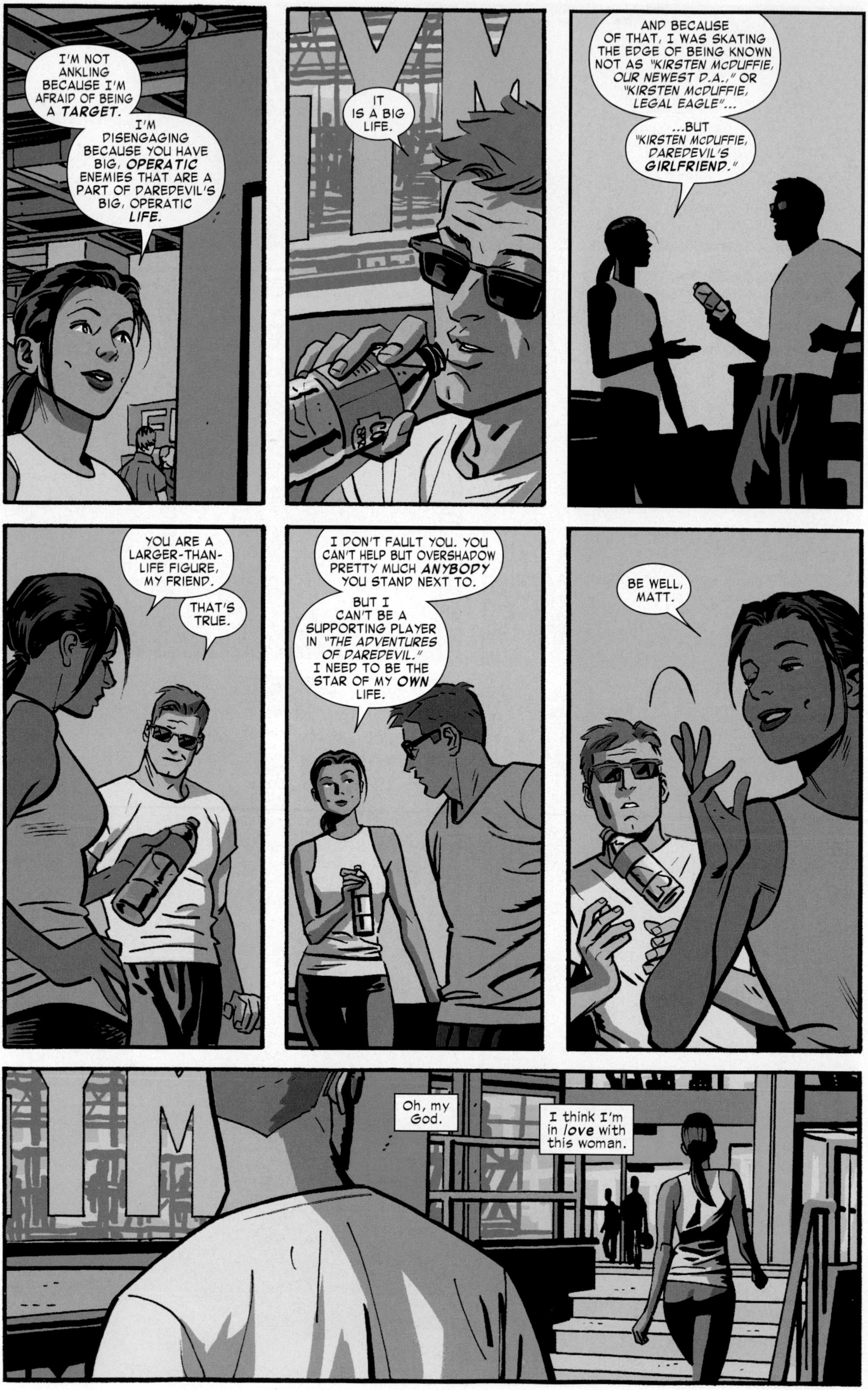
I'M NOT ANKLING BECAUSE I'M AFRAID OF BEING A TARGET.
I'M DISENGAGING BECAUSE YOU HAVE BIG, OPERATIC ENEMIES THAT ARE A PART OF DAREDEVIL'S BIG, OPERATIC LIFE.
IT IS A BIG LIFE.
AND BECAUSE OF THAT, I WAS SKATING THE EDGE OF BEING KNOWN NOT AS "KIRSTEN McDUFFIE, OUR NEWEST D.A.," OR "KIRSTEN McDUFFIE, LEGAL EAGLE"...
...BUT "KIRSTEN McDUFFIE, DAREDEVIL'S GIRLFRIEND."
YOU ARE A LARGER-THAN-LIFE FIGURE, MY FRIEND.
THAT'S TRUE.
I DON'T FAULT YOU. YOU CAN'T HELP BUT OVERSHADOW PRETTY MUCH ANYBODY YOU STAND NEXT TO.
BUT I CAN'T BE A SUPPORTING PLAYER IN "THE ADVENTURES OF DAREDEVIL." I NEED TO BE THE STAR OF MY OWN LIFE.
BE WELL, MATT.
Oh, my God.
I think I'm in love with this woman.

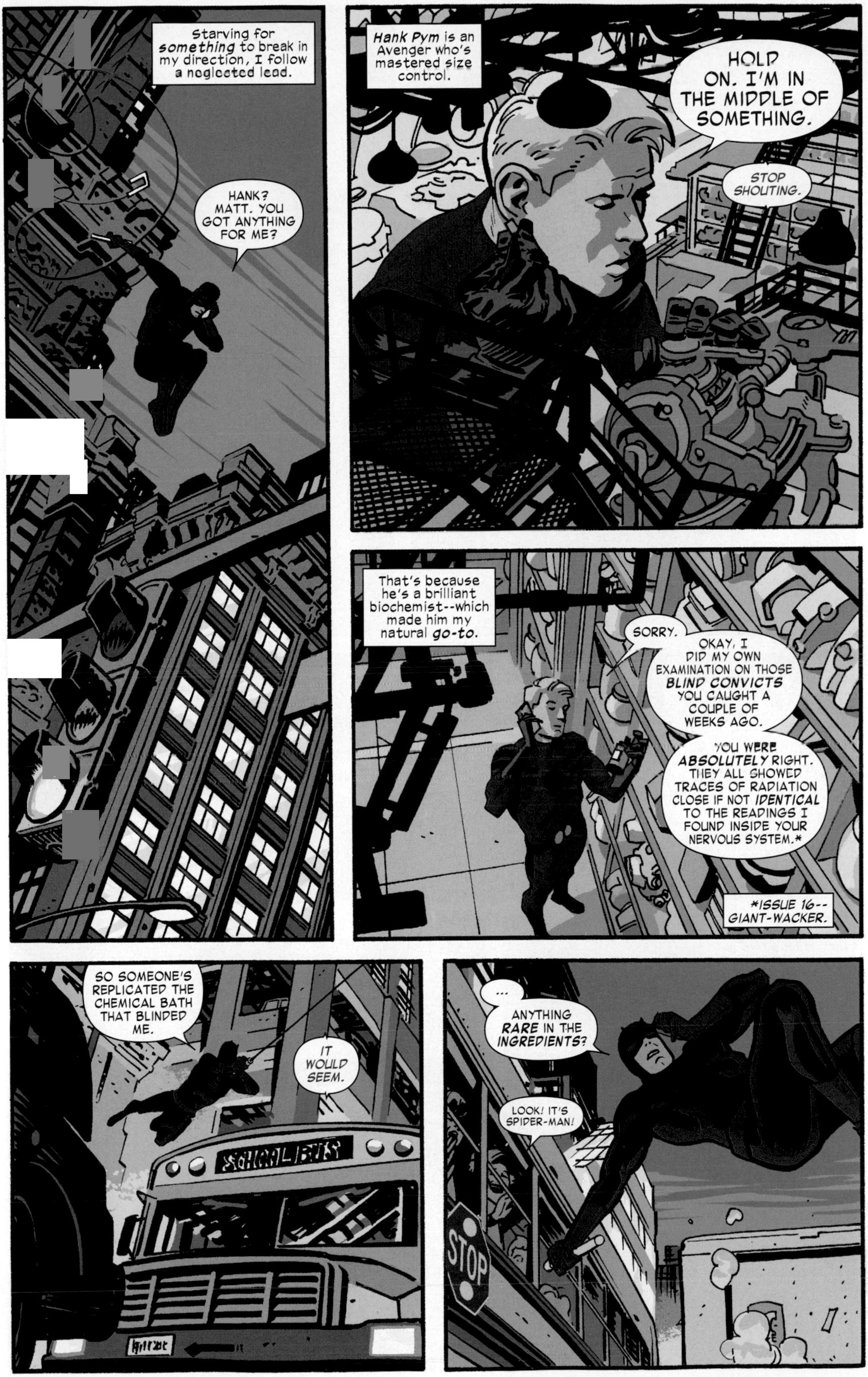
Starving for *something* to break in my direction, I follow a neglected lead.
HANK? MATT. YOU GOT ANYTHING FOR ME?
Hank Pym is an Avenger who's mastered size control.
HOLD ON. I'M IN THE MIDDLE OF SOMETHING.
STOP SHOUTING.
That's because he's a brilliant biochemist--which made him my natural *go-to*.
SORRY.
OKAY, I DID MY OWN EXAMINATION ON THOSE *BLIND CONVICTS* YOU CAUGHT A COUPLE OF WEEKS AGO.
YOU WERE *ABSOLUTELY* RIGHT. THEY ALL SHOWED TRACES OF RADIATION CLOSE IF NOT *IDENTICAL* TO THE READINGS I FOUND INSIDE YOUR NERVOUS SYSTEM.*
*ISSUE 16-- GIANT-WACKER.
SO SOMEONE'S REPLICATED THE CHEMICAL BATH THAT BLINDED ME.
IT WOULD SEEM.
SCHOOL BUS
...
ANYTHING *RARE* IN THE *INGREDIENTS*?
LOOK! IT'S SPIDER-MAN!
STOP

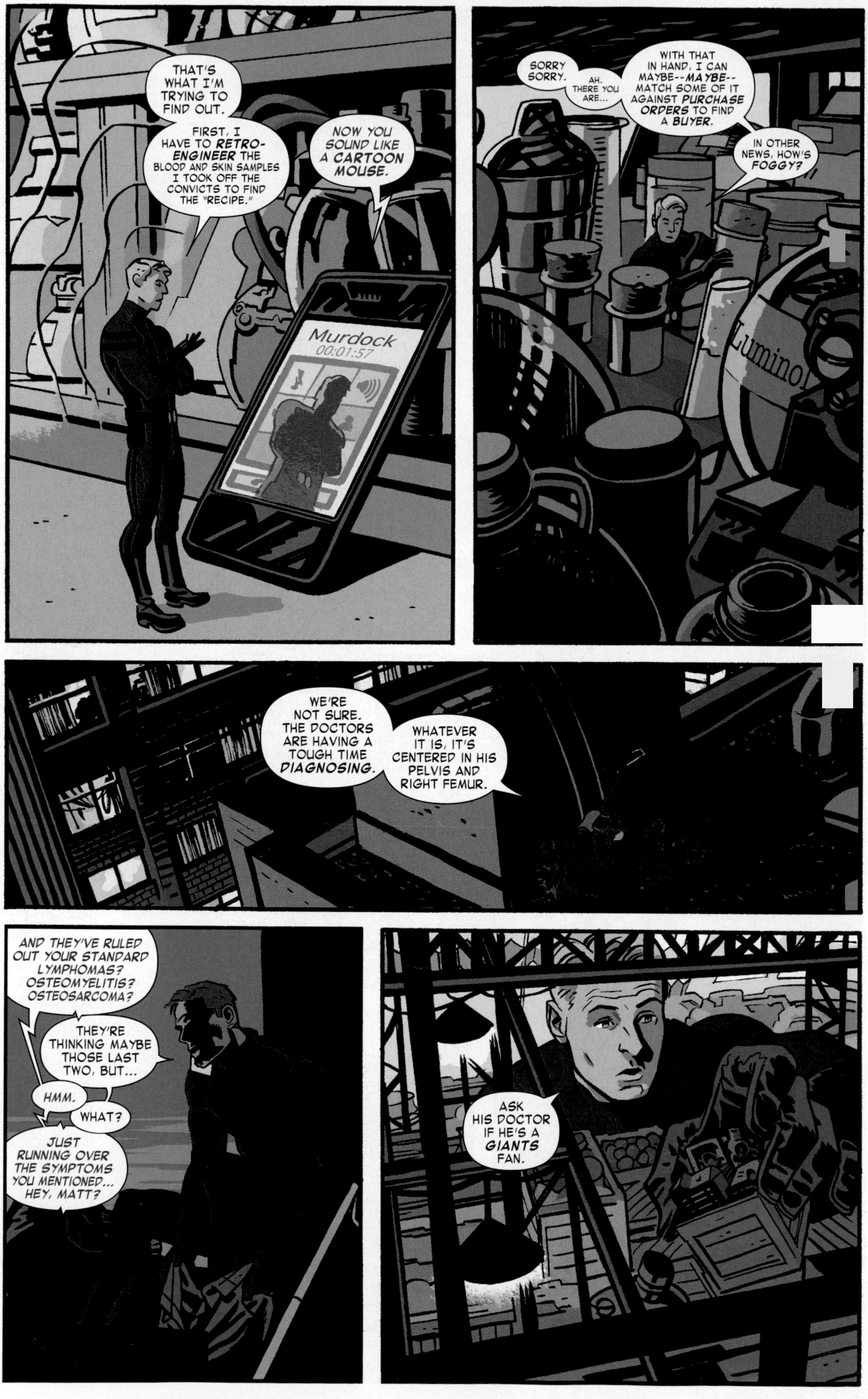
THAT'S WHAT I'M TRYING TO FIND OUT.
FIRST, I HAVE TO RETRO-ENGINEER THE BLOOD AND SKIN SAMPLES I TOOK OFF THE CONVICTS TO FIND THE "RECIPE."
NOW YOU SOUND LIKE A CARTOON MOUSE.
Murdock
00:01:57
SORRY SORRY.
AH. THERE YOU ARE...
WITH THAT IN HAND, I CAN MAYBE--MAYBE--MATCH SOME OF IT AGAINST PURCHASE ORDERS TO FIND A BUYER.
IN OTHER NEWS, HOW'S FOGGY?
Luminol
WE'RE NOT SURE. THE DOCTORS ARE HAVING A TOUGH TIME DIAGNOSING.
WHATEVER IT IS, IT'S CENTERED IN HIS PELVIS AND RIGHT FEMUR.
AND THEY'VE RULED OUT YOUR STANDARD LYMPHOMAS? OSTEOMYELITIS? OSTEOSARCOMA?
THEY'RE THINKING MAYBE THOSE LAST TWO, BUT...
HMM.
WHAT?
JUST RUNNING OVER THE SYMPTOMS YOU MENTIONED... HEY, MATT?
ASK HIS DOCTOR IF HE'S A GIANTS FAN.

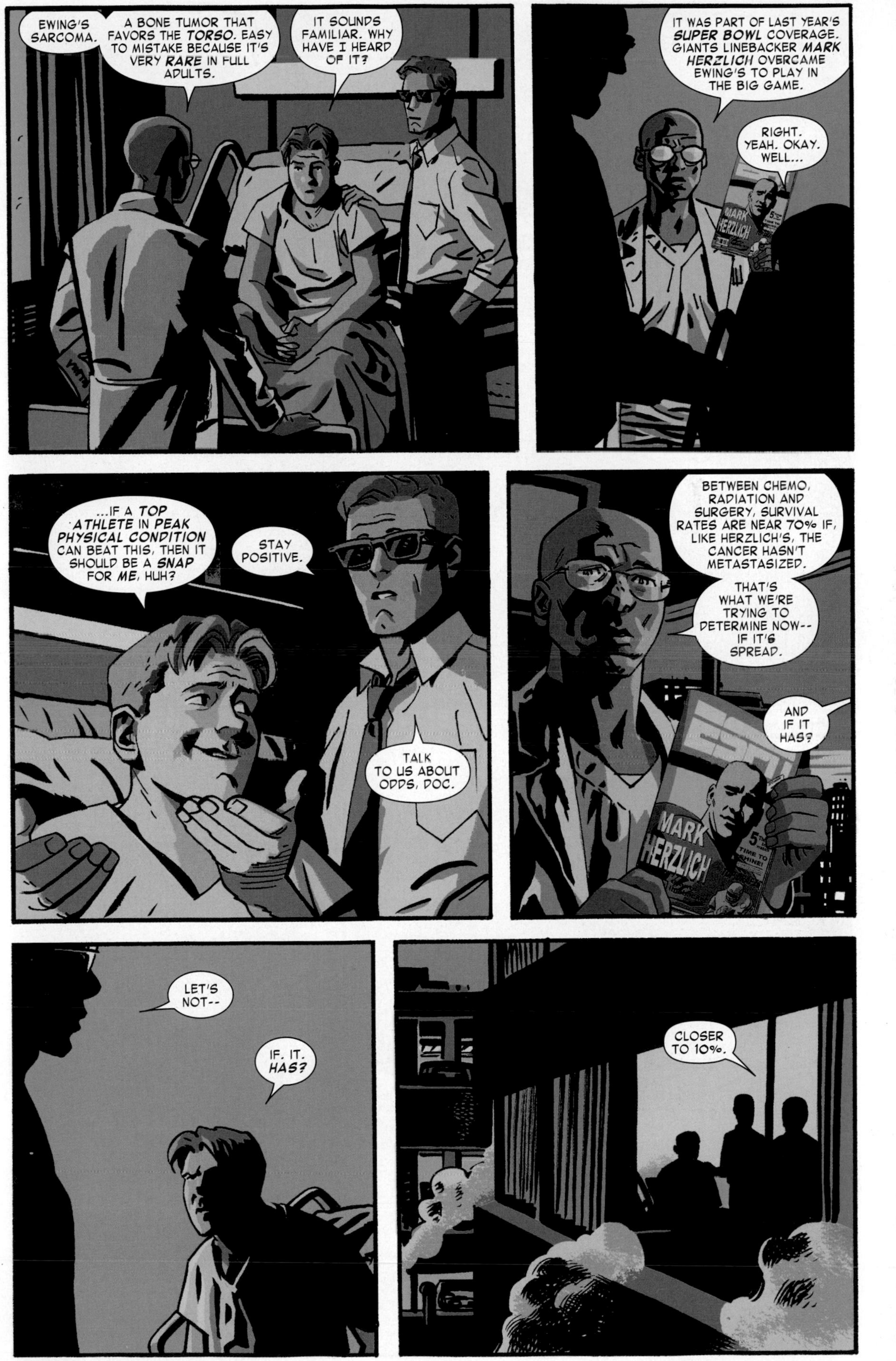
EWING'S SARCOMA.
A BONE TUMOR THAT FAVORS THE *TORSO*. EASY TO MISTAKE BECAUSE IT'S VERY *RARE* IN FULL ADULTS.
IT SOUNDS FAMILIAR. WHY HAVE I HEARD OF IT?
IT WAS PART OF LAST YEAR'S *SUPER BOWL* COVERAGE. GIANTS LINEBACKER *MARK HERZLICH* OVERCAME EWING'S TO PLAY IN THE BIG GAME.
RIGHT. YEAH. OKAY. WELL...
MARK HERZLICH
...IF A *TOP ATHLETE* IN *PEAK PHYSICAL CONDITION* CAN BEAT THIS, THEN IT SHOULD BE A *SNAP* FOR *ME*, HUH?
STAY POSITIVE.
TALK TO US ABOUT ODDS, DOC.
BETWEEN CHEMO, RADIATION AND SURGERY, SURVIVAL RATES ARE NEAR 70% IF, LIKE HERZLICH'S, THE CANCER HASN'T METASTASIZED.
THAT'S WHAT WE'RE TRYING TO DETERMINE NOW-- IF IT'S SPREAD.
AND IF IT HAS?
MARK HERZLICH
TIME TO SHINE!
LET'S NOT--
IF. IT. *HAS?*
CLOSER TO 10%.

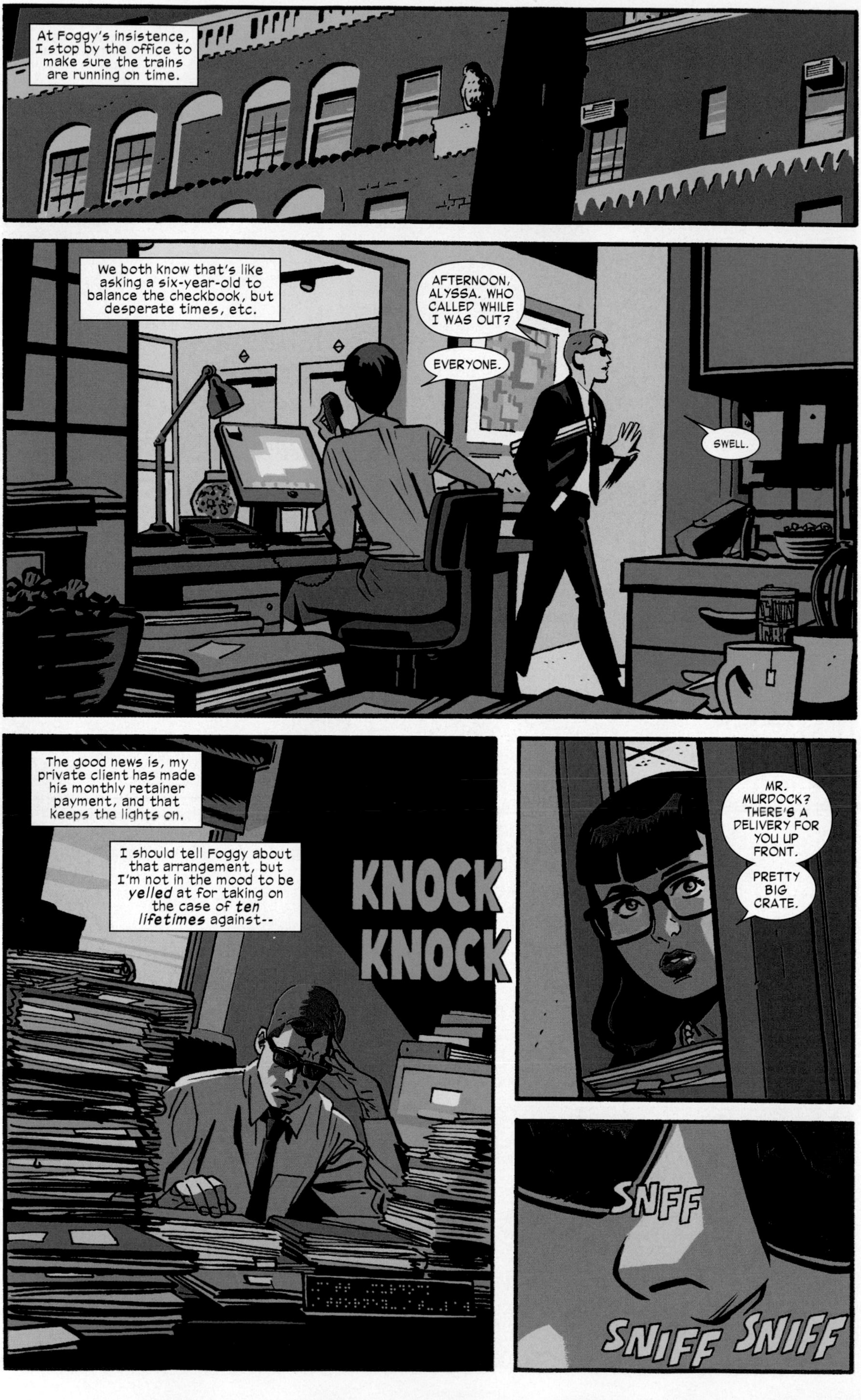

At Foggy's insistence, I stop by the office to make sure the trains are running on time.
We both know that's like asking a six-year-old to balance the checkbook, but desperate times, etc.
AFTERNOON, ALYSSA. WHO CALLED WHILE I WAS OUT?
EVERYONE.
SWELL.
The good news is, my private client has made his monthly retainer payment, and that keeps the lights on.
I should tell Foggy about that arrangement, but I'm not in the mood to be *yelled* at for taking on the case of *ten lifetimes* against--
KNOCK KNOCK
MR. MURDOCK? THERE'S A DELIVERY FOR YOU UP FRONT.
PRETTY BIG CRATE.
SNFF
SNIFF SNIFF

The smell--!

DON'T OPEN THAT!

PRIVATE

Someone's trying to make more *Daredevils* with a uniquely odorous *chemical stew.*

skritch

They tried it on *humans.*

WHAT'S *IN* THERE?

NO LABEL.

GO GET A CROWBAR.

ORDER A DISHWASHER?

skritch

SKRITCH

SKRITCH

But you *never* test on *humans* first.

GET AWAY FROM THERE!

DON'T OPEN THE BOX!

MR. MURDOCK, WHAT'S WRONG--?

NELSON & MURDOCK
LAW OFFICES
NEW YORK, NY

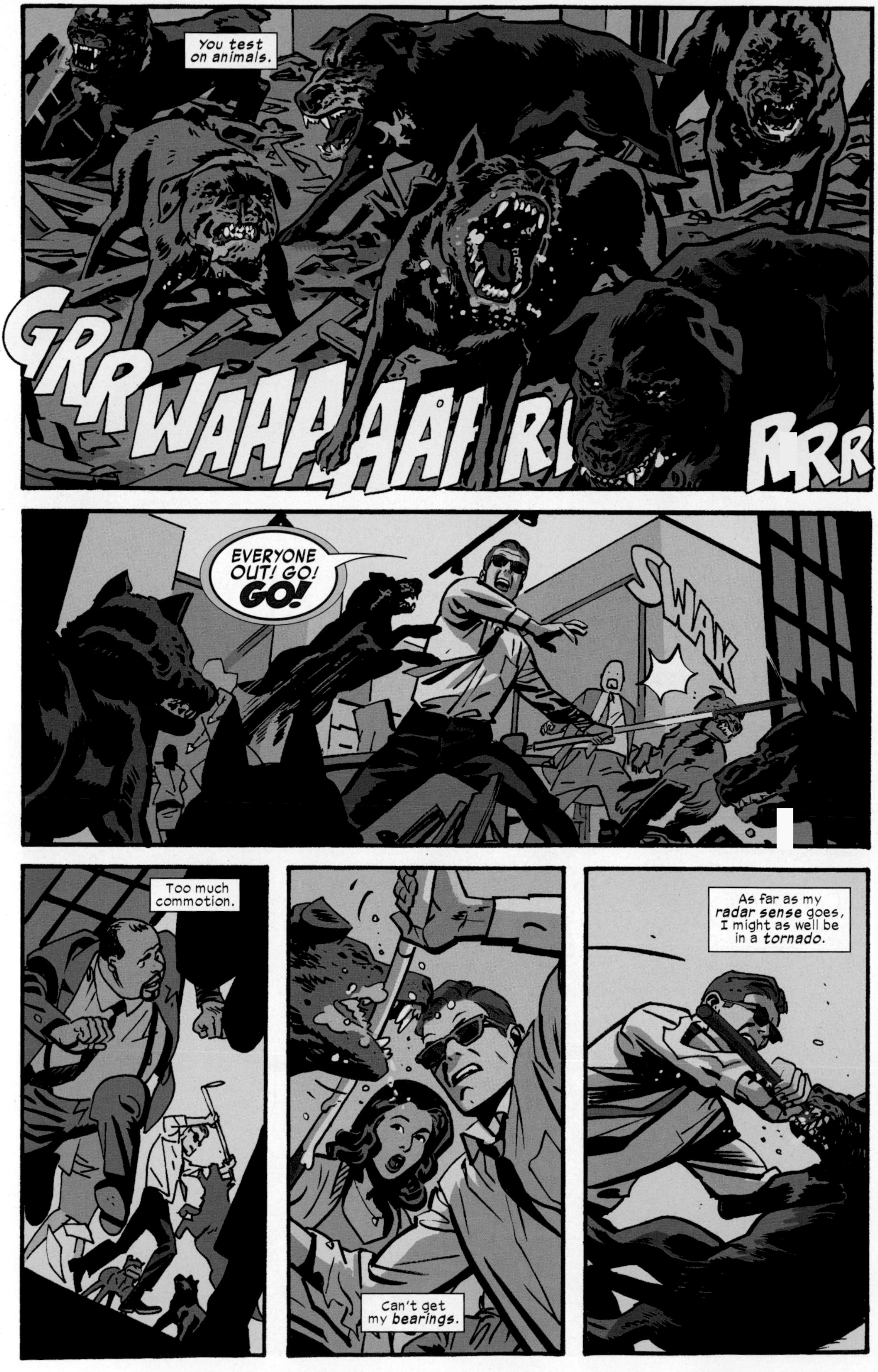
You test on animals.
GRRWAAAAAARRRRRR
EVERYONE OUT! GO! GO!
SWAK
Too much commotion.
Can't get my *bearings*.
As far as my *radar sense* goes, I might as well be in a *tornado*.

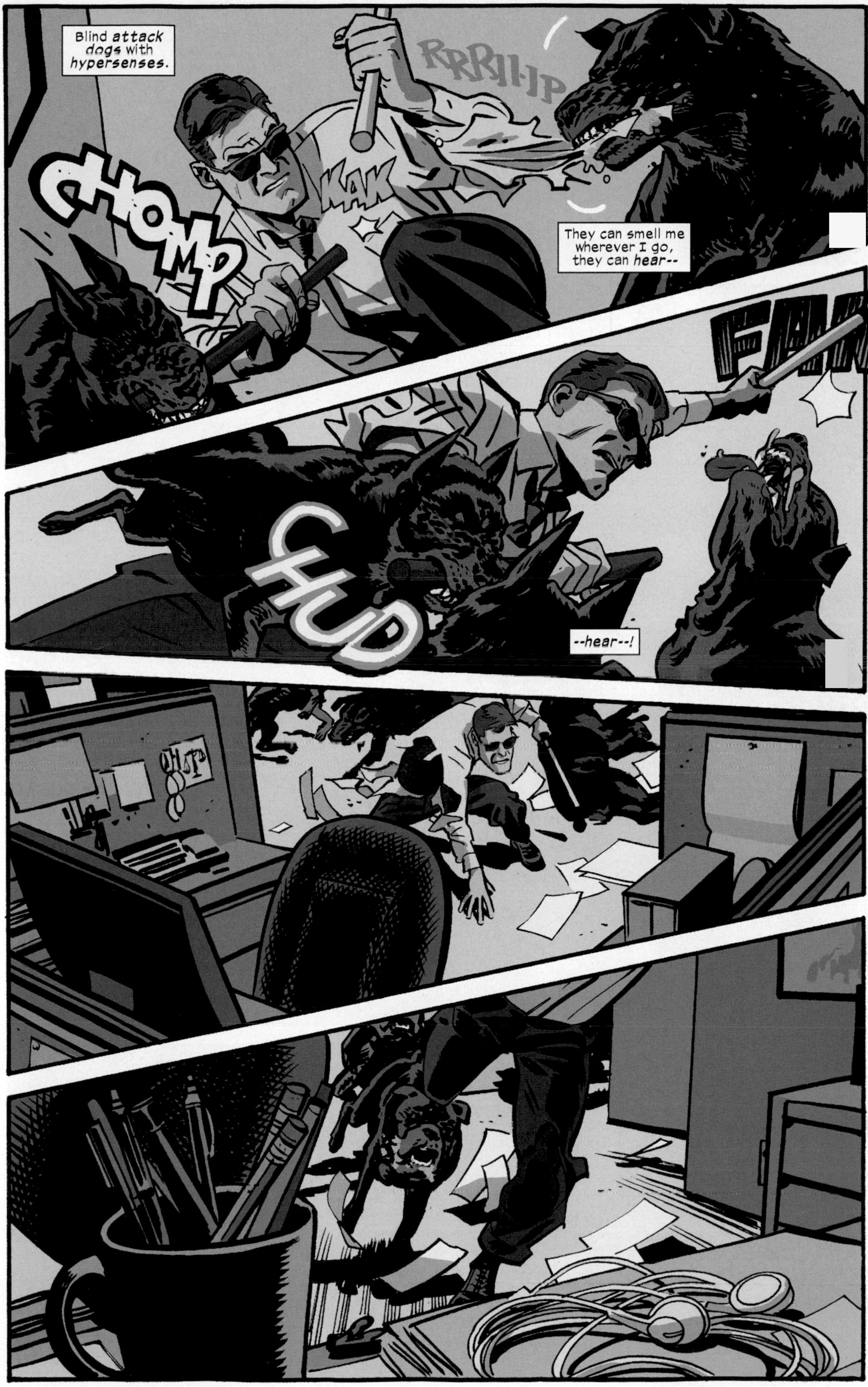
Blind attack dogs with hypersenses.
RRRIII-IP
CHOMP
KAK
They can smell me wherever I go, they can hear--
FAAK
CHUD
--hear--!

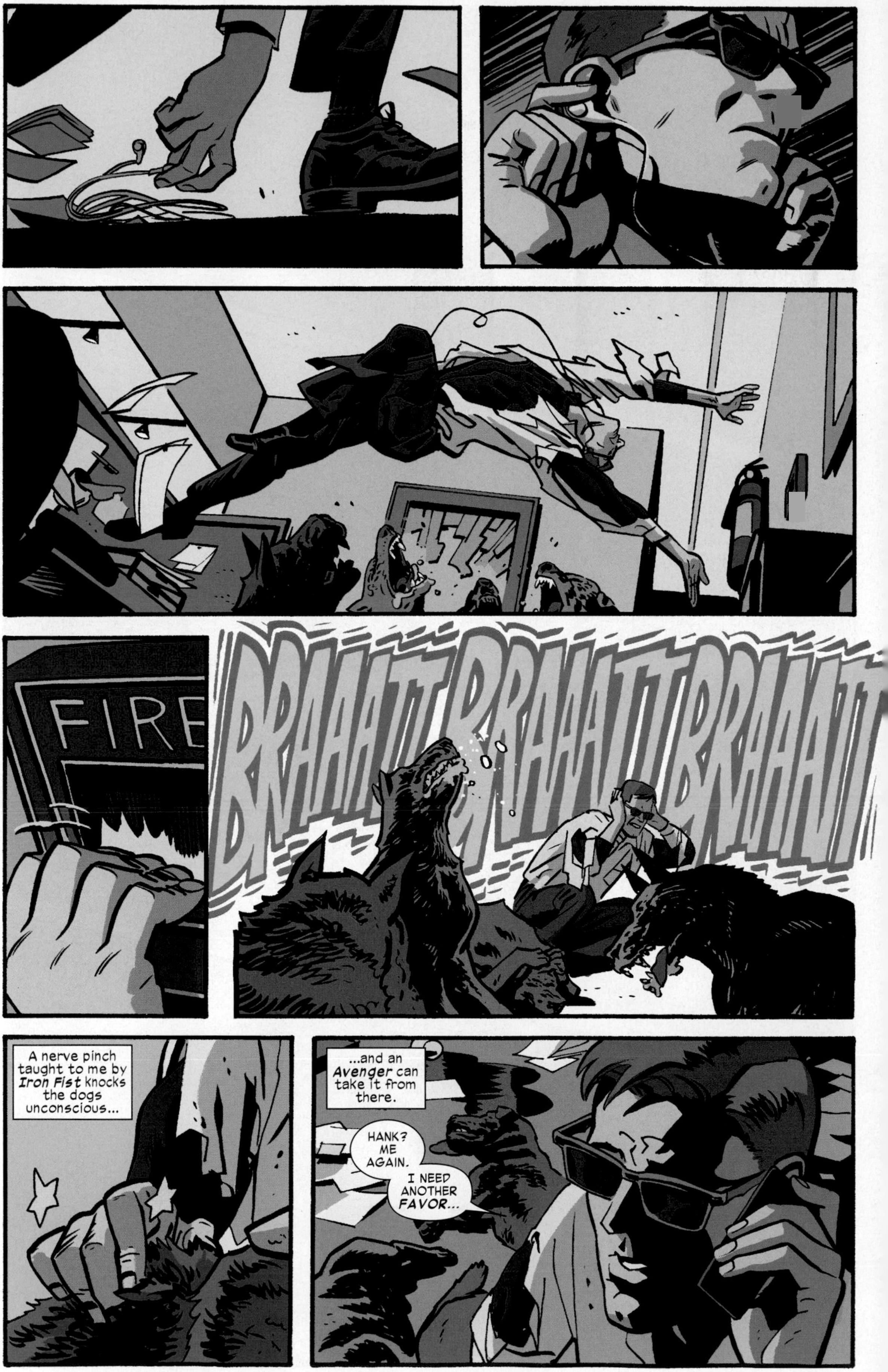
FIRE
BRAAAT! BRAAAT! BRAAAT!
A nerve pinch taught to me by Iron Fist knocks the dogs unconscious...
...and an Avenger can take it from there.
HANK? ME AGAIN.
I NEED ANOTHER FAVOR...

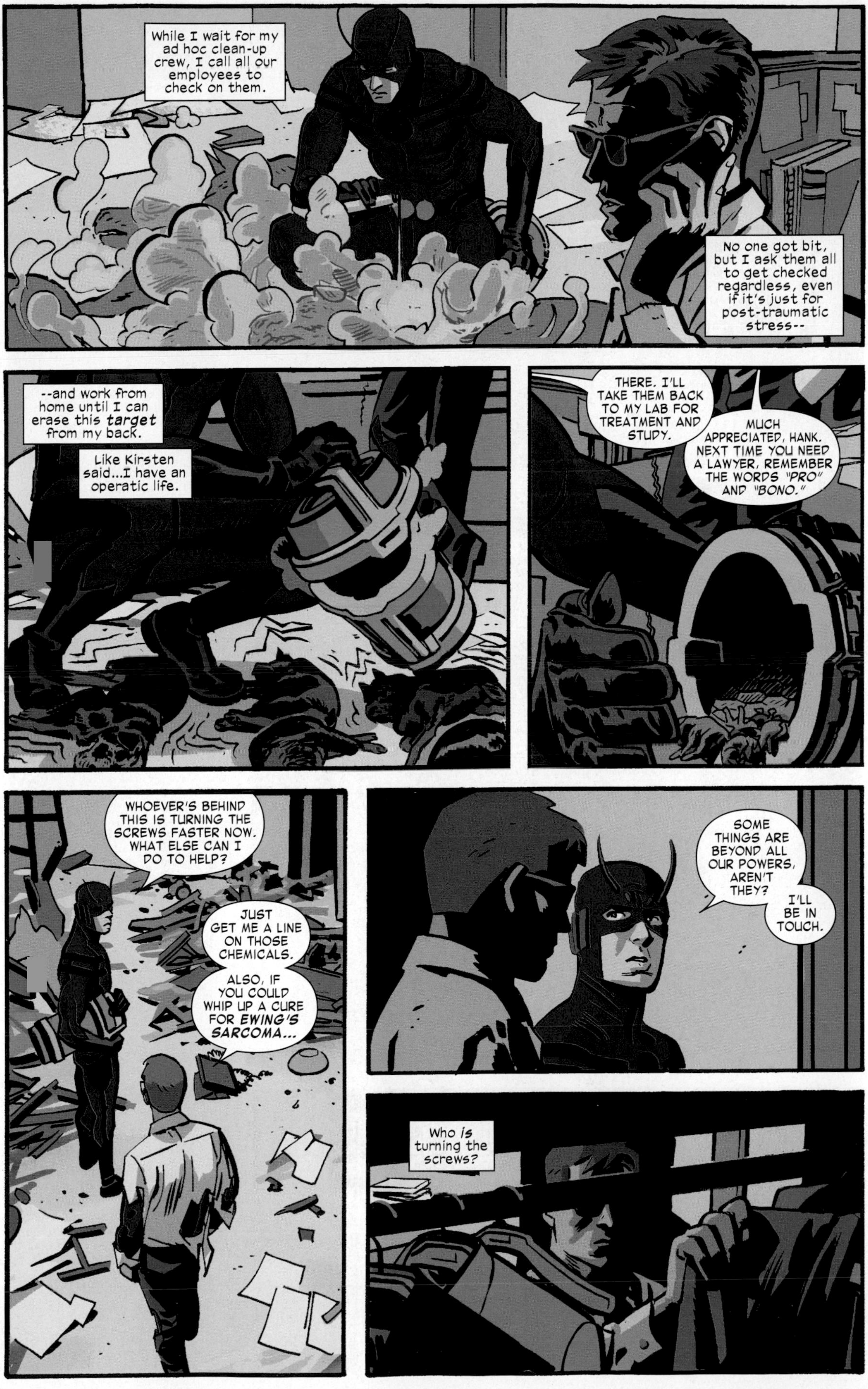
While I wait for my ad hoc clean-up crew, I call all our employees to check on them.
No one got bit, but I ask them all to get checked regardless, even if it's just for post-traumatic stress--
--and work from home until I can erase this *target* from my back.
Like Kirsten said...I have an operatic life.
THERE. I'LL TAKE THEM BACK TO MY LAB FOR TREATMENT AND STUDY.
MUCH APPRECIATED, HANK. NEXT TIME YOU NEED A LAWYER, REMEMBER THE WORDS *"PRO"* AND *"BONO."*
WHOEVER'S BEHIND THIS IS TURNING THE SCREWS FASTER NOW. WHAT ELSE CAN I DO TO HELP?
JUST GET ME A LINE ON THOSE CHEMICALS.
ALSO, IF YOU COULD WHIP UP A CURE FOR *EWING'S SARCOMA...*
SOME THINGS ARE BEYOND ALL OUR POWERS, AREN'T THEY?
I'LL BE IN TOUCH.
Who *is* turning the screws?

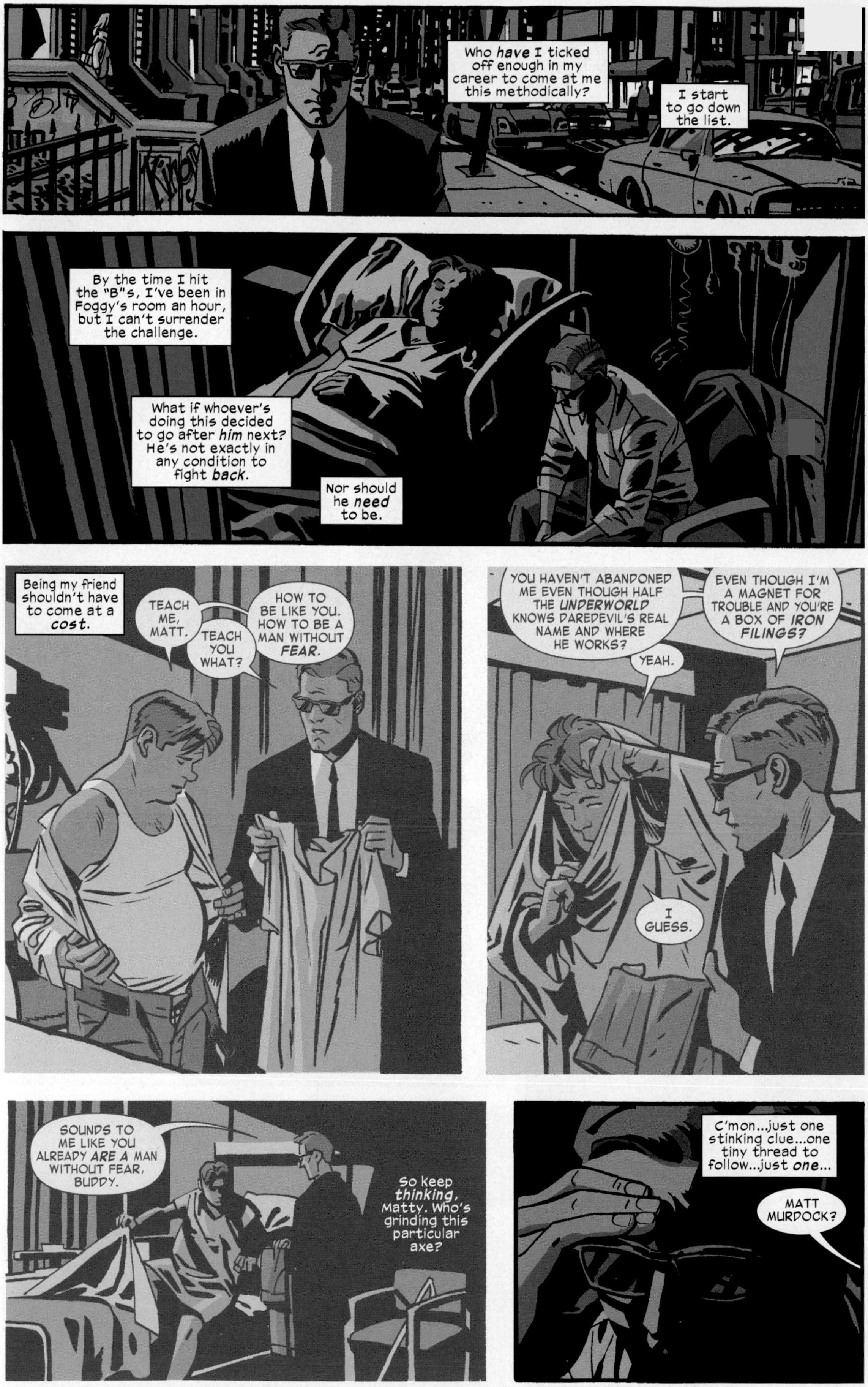
Who *have* I ticked off enough in my career to come at me this methodically?
I start to go down the list.
By the time I hit the "B"s, I've been in Foggy's room an hour, but I can't surrender the challenge.
What if whoever's doing this decided to go after *him* next? He's not exactly in any condition to fight *back*.
Nor should he *need* to be.
Being my friend shouldn't have to come at a *cost*.
TEACH ME, MATT.
TEACH YOU WHAT?
HOW TO BE LIKE YOU. HOW TO BE A MAN WITHOUT *FEAR*.
YOU HAVEN'T ABANDONED ME EVEN THOUGH HALF THE *UNDERWORLD* KNOWS DAREDEVIL'S REAL NAME AND WHERE HE WORKS?
YEAH.
EVEN THOUGH I'M A MAGNET FOR TROUBLE AND YOU'RE A BOX OF *IRON FILINGS?*
I GUESS.
SOUNDS TO ME LIKE YOU ALREADY *ARE A* MAN WITHOUT FEAR, BUDDY.
So keep *thinking*, Matty. Who's grinding this particular axe?
C'mon...just one stinking clue...one tiny thread to follow...just *one*...
MATT MURDOCK?

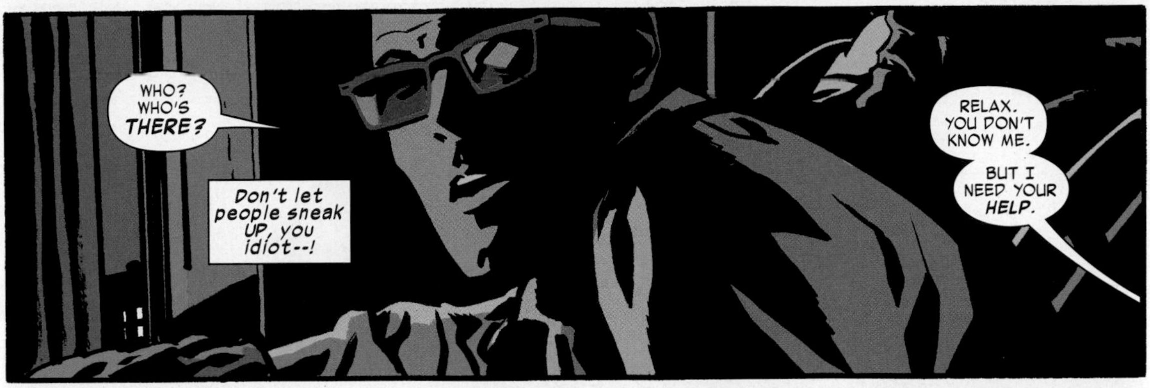
WHO? WHO'S THERE?
Don't let people sneak UP, you idiot--!
RELAX. YOU DON'T KNOW ME.
BUT I NEED YOUR HELP.

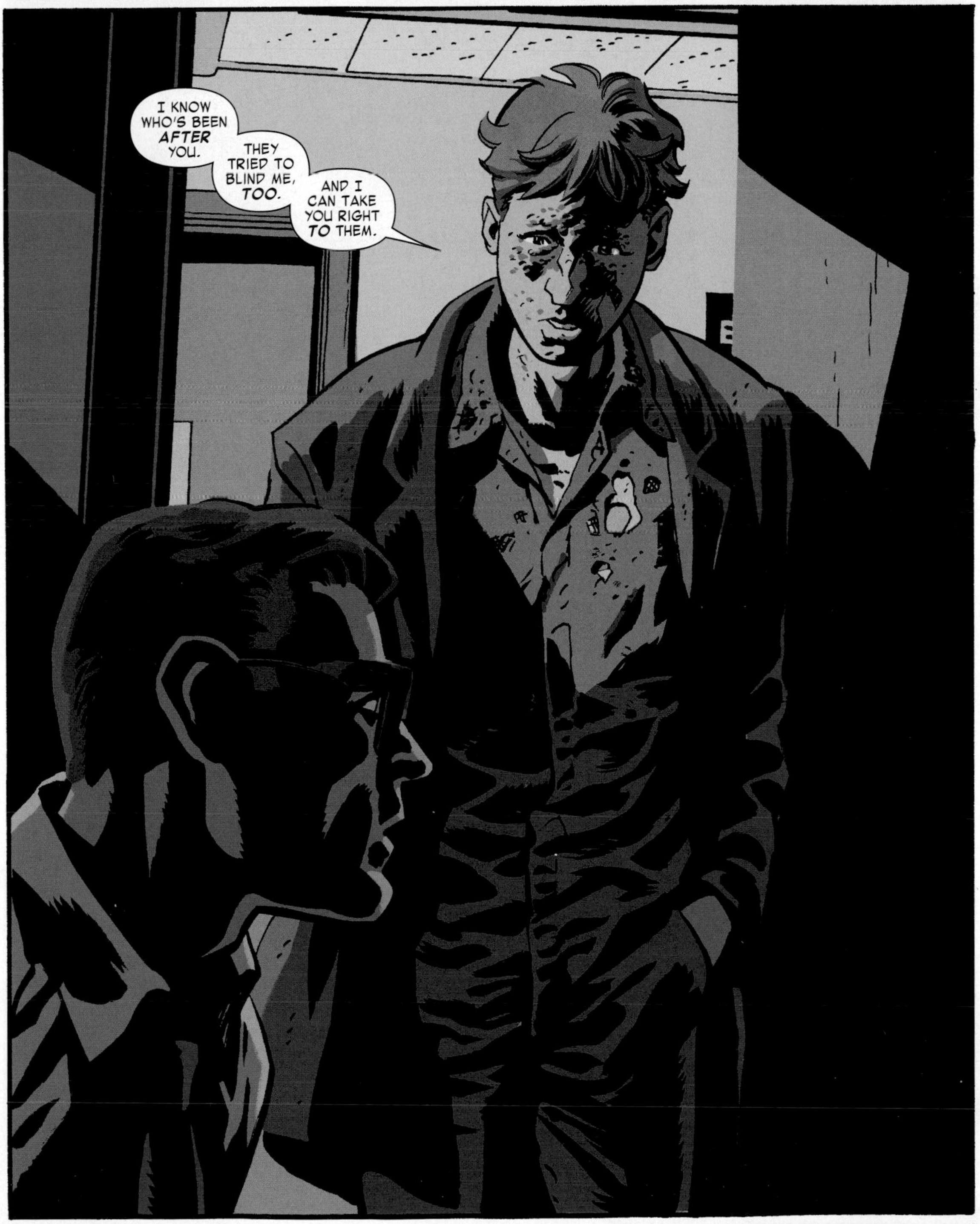
I KNOW WHO'S BEEN AFTER YOU.
THEY TRIED TO BLIND ME, TOO.
AND I CAN TAKE YOU RIGHT TO THEM.

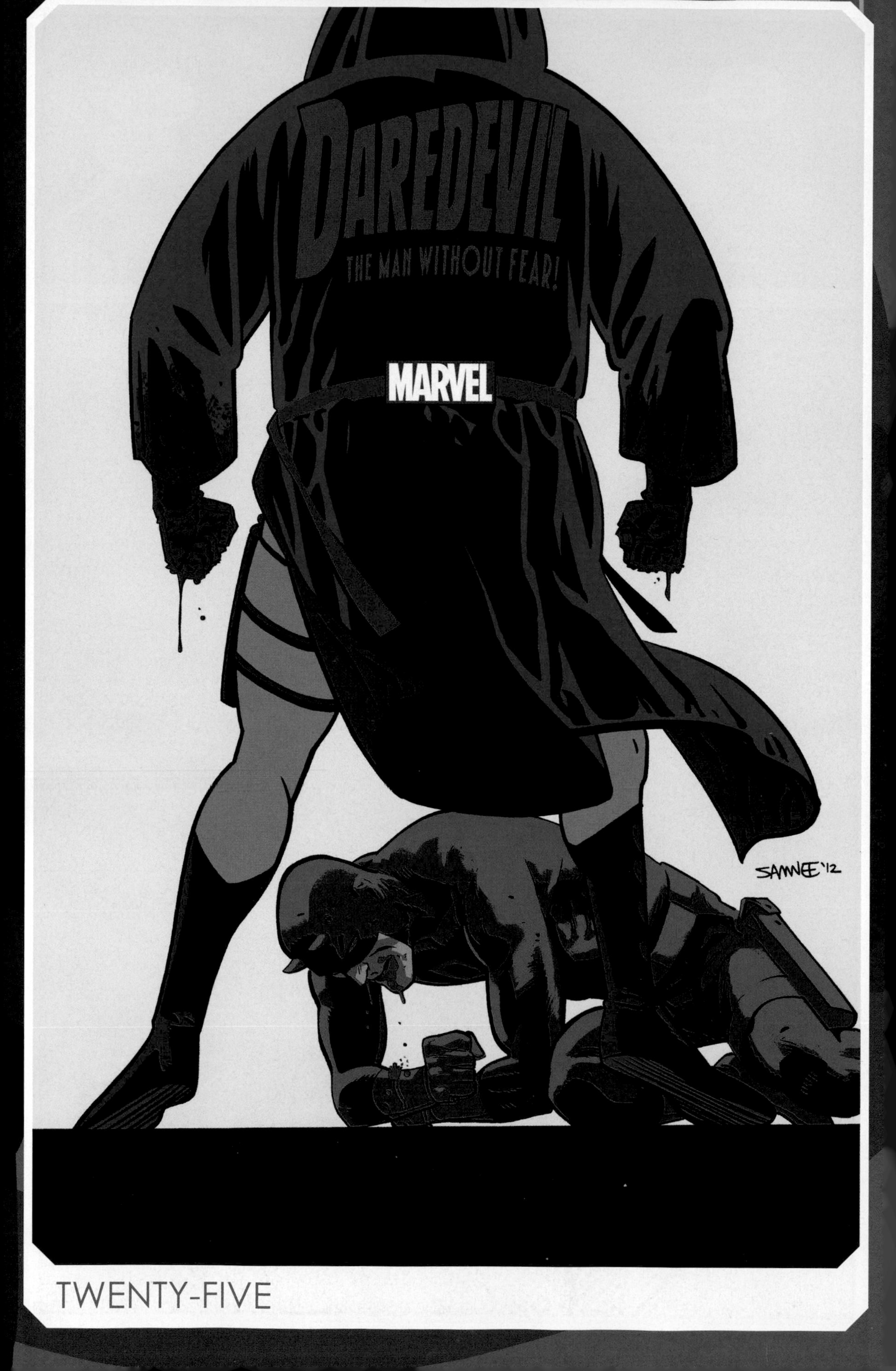
DAREDEVIL
THE MAN WITHOUT FEAR!
MARVEL
SAMNEE '12

TWENTY-FIVE

Cross-exam.

YOU SAY WHOEVER'S AFTER *ME* EXPERIMENTED ON *YOU*, MR...?

NAME'S LARRY. ON A *BUNCH* OF US. PULLED US OUT OF CITY SHELTERS, PAID US FOR "MEDICAL TESTING." NOTHING "MEDICAL" ABOUT IT.

HIT US WITH *CHEMICALS*, *BLINDED* THOSE THEY DIDN'T *KILL*...

I BROKE AWAY. BEEN HIDIN' IN *ALLEYS* EVER *SINCE*, BUT THEY'RE *GONNA FIND* ME. YOU HELP *ME*, I'LL HELP *YOU* GET THEM FIRST.

Body odor and stomach rumblings back up the "*hiding and homeless*" claim.

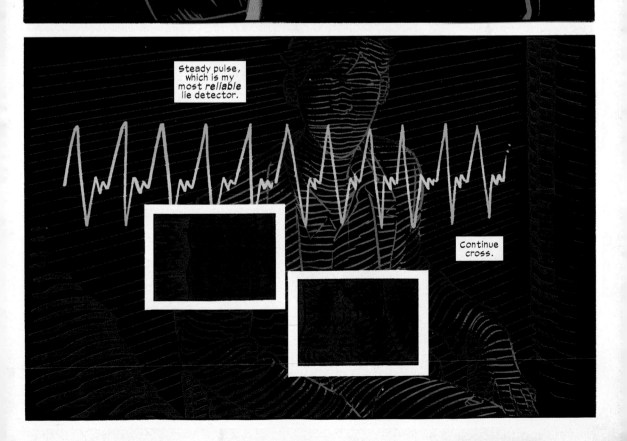

Steady pulse, which is my most *reliable* lie detector.

Continue cross.

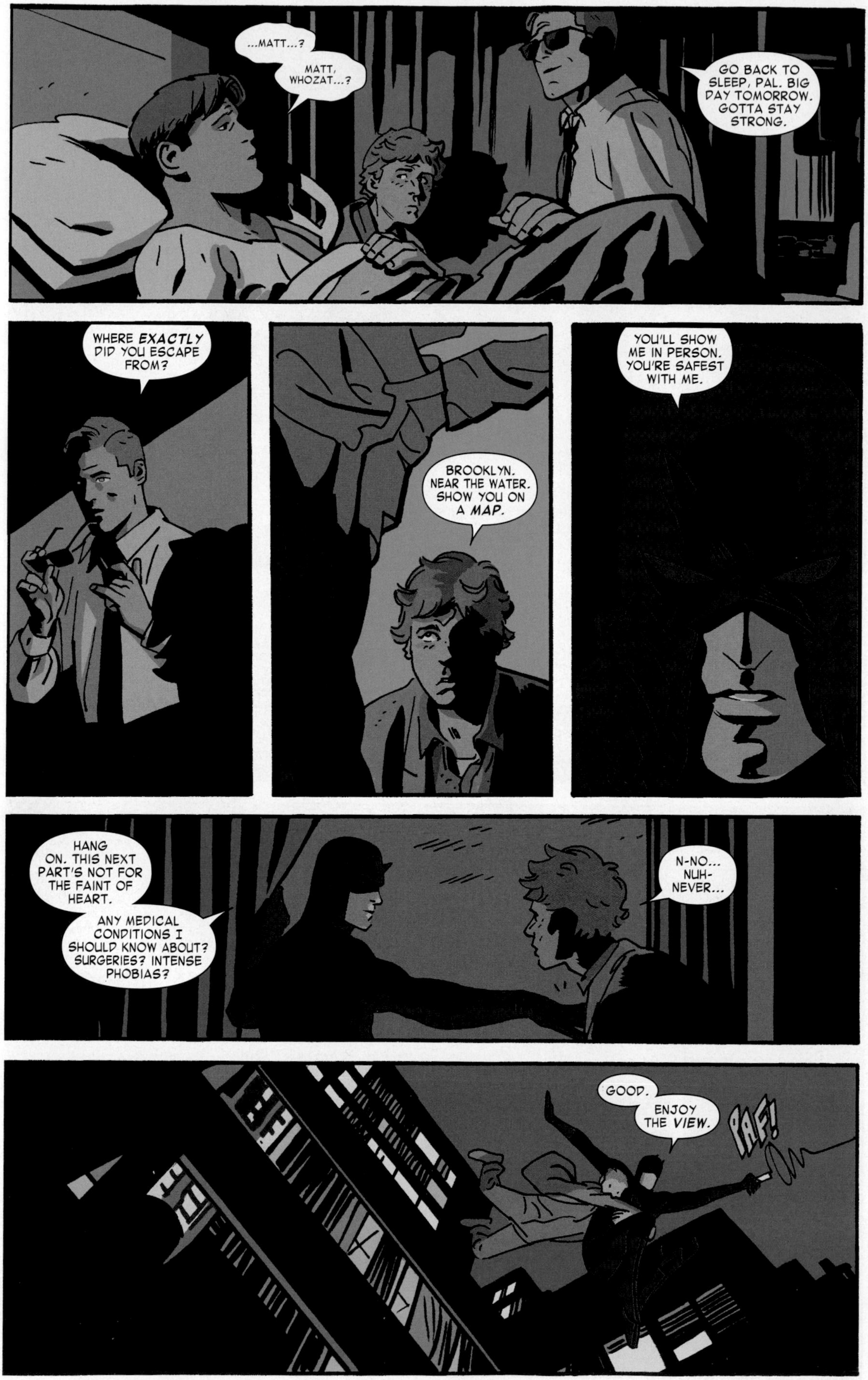
...MATT...?
MATT, WHOZAT...?
GO BACK TO SLEEP, PAL. BIG DAY TOMORROW. GOTTA STAY STRONG.
WHERE EXACTLY DID YOU ESCAPE FROM?
BROOKLYN. NEAR THE WATER. SHOW YOU ON A MAP.
YOU'LL SHOW ME IN PERSON. YOU'RE SAFEST WITH ME.
HANG ON. THIS NEXT PART'S NOT FOR THE FAINT OF HEART.
ANY MEDICAL CONDITIONS I SHOULD KNOW ABOUT? SURGERIES? INTENSE PHOBIAS?
N-NO... NUH- NEVER...
GOOD.
ENJOY THE VIEW.
PAF!

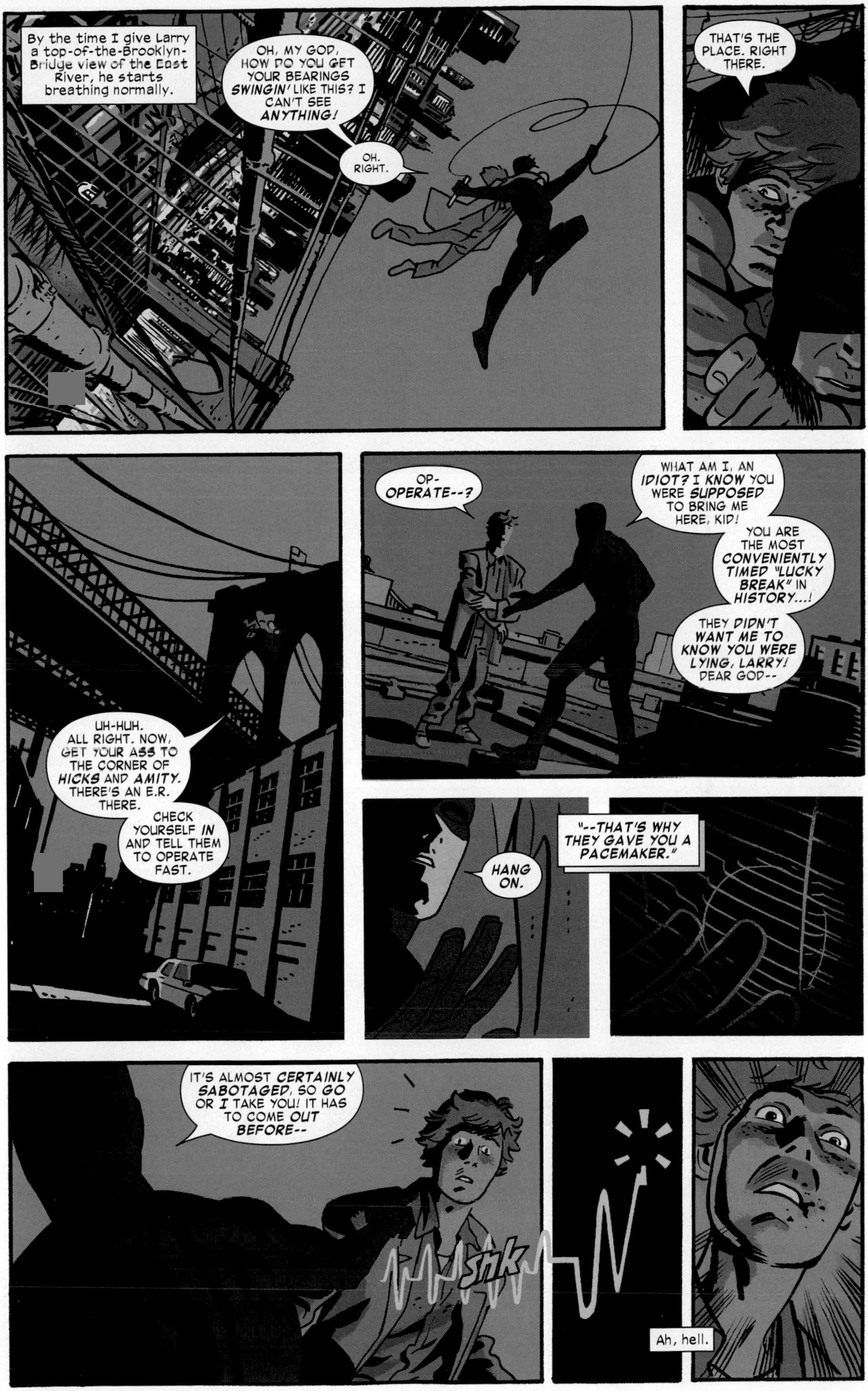
By the time I give Larry a top-of-the-Brooklyn-Bridge view of the East River, he starts breathing normally.
OH, MY GOD, HOW DO YOU GET YOUR BEARINGS SWINGIN' LIKE THIS? I CAN'T SEE ANYTHING!
OH. RIGHT.
THAT'S THE PLACE. RIGHT THERE.
UH-HUH. ALL RIGHT. NOW, GET YOUR ASS TO THE CORNER OF HICKS AND AMITY. THERE'S AN E.R. THERE.
CHECK YOURSELF IN AND TELL THEM TO OPERATE FAST.
OP- OPERATE--?
WHAT AM I, AN IDIOT? I KNOW YOU WERE SUPPOSED TO BRING ME HERE, KID!
YOU ARE THE MOST CONVENIENTLY TIMED "LUCKY BREAK" IN HISTORY...!
THEY DIDN'T WANT ME TO KNOW YOU WERE LYING, LARRY! DEAR GOD--
HANG ON.
"--THAT'S WHY THEY GAVE YOU A PACEMAKER."
IT'S ALMOST CERTAINLY SABOTAGED, SO GO OR I TAKE YOU! IT HAS TO COME OUT BEFORE--
SHK
Ah, hell.

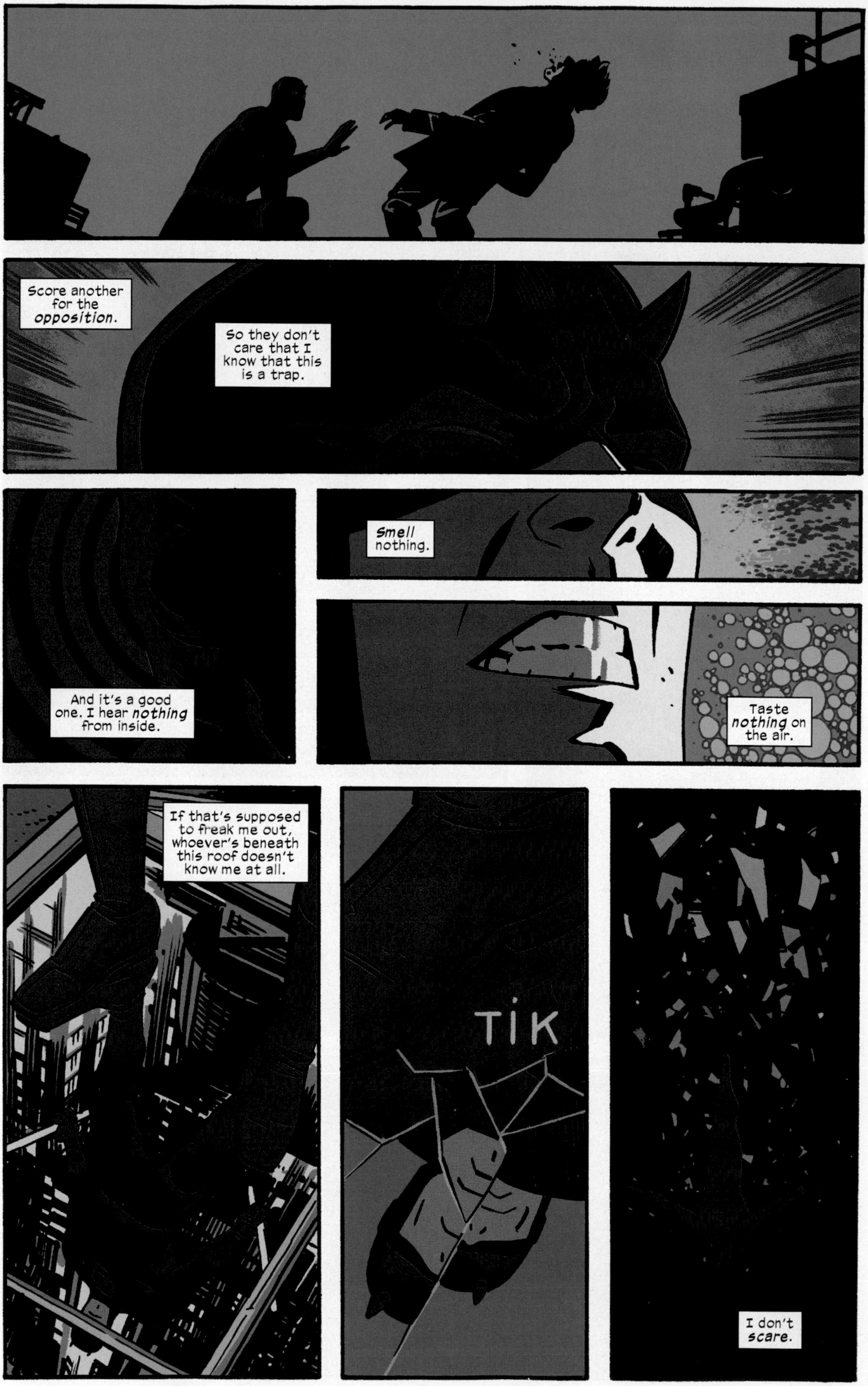
Score another for the *opposition*.
So they don't care that I know that this is a trap.
And it's a good one. I hear *nothing* from inside.
Smell nothing.
Taste *nothing* on the air.
If that's supposed to freak me out, whoever's beneath this roof doesn't know me at all.
TIK
I don't *scare*.

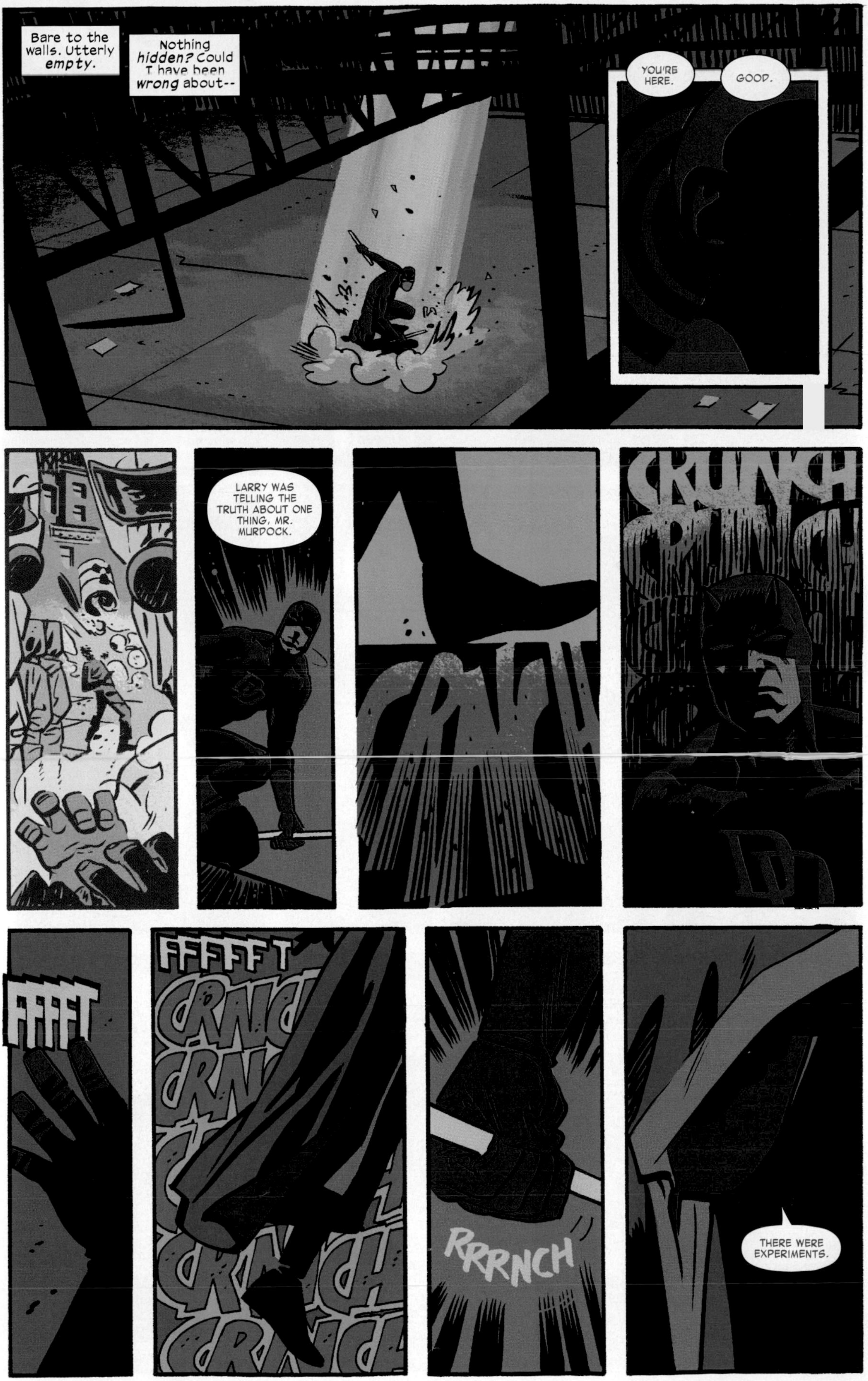
Bare to the walls. Utterly *empty*.
Nothing *hidden?* Could I have been *wrong* about--
YOU'RE HERE.
GOOD.
LARRY WAS TELLING THE TRUTH ABOUT ONE THING, MR. MURDOCK.
CRNCH
CRUNCH
FFFFT
FFFFFT
CRNCH
RRRNCH
THERE WERE EXPERIMENTS.

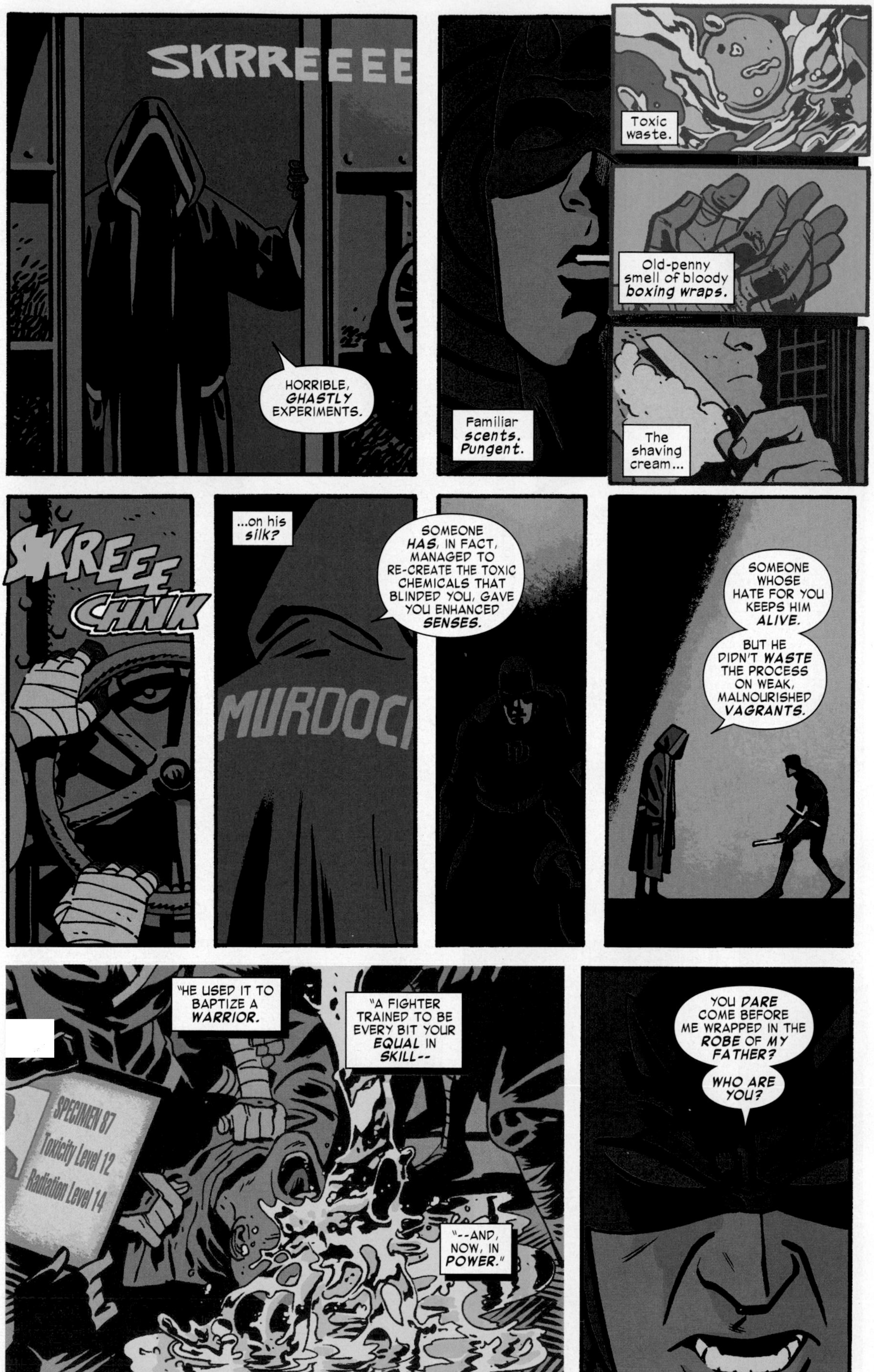
SKRREEEE
HORRIBLE, GHASTLY EXPERIMENTS.
Familiar scents. Pungent.
Toxic waste.
Old-penny smell of bloody boxing wraps.
The shaving cream...
SKREEE
CHNK
...on his silk?
MURDOCK
SOMEONE HAS, IN FACT, MANAGED TO RE-CREATE THE TOXIC CHEMICALS THAT BLINDED YOU, GAVE YOU ENHANCED SENSES.
SOMEONE WHOSE HATE FOR YOU KEEPS HIM ALIVE.
BUT HE DIDN'T WASTE THE PROCESS ON WEAK, MALNOURISHED VAGRANTS.
"HE USED IT TO BAPTIZE A WARRIOR.
"A FIGHTER TRAINED TO BE EVERY BIT YOUR EQUAL IN SKILL--
SPECIMEN 87
Toxicity Level 12
Radiation Level 14
"--AND, NOW, IN POWER."
YOU DARE COME BEFORE ME WRAPPED IN THE ROBE OF MY FATHER?
WHO ARE YOU?

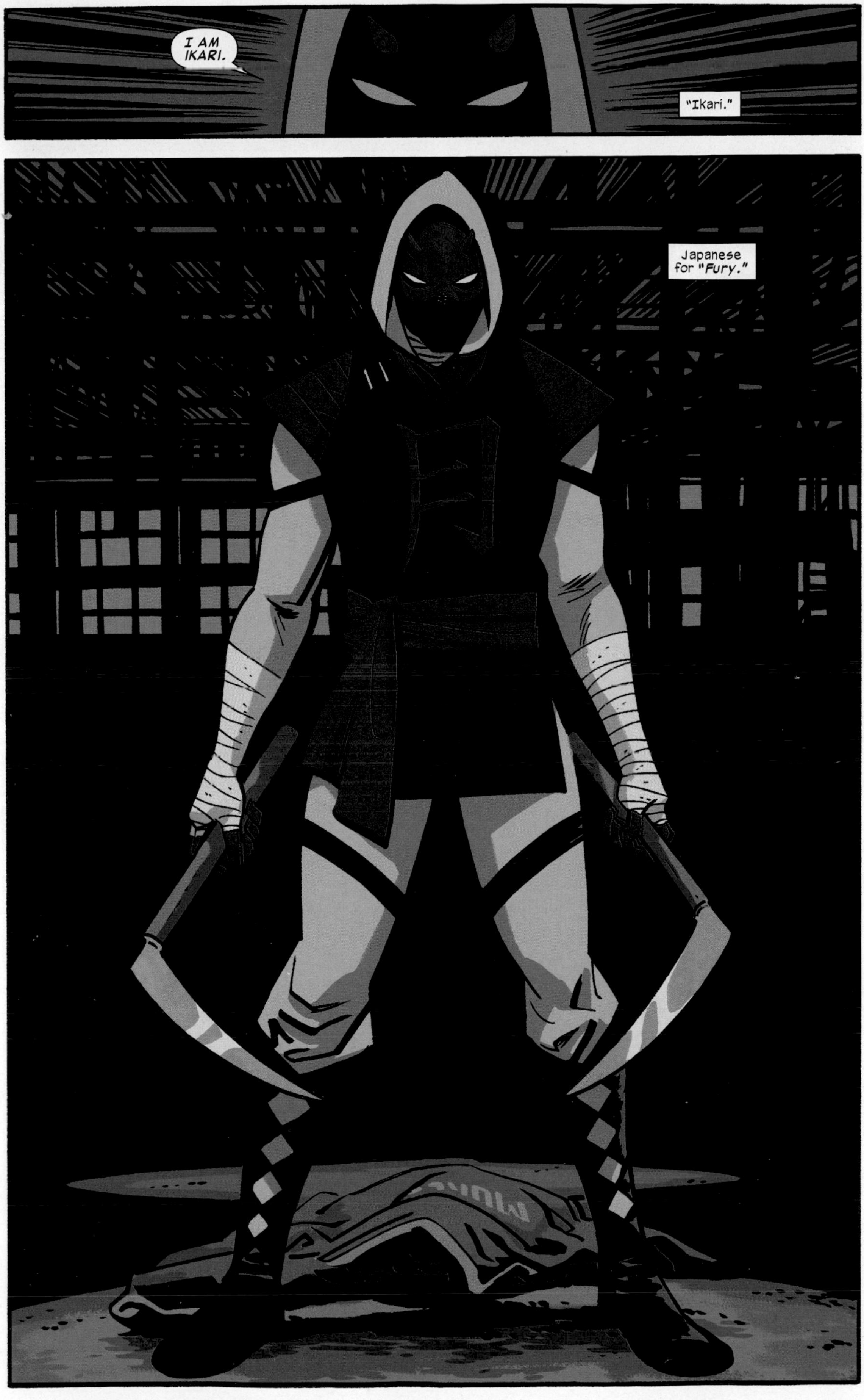
I AM IKARI.
"Ikari."
Japanese for "Fury."

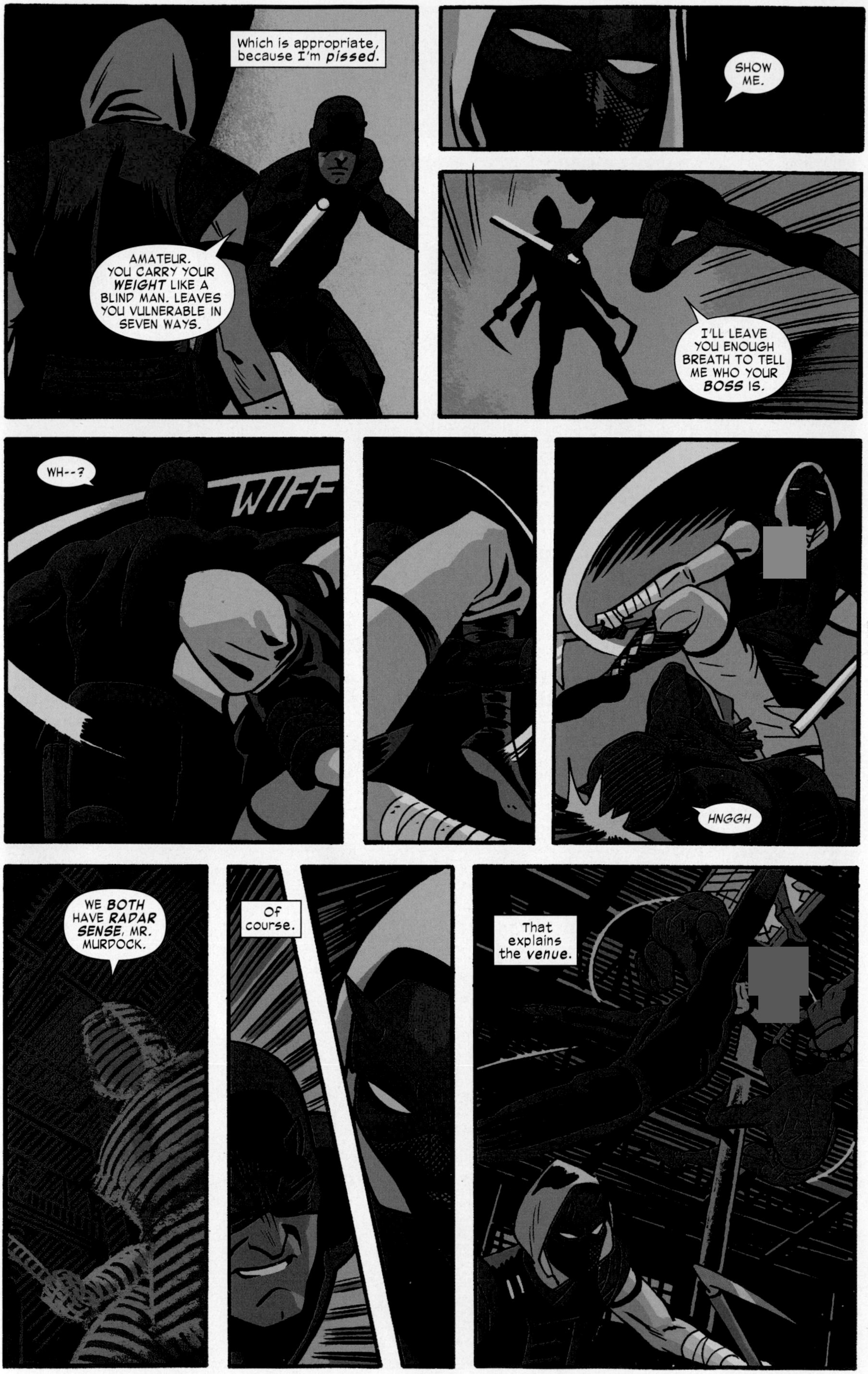
Which is appropriate, because I'm *pissed*.
AMATEUR. YOU CARRY YOUR **WEIGHT** LIKE A BLIND MAN. LEAVES YOU VULNERABLE IN SEVEN WAYS.
SHOW ME.
I'LL LEAVE YOU ENOUGH BREATH TO TELL ME WHO YOUR **BOSS** IS.
WH--?
WIFF
HNGGH
WE **BOTH** HAVE **RADAR SENSE**, MR. MURDOCK.
Of course.
That explains the *venue*.

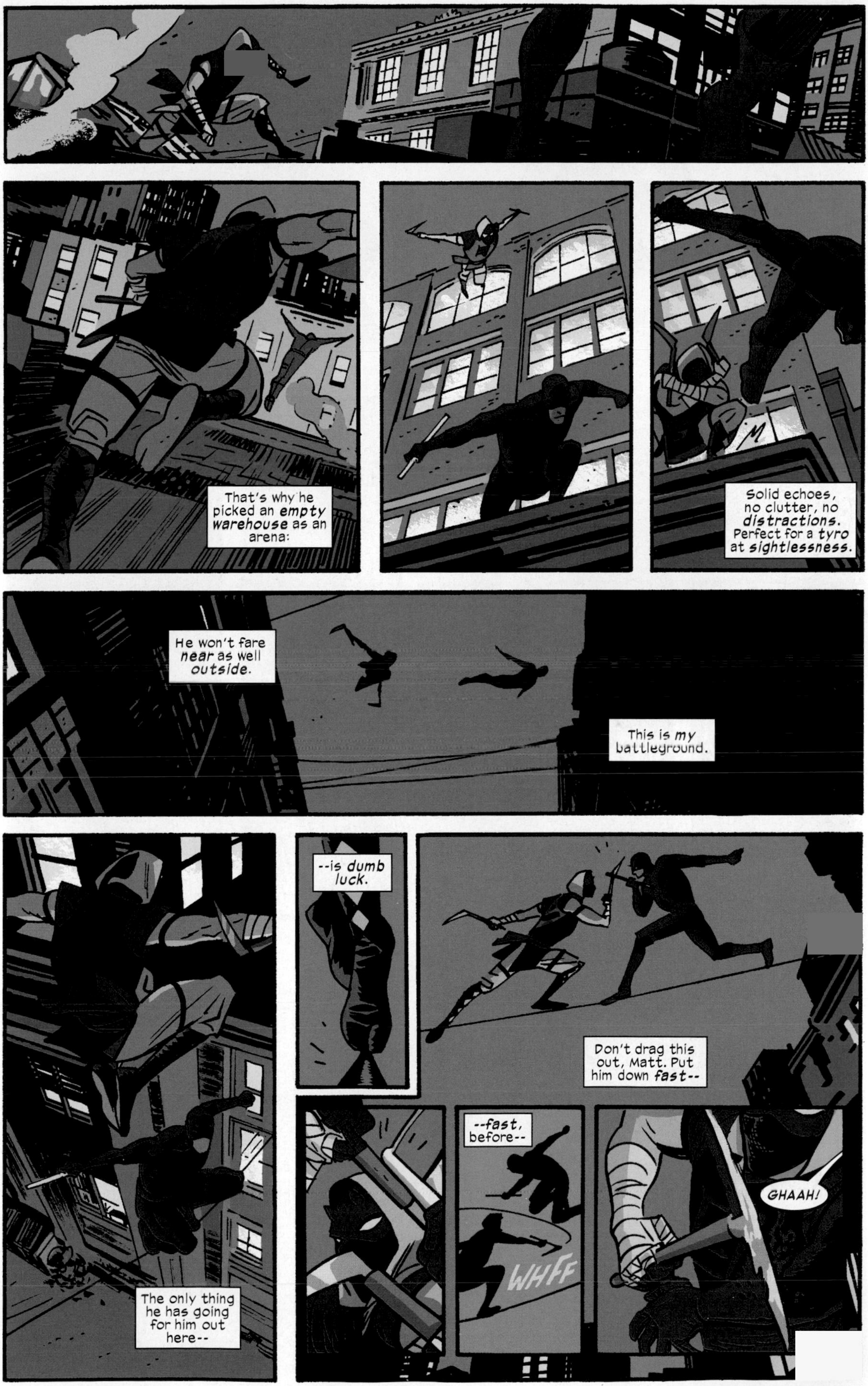
That's why he picked an empty warehouse as an arena:
Solid echoes, no clutter, no distractions. Perfect for a tyro at sightlessness.
He won't fare near as well outside.
This is my battleground.
The only thing he has going for him out here--
--is dumb luck.
Don't drag this out, Matt. Put him down fast--
--fast, before--
WHFF
GHAAH!

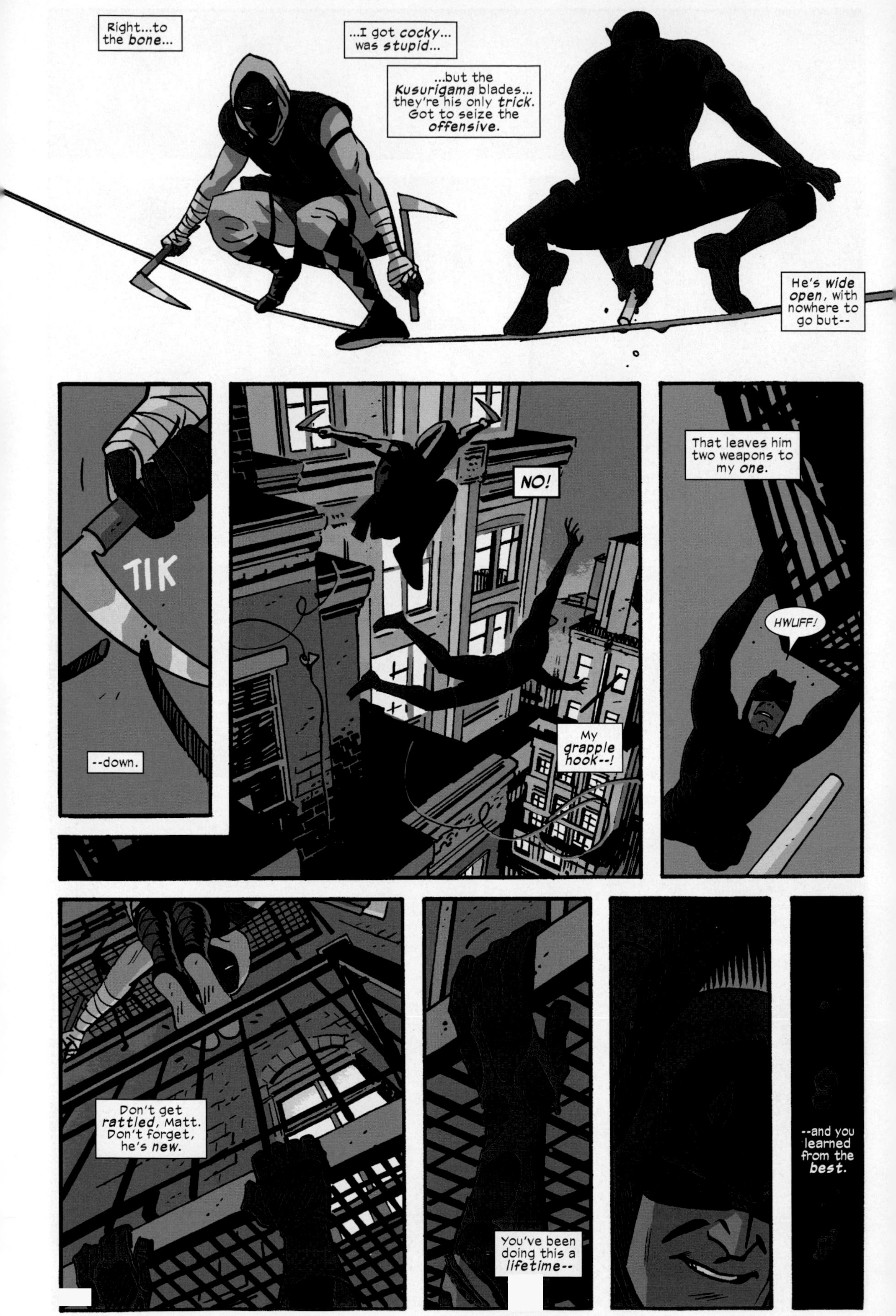

Right...to the *bone*...
...I got *cocky*... was *stupid*...
...but the *Kusurigama* blades... they're his only *trick*. Got to seize the *offensive*.
He's *wide open*, with nowhere to go but--
TIK
--down.
NO!
My *grapple hook*--!
That leaves him two weapons to my *one*.
HWUFF!
Don't get *rattled*, Matt. Don't forget, he's *new*.
You've been doing this a *lifetime*--
--and you learned from the *best*.

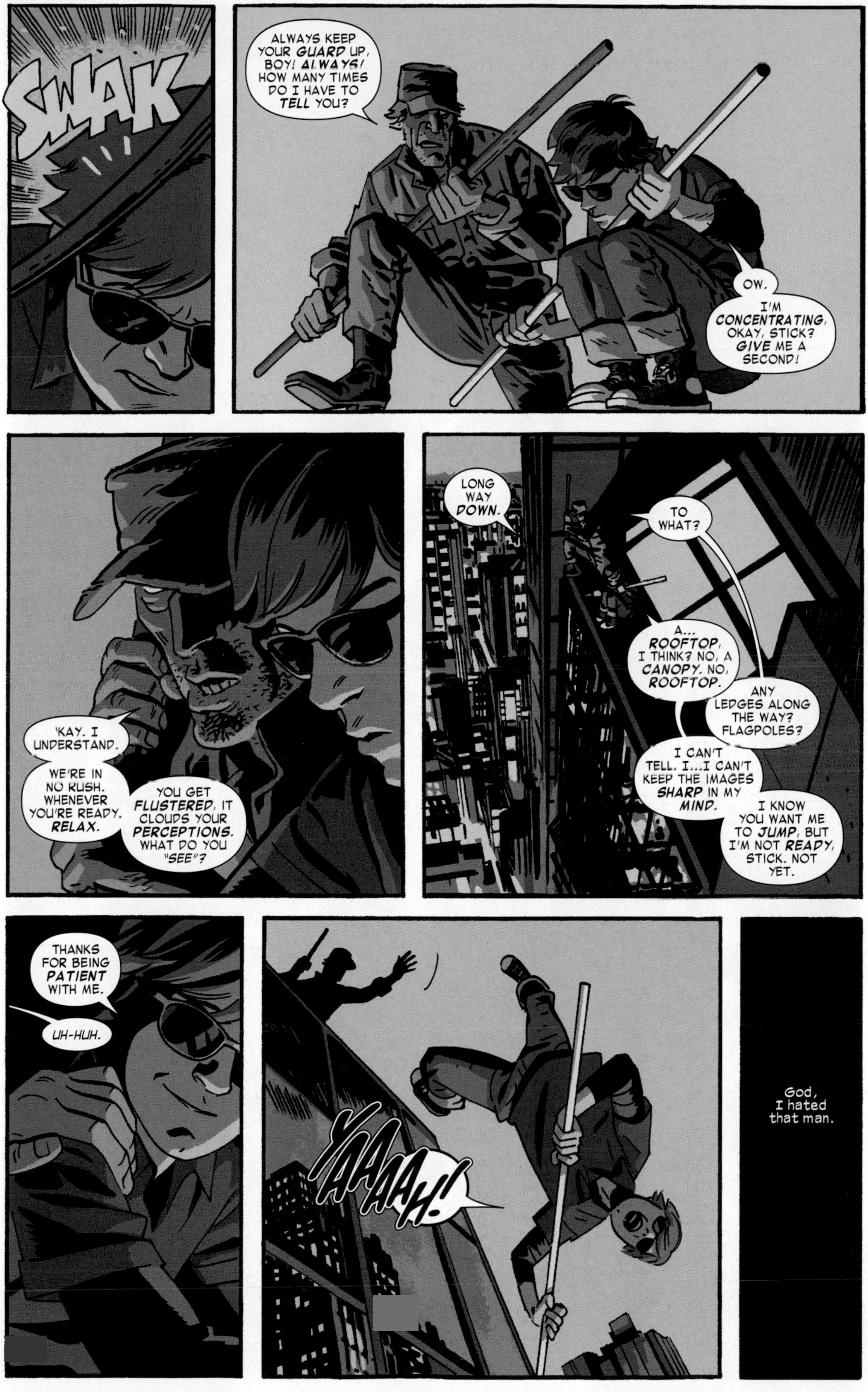
SWAK
ALWAYS KEEP YOUR GUARD UP, BOY! ALWAYS! HOW MANY TIMES DO I HAVE TO TELL YOU?
OW.
I'M CONCENTRATING, OKAY, STICK? GIVE ME A SECOND!
'KAY. I UNDERSTAND.
WE'RE IN NO RUSH. WHENEVER YOU'RE READY. RELAX.
YOU GET FLUSTERED, IT CLOUDS YOUR PERCEPTIONS. WHAT DO YOU "SEE"?
LONG WAY DOWN.
TO WHAT?
A... ROOFTOP, I THINK? NO, A CANOPY. NO, ROOFTOP.
ANY LEDGES ALONG THE WAY? FLAGPOLES?
I CAN'T TELL. I...I CAN'T KEEP THE IMAGES SHARP IN MY MIND.
I KNOW YOU WANT ME TO JUMP, BUT I'M NOT READY, STICK. NOT YET.
THANKS FOR BEING PATIENT WITH ME.
UH-HUH.
YAAAAAH!
God, I hated that man.

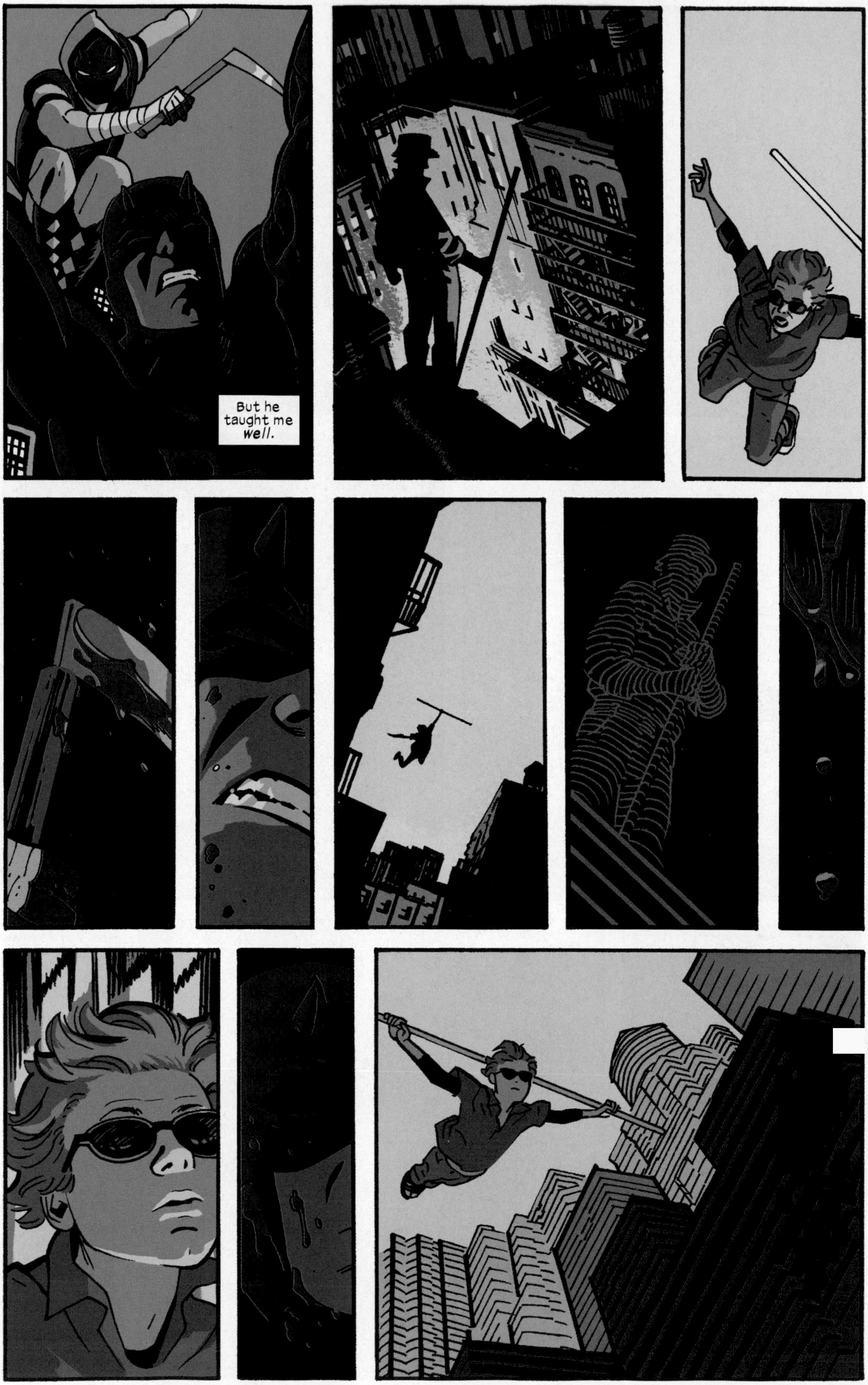
But he taught me *well*.

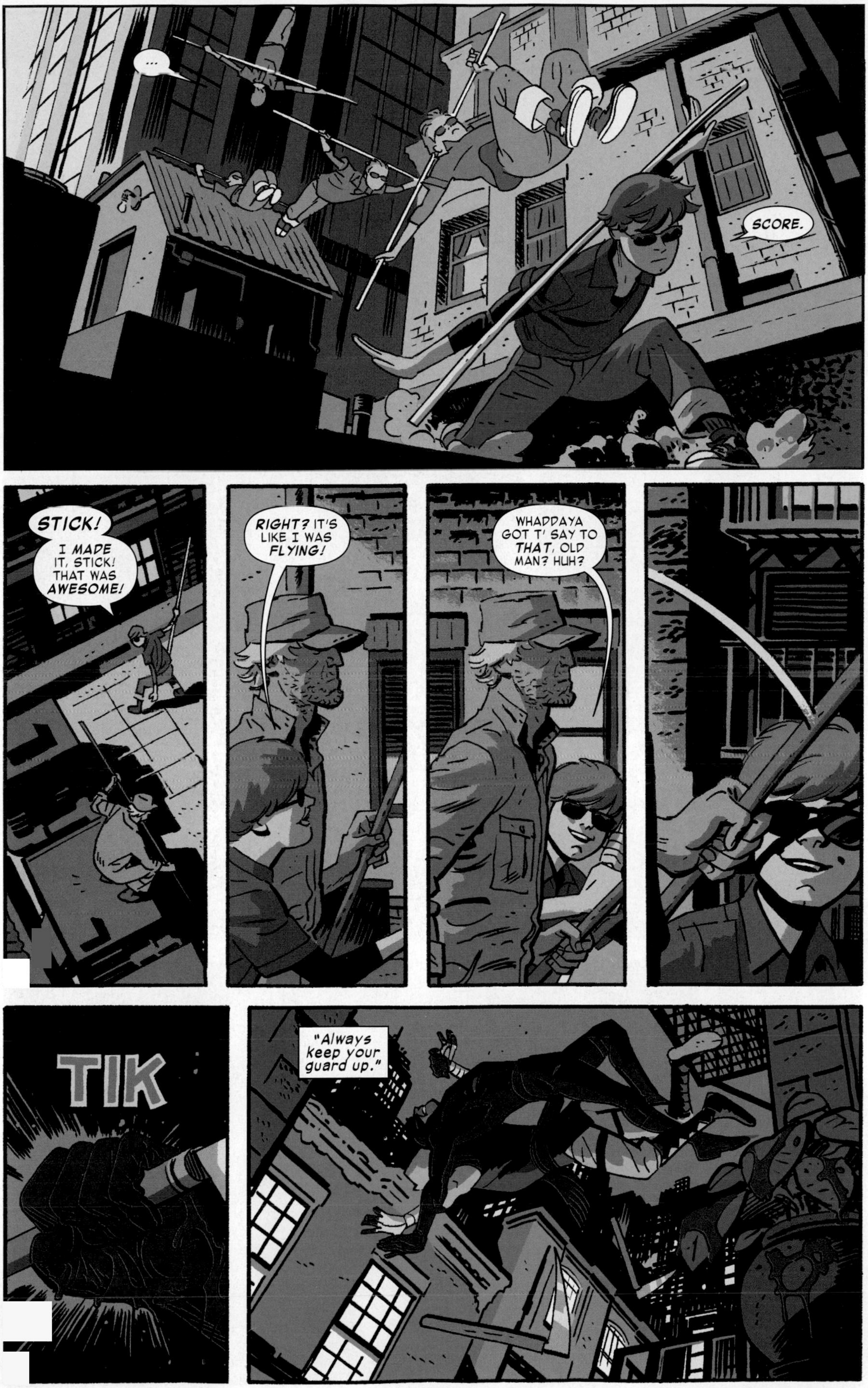
...
SCORE.
STICK!
I MADE IT, STICK! THAT WAS AWESOME!
RIGHT? IT'S LIKE I WAS FLYING!
WHADDAYA GOT T' SAY TO THAT, OLD MAN? HUH?
TIK
"Always keep your guard up."

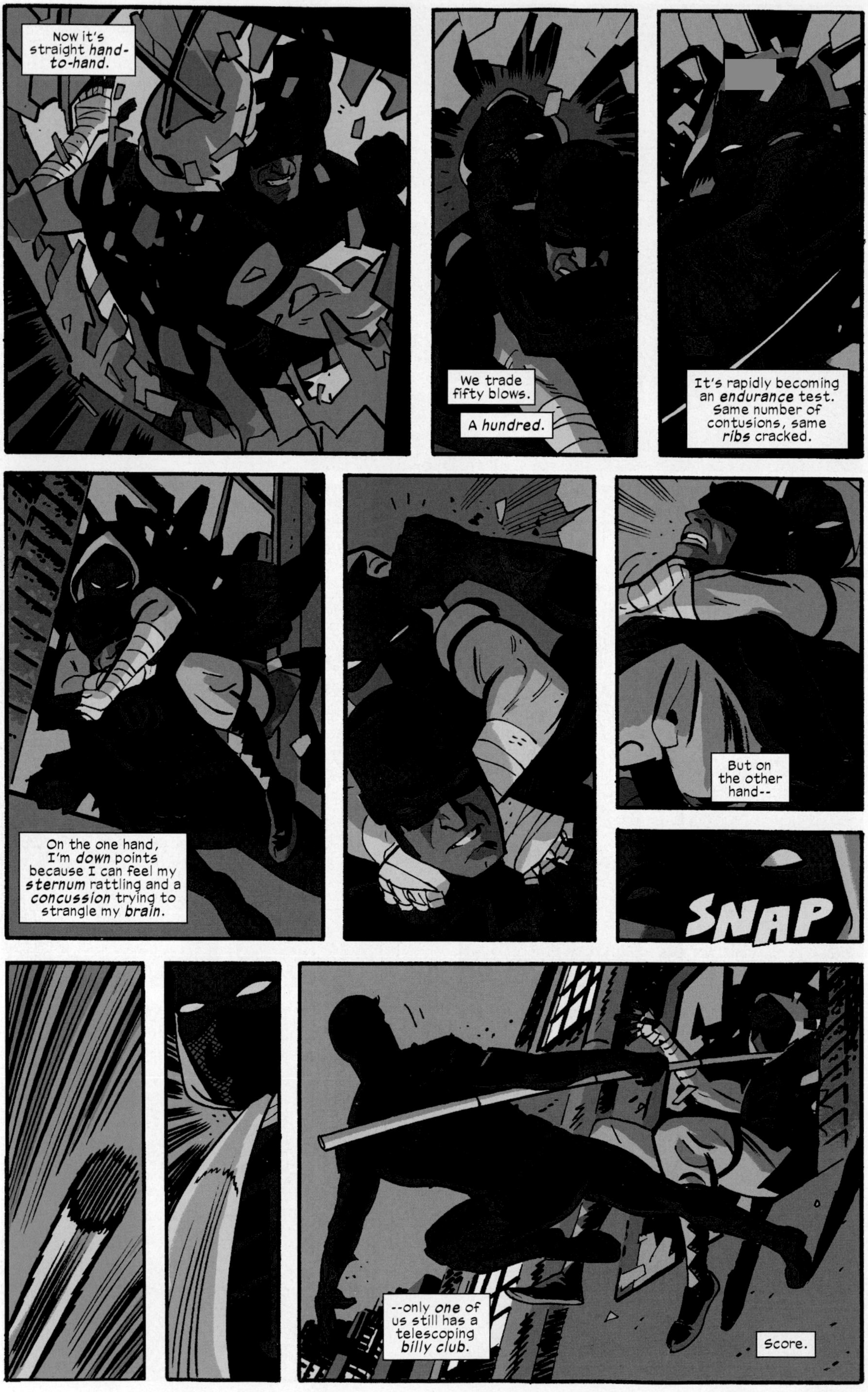

Now it's straight *hand-to-hand*.
We trade fifty blows.
A *hundred*.
It's rapidly becoming an *endurance* test. Same number of contusions, same *ribs* cracked.
On the one hand, I'm *down* points because I can feel my *sternum* rattling and a *concussion* trying to strangle my *brain*.
But on the other hand--
SNAP
--only *one* of us still has a telescoping *billy club*.
Score.

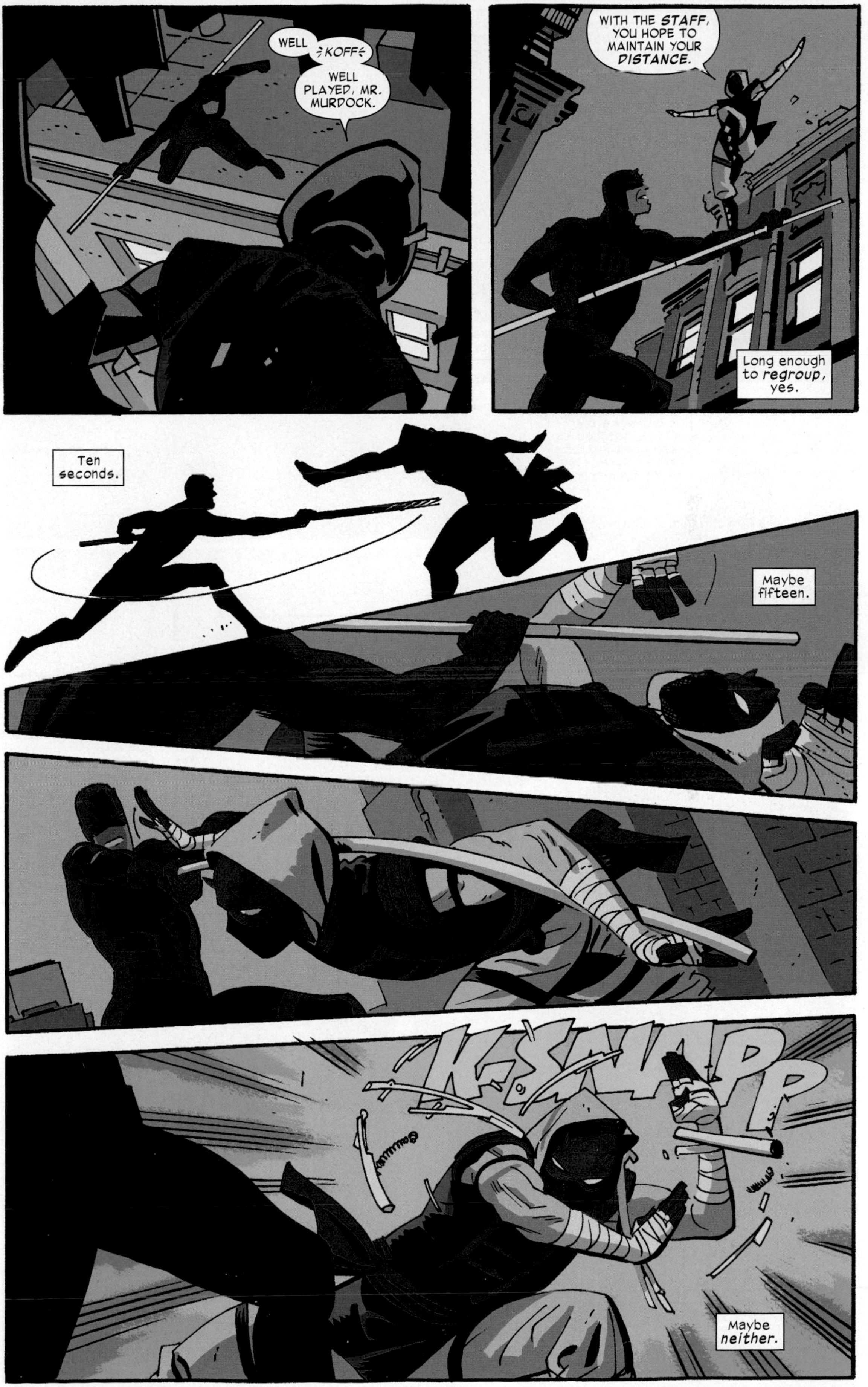

WELL
KOFF
WELL PLAYED, MR. MURDOCK.
WITH THE STAFF, YOU HOPE TO MAINTAIN YOUR DISTANCE.
Long enough to regroup, yes.
Ten seconds.
Maybe fifteen.
K-SNAPP
Maybe neither.

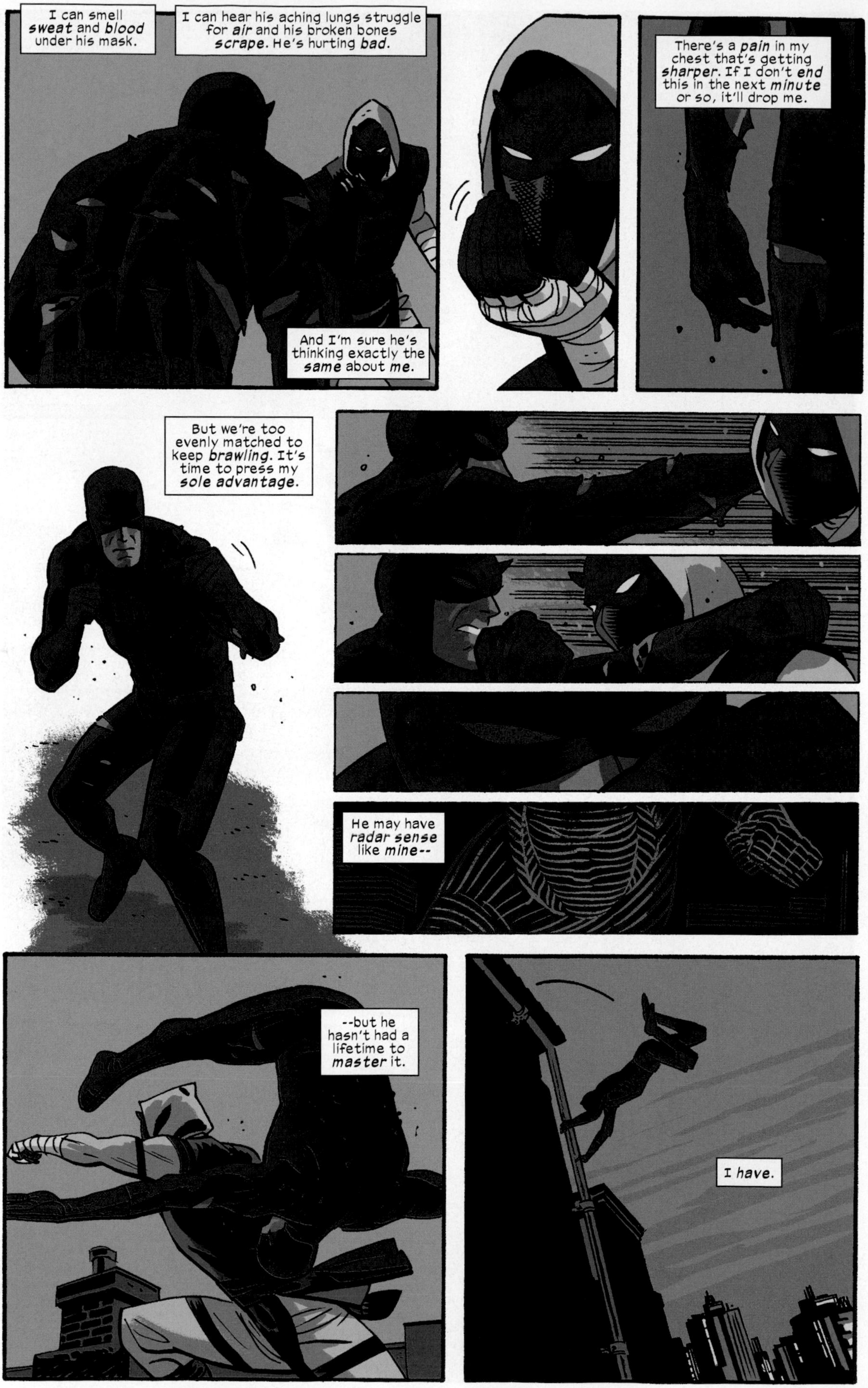
I can smell sweat and blood under his mask.
I can hear his aching lungs struggle for air and his broken bones scrape. He's hurting bad.
And I'm sure he's thinking exactly the same about me.
There's a pain in my chest that's getting sharper. If I don't end this in the next minute or so, it'll drop me.
But we're too evenly matched to keep brawling. It's time to press my sole advantage.
He may have radar sense like mine--
--but he hasn't had a lifetime to master it.
I have.

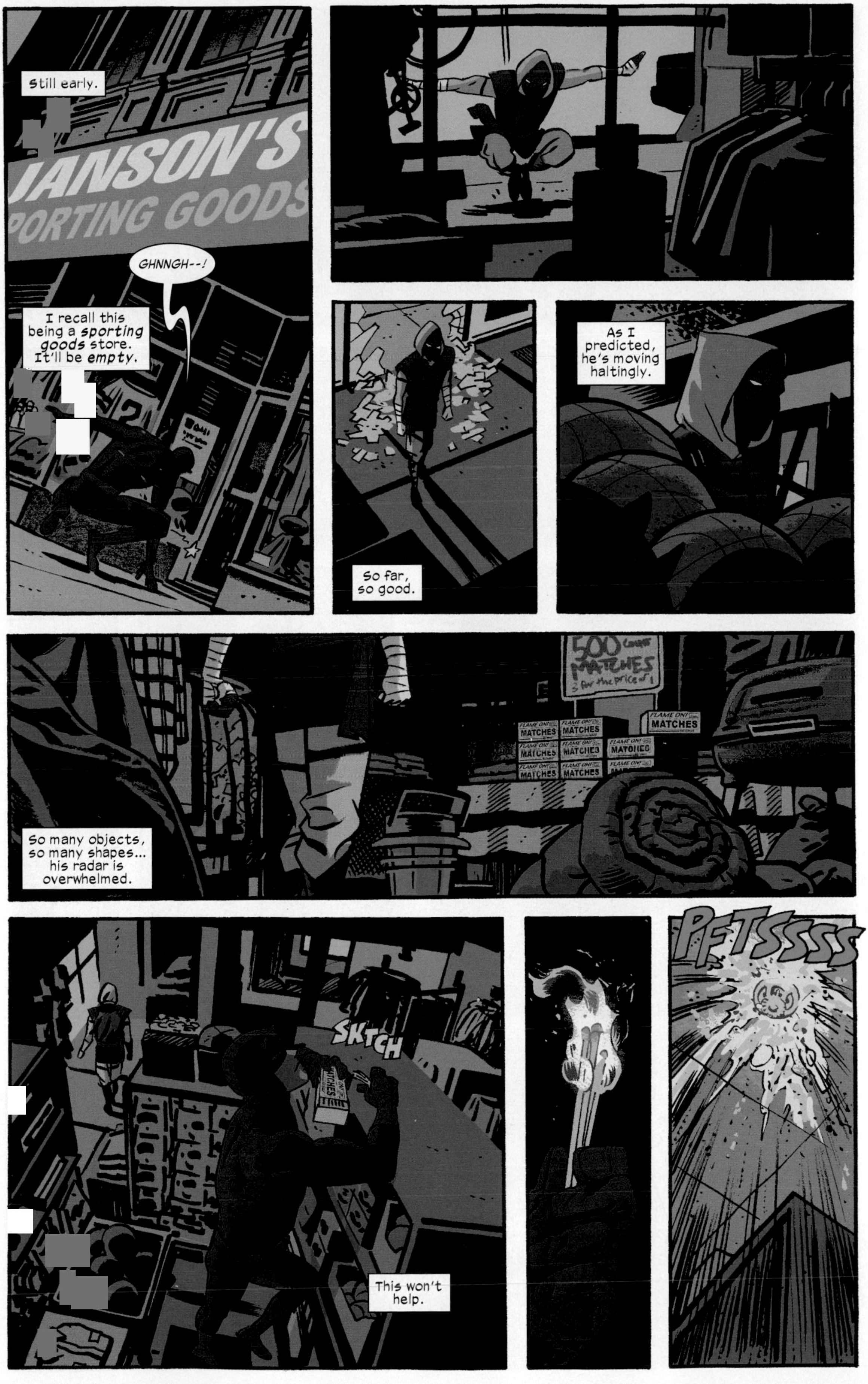
Still early.
JANSON'S
SPORTING GOODS
GHNNGH--!
I recall this being a sporting goods store. It'll be empty.
So far, so good.
As I predicted, he's moving haltingly.
500 COUNT
MATCHES
3 for the price of 1
FLAME ON!
MATCHES
So many objects, so many shapes... his radar is overwhelmed.
SKTCH
This won't help.
PFTSSSS

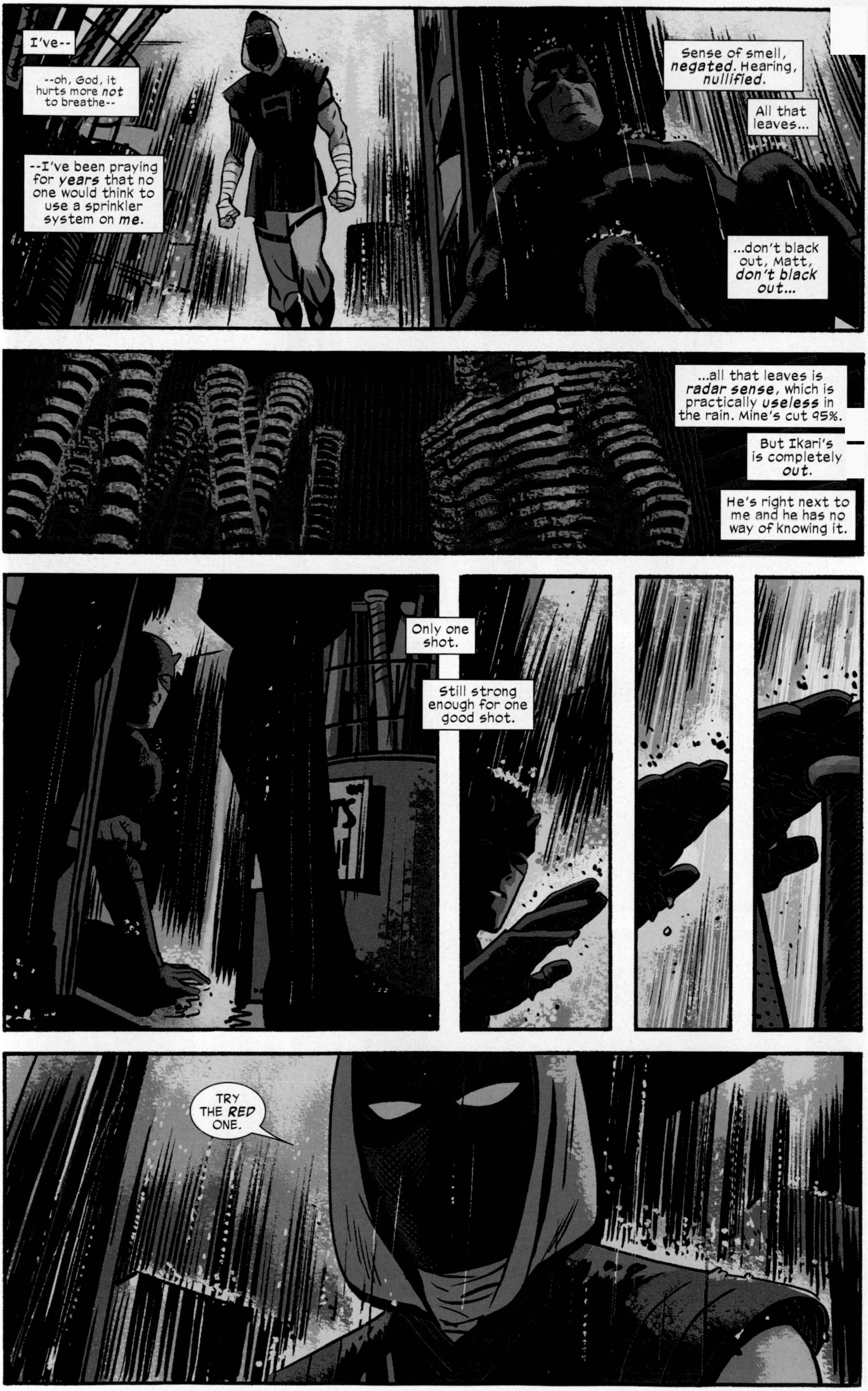
I've--
--oh, God, it hurts more *not* to breathe--
--I've been praying for *years* that no one would think to use a sprinkler system on *me*.
Sense of smell, *negated*. Hearing, *nullified*.
All that leaves...
...don't black out, Matt, *don't black out*...
...all that leaves is *radar sense*, which is practically *useless* in the rain. Mine's cut 95%.
But Ikari's is completely *out*.
He's right next to me and he has no way of knowing it.
Only one shot.
Still strong enough for one good shot.
TRY THE *RED* ONE.

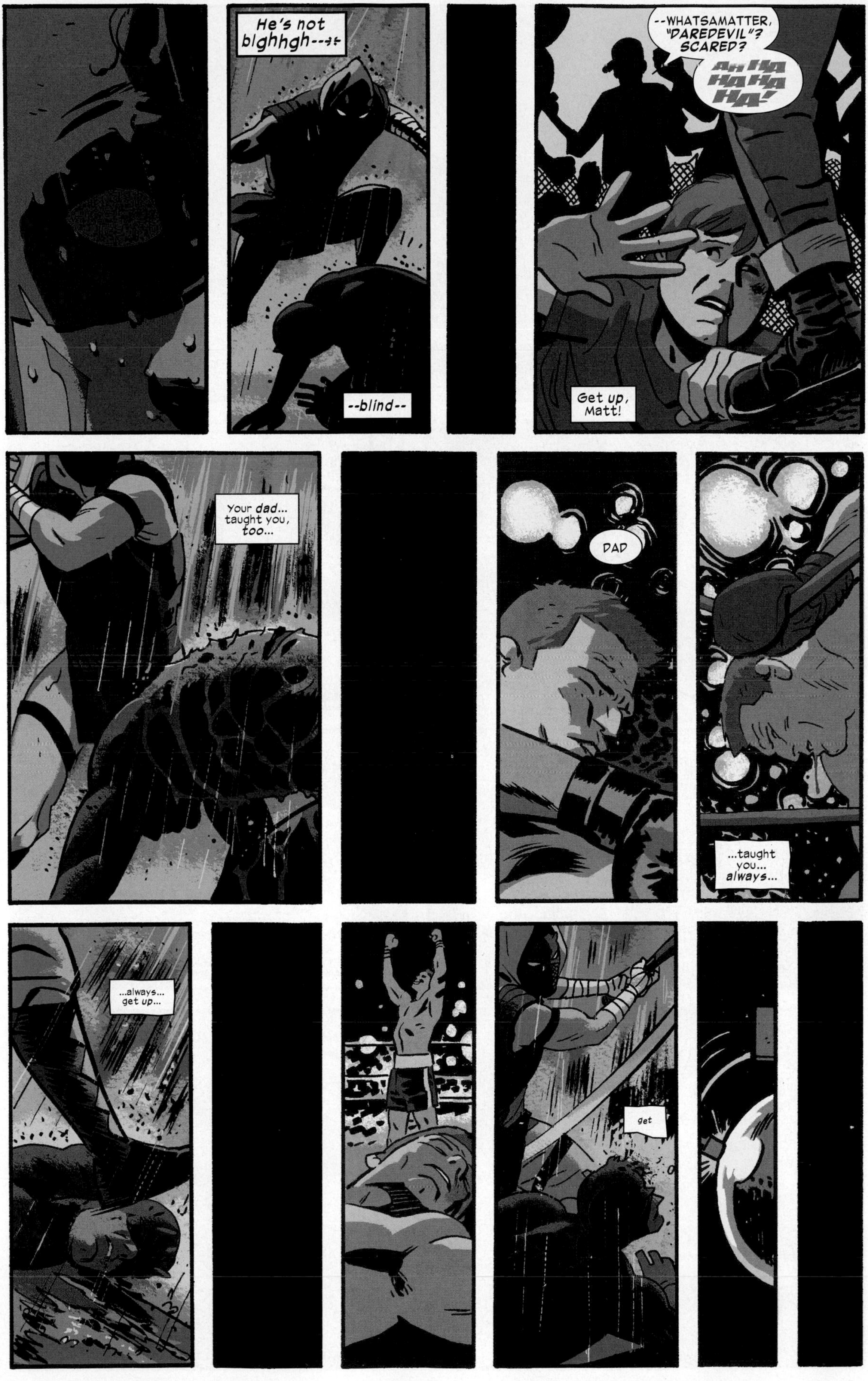
He's not blghhgh--
--blind--
--WHATSAMATTER, "DAREDEVIL"? SCARED?
AH HA HA HA HA!
Get up, Matt!
Your dad... taught you, too...
DAD
...taught you... always...
...always... get up...
get

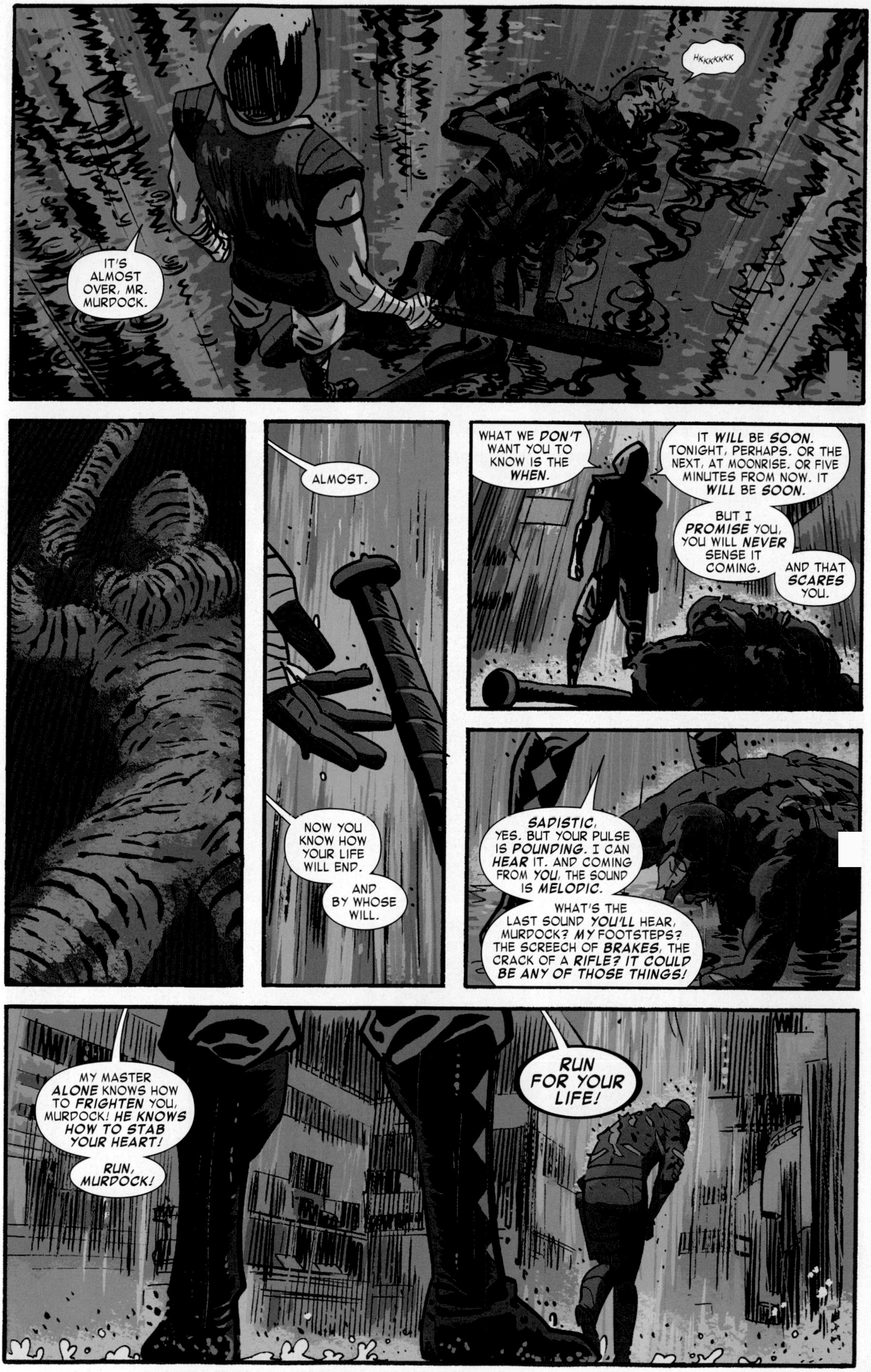
HKKKKKK
IT'S ALMOST OVER, MR. MURDOCK.
ALMOST.
NOW YOU KNOW HOW YOUR LIFE WILL END.
AND BY WHOSE WILL.
WHAT WE DON'T WANT YOU TO KNOW IS THE WHEN.
IT WILL BE SOON. TONIGHT, PERHAPS. OR THE NEXT, AT MOONRISE. OR FIVE MINUTES FROM NOW. IT WILL BE SOON.
BUT I PROMISE YOU, YOU WILL NEVER SENSE IT COMING.
AND THAT SCARES YOU.
SADISTIC, YES. BUT YOUR PULSE IS POUNDING. I CAN HEAR IT. AND COMING FROM YOU, THE SOUND IS MELODIC.
WHAT'S THE LAST SOUND YOU'LL HEAR, MURDOCK? MY FOOTSTEPS? THE SCREECH OF BRAKES, THE CRACK OF A RIFLE? IT COULD BE ANY OF THOSE THINGS!
MY MASTER ALONE KNOWS HOW TO FRIGHTEN YOU, MURDOCK! HE KNOWS HOW TO STAB YOUR HEART!
RUN, MURDOCK!
RUN FOR YOUR LIFE!

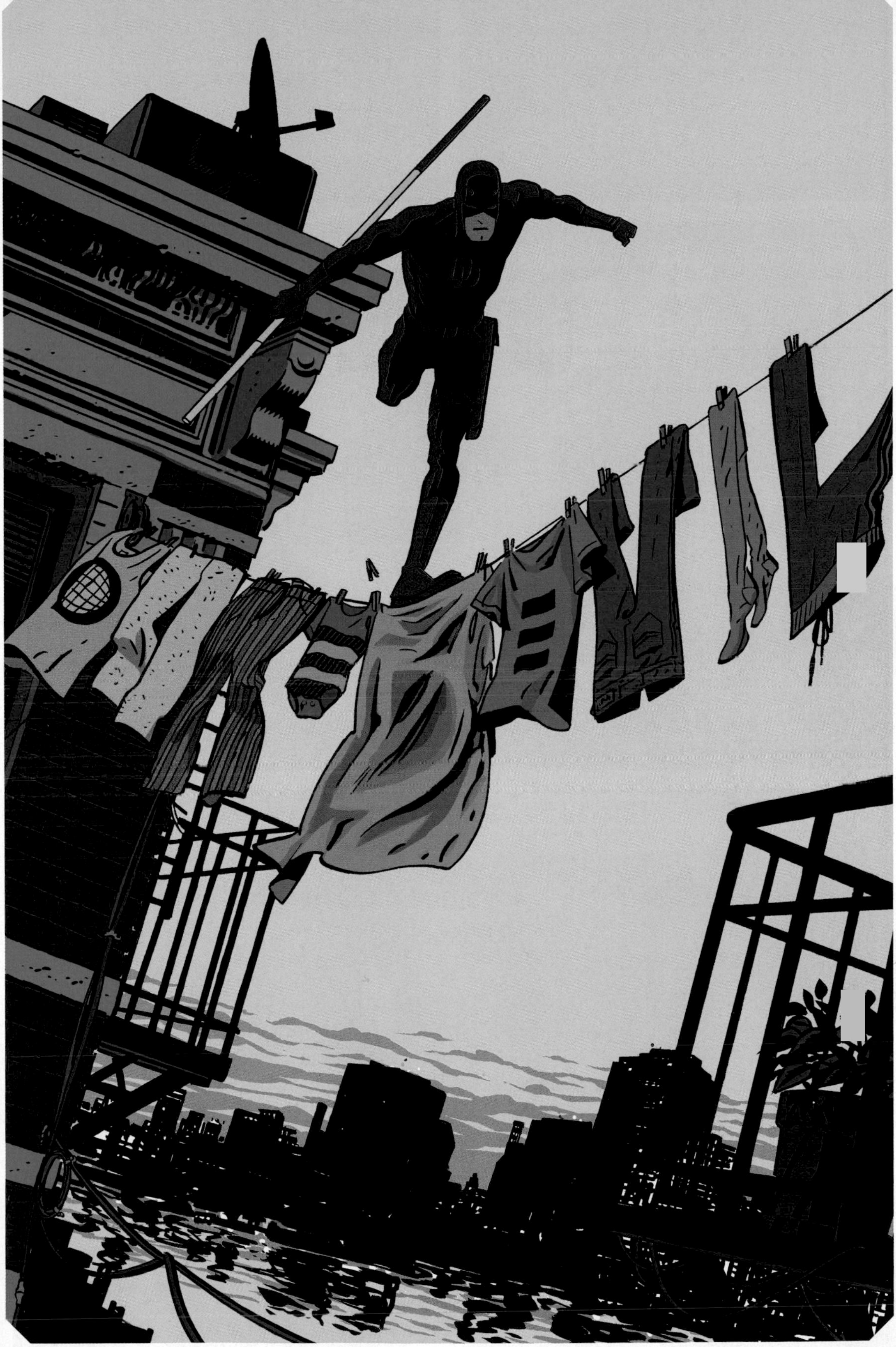

TWENTY-SIX

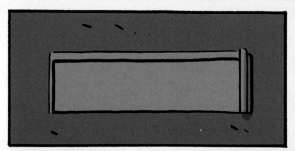

sktt

IT'S DONE.

IS--HE-- DEAD...?

NOT YET.

SPLENDID...

YOU SHOULD HAVE SEEN HIM SCRAMBLE TO GET AWAY. LIKE A WHIPPED DOG.

AND HE DOESN'T EVEN KNOW WHO'S BEHIND THE ATTACK.

WHY WOULD HE?

AS FAR AS THE WORLD IS CONCERNED--

DON'T-- SPIT--THE-- WORDS...

WHAT-- WAS--DONE-- TO--ME--WAS-- NOT--A-- SETBACK...

...BUT--A-- GIFT...

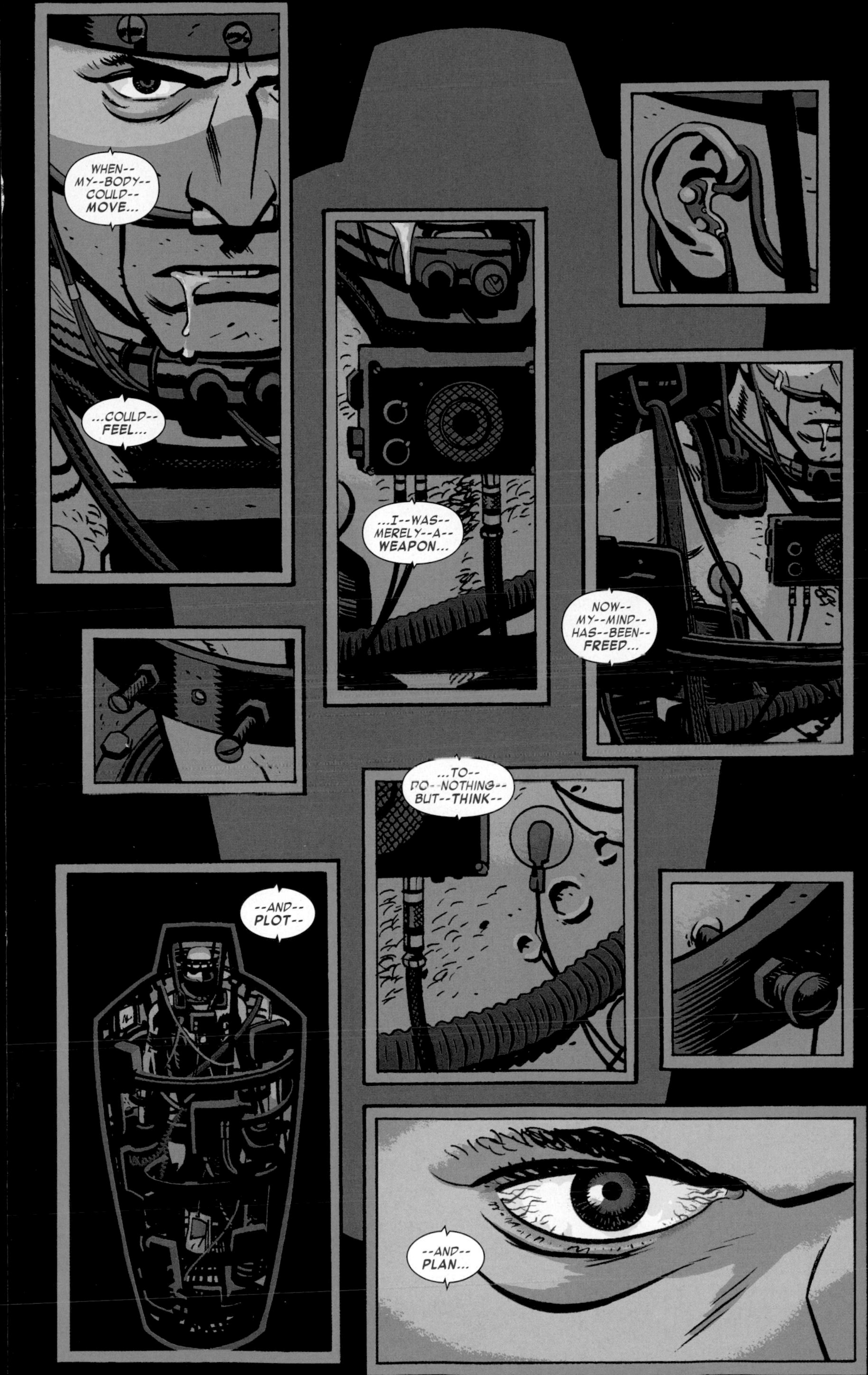
WHEN--
MY--BODY--
COULD--
MOVE...
...COULD--
FEEL...
...I--WAS--
MERELY--A--
WEAPON...
NOW--
MY--MIND--
HAS--BEEN--
FREED...
...TO--
DO--NOTHING--
BUT--THINK--
--AND--
PLOT--
--AND--
PLAN...

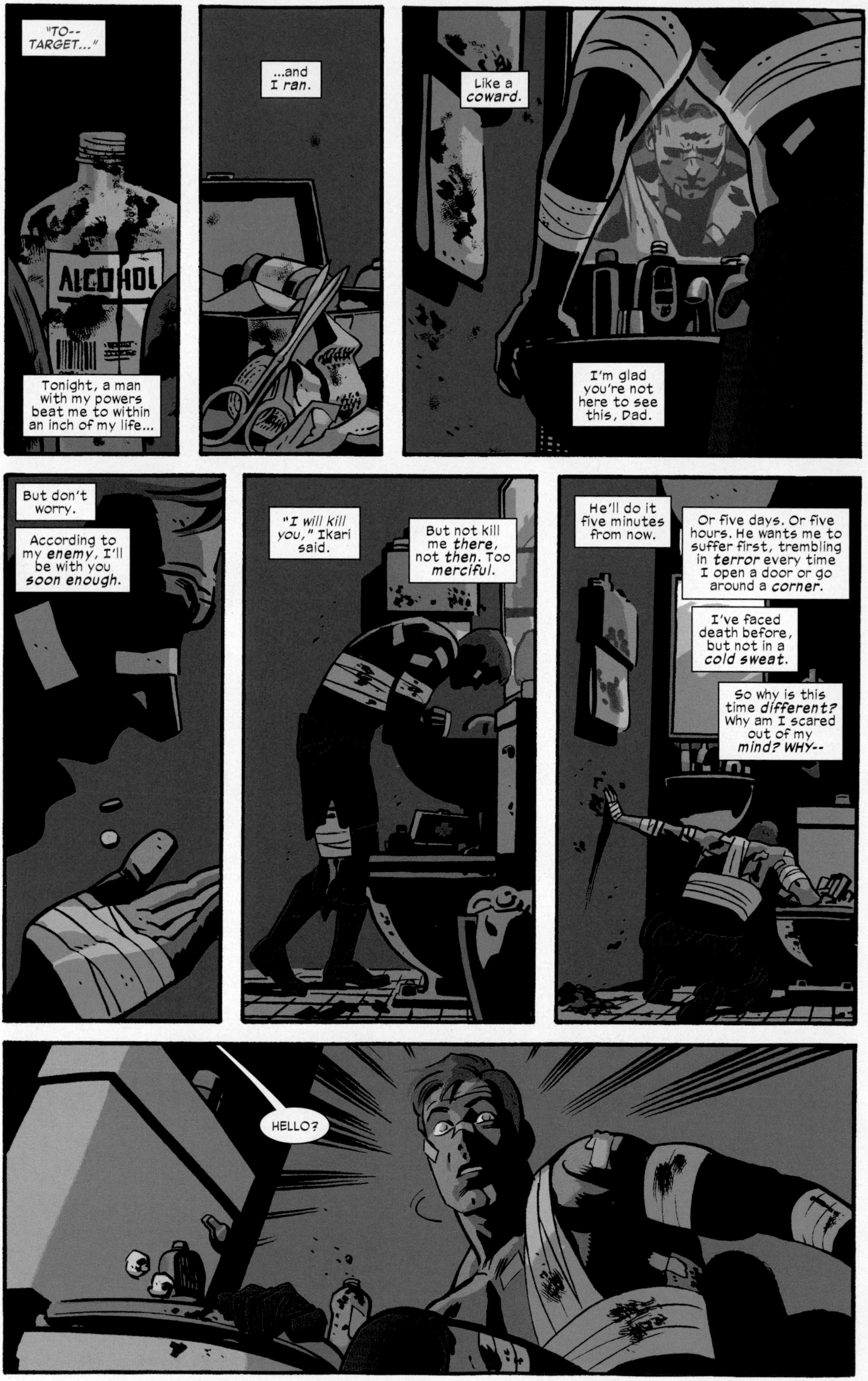
"TO--
TARGET..."
Tonight, a man with my powers beat me to within an inch of my life...
...and I ran.
Like a coward.
I'm glad you're not here to see this, Dad.
But don't worry.
According to my enemy, I'll be with you soon enough.
"I will kill you," Ikari said.
But not kill me there, not then. Too merciful.
He'll do it five minutes from now.
Or five days. Or five hours. He wants me to suffer first, trembling in terror every time I open a door or go around a corner.
I've faced death before, but not in a cold sweat.
So why is this time different? Why am I scared out of my mind? WHY--
HELLO?

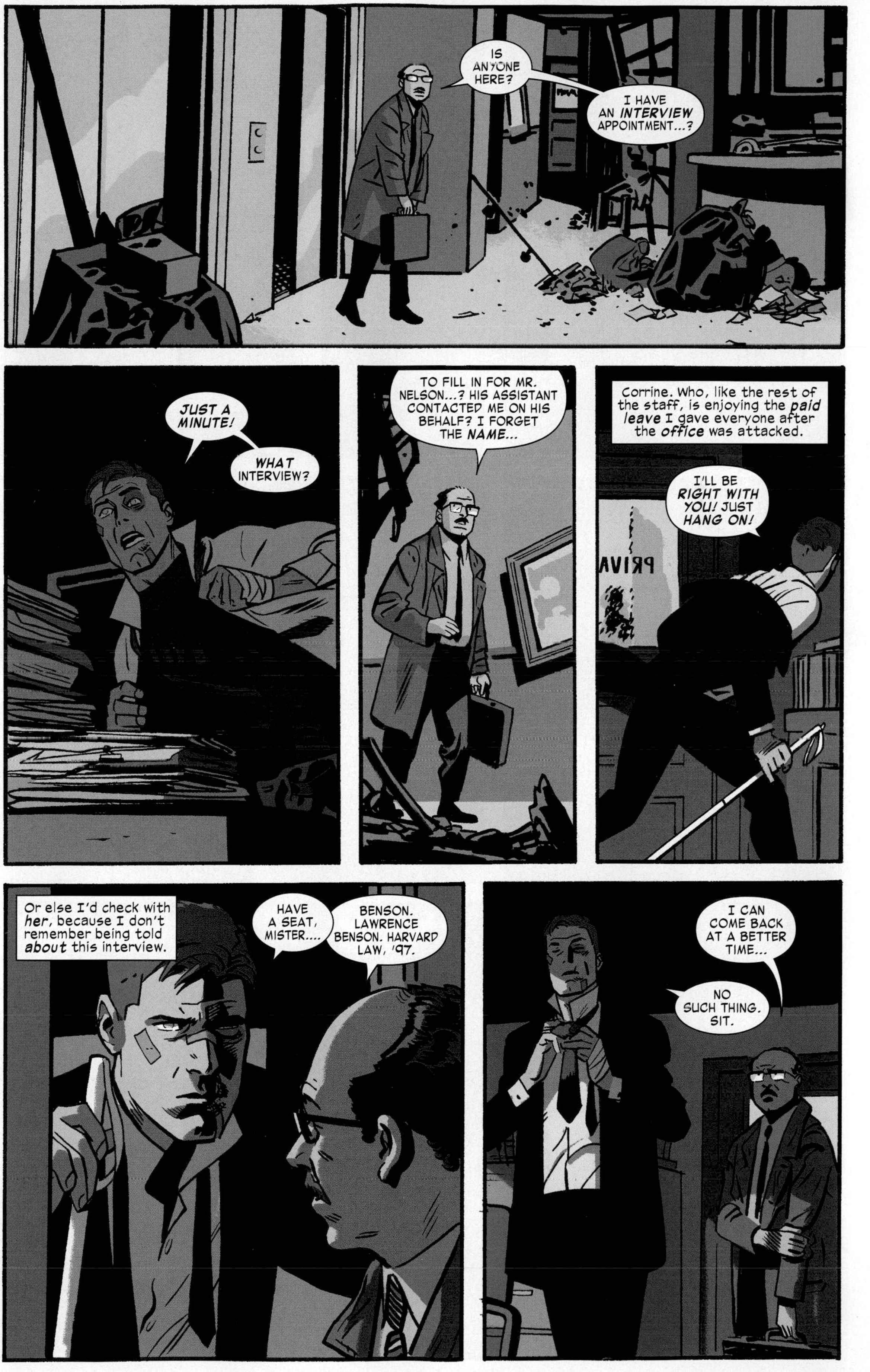
IS ANYONE HERE?
I HAVE AN INTERVIEW APPOINTMENT...?
JUST A MINUTE!
WHAT INTERVIEW?
TO FILL IN FOR MR. NELSON...? HIS ASSISTANT CONTACTED ME ON HIS BEHALF? I FORGET THE NAME...
Corrine. Who, like the rest of the staff, is enjoying the paid leave I gave everyone after the office was attacked.
I'LL BE RIGHT WITH YOU! JUST HANG ON!
PRIVA
Or else I'd check with her, because I don't remember being told about this interview.
HAVE A SEAT, MISTER....
BENSON. LAWRENCE BENSON. HARVARD LAW, '97.
I CAN COME BACK AT A BETTER TIME...
NO SUCH THING. SIT.

YOU MUST BE *MATT MURDOCK.* I KNOW ALL ABOUT YOU.

WHAT DO YOU MEAN BY *THAT?*

NOTHING! I'VE... FOLLOWED YOUR *CAREER!*

CAN...CAN YOU TELL ME MORE ABOUT WHAT YOU'D *NEED* ME FOR?

Wouldn't Corrine have covered that in the pre-interview? Maybe. Maybe not.

MY PARTNER'S BEGINNING AGGRESSIVE TREATMENT FOR HIS CANCER. SOMEONE HAS TO ASSUME HIS...

...HIS CASELOAD...

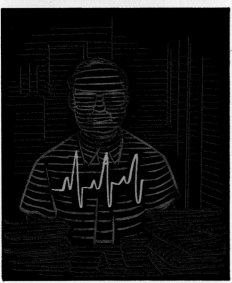

THIS IS JUST A JOB INTERVIEW, MR. BENSON, NOT A CROSS-EXAM. WHY SO NERVOUS?

WHO, ME? I'M FINE.

A lie.

But it could be the interview.

On the other hand, Ikari promised that I could die at any moment.

CHK

Not necessarily by his direct hand.

What's in the *briefcase,* Mr. Benson...?

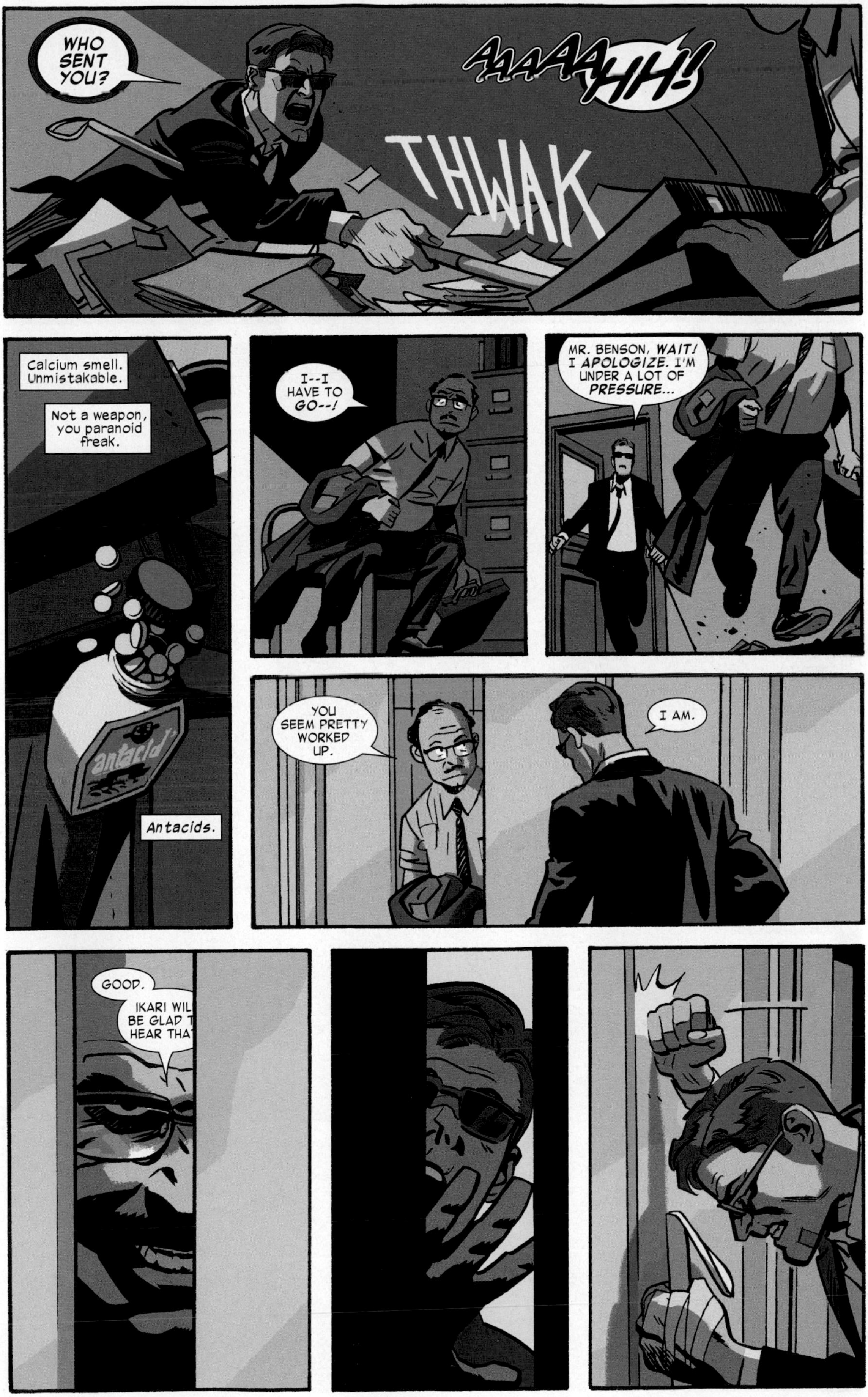
WHO SENT YOU?
AAAAAHH!
THWAK
Calcium smell. Unmistakable.
Not a weapon, you paranoid freak.
Antacids.
I--I HAVE TO GO--!
MR. BENSON, WAIT! I APOLOGIZE. I'M UNDER A LOT OF PRESSURE...
YOU SEEM PRETTY WORKED UP.
I AM.
GOOD.
IKARI WIL BE GLAD T HEAR THA

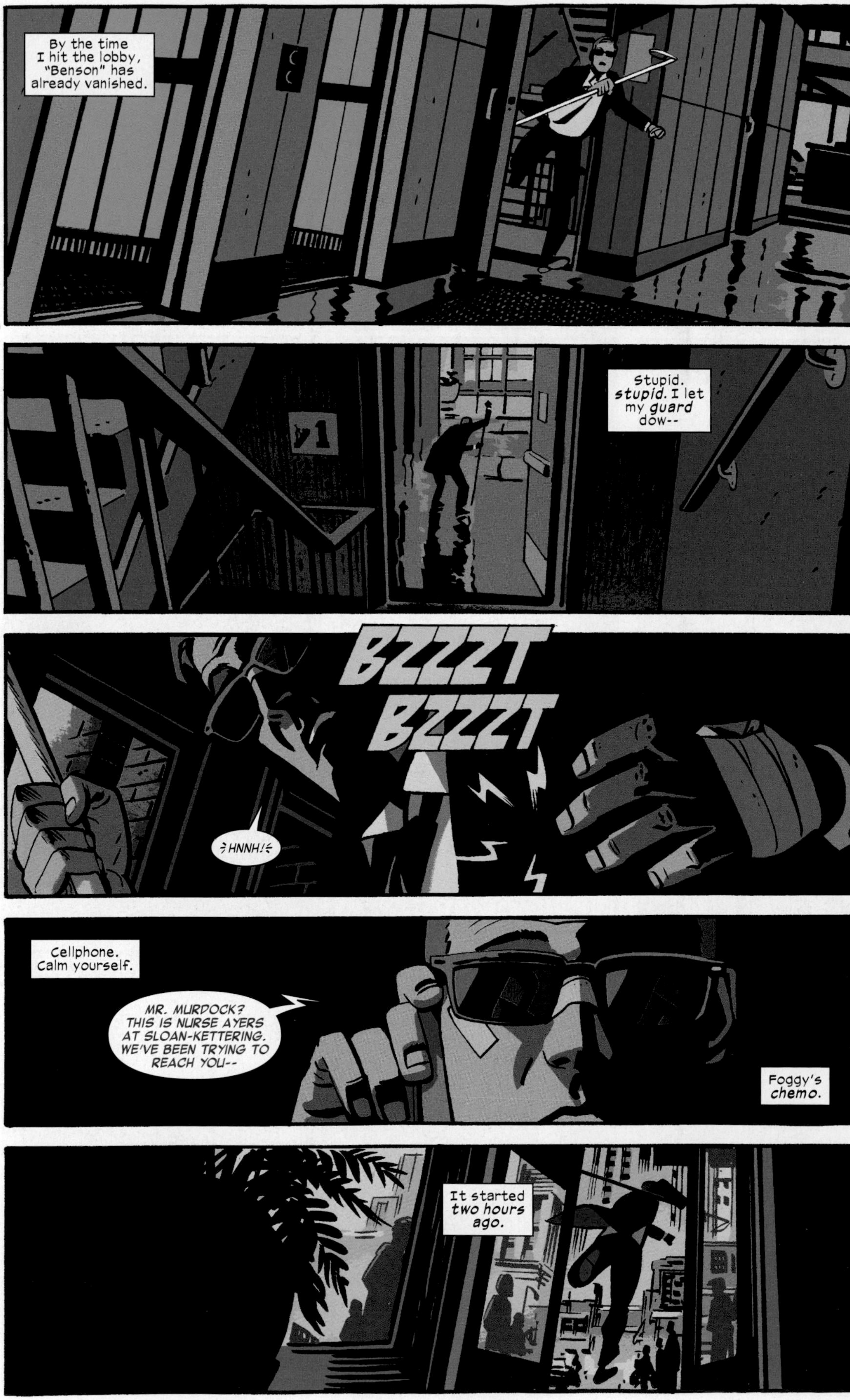
By the time I hit the lobby, "Benson" has already vanished.
Stupid. *stupid.* I let my *guard* dow--
BZZZT BZZZT
HNNH!
Cellphone. Calm yourself.
MR. MURDOCK? THIS IS NURSE AYERS AT SLOAN-KETTERING. WE'VE BEEN TRYING TO REACH YOU--
Foggy's *chemo.*
It started *two hours* ago.

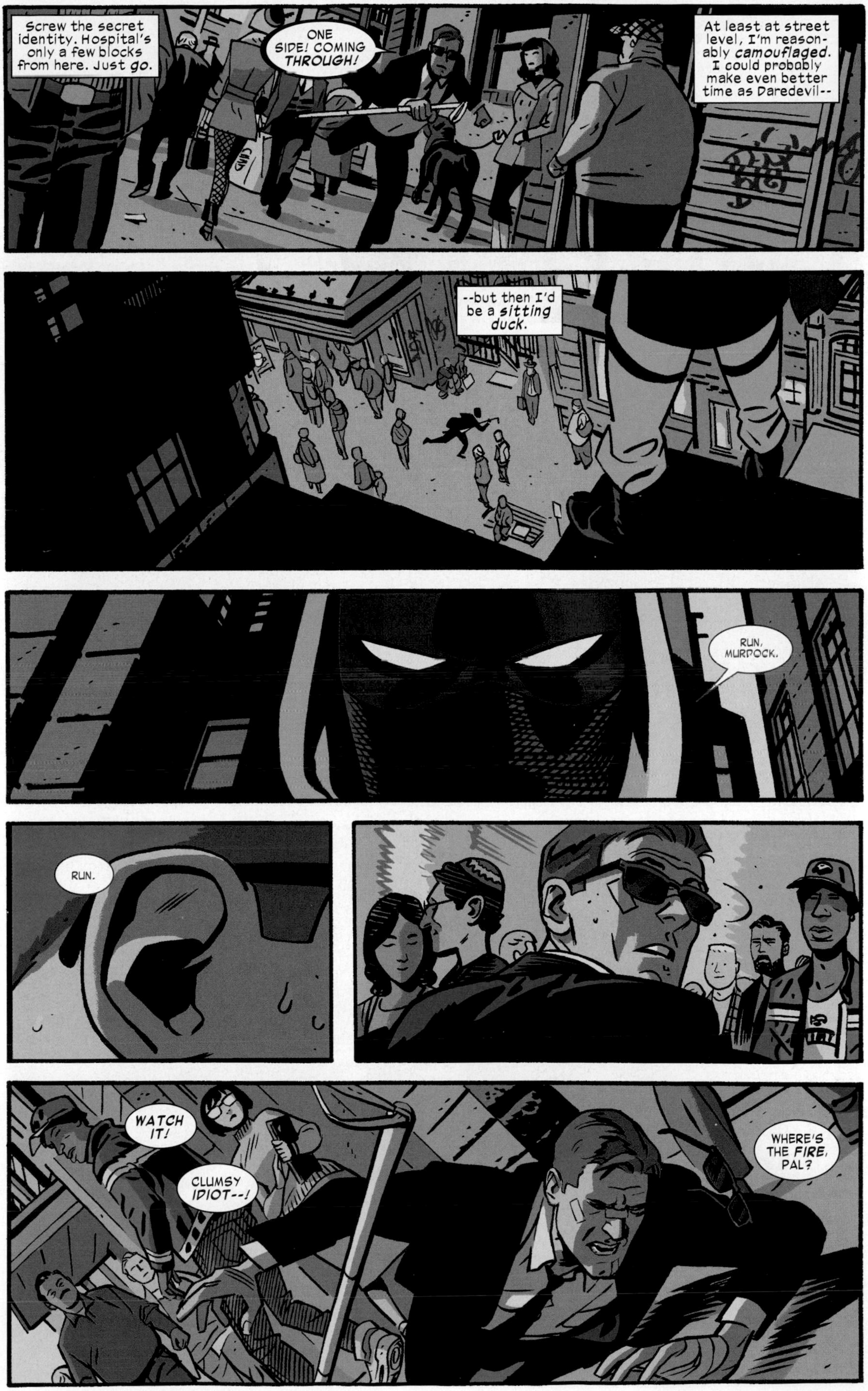
Screw the secret identity. Hospital's only a few blocks from here. Just go.
ONE SIDE! COMING THROUGH!
At least at street level, I'm reasonably camouflaged. I could probably make even better time as Daredevil--
--but then I'd be a sitting duck.
RUN, MURDOCK.
RUN.
WATCH IT!
CLUMSY IDIOT--!
WHERE'S THE FIRE, PAL?

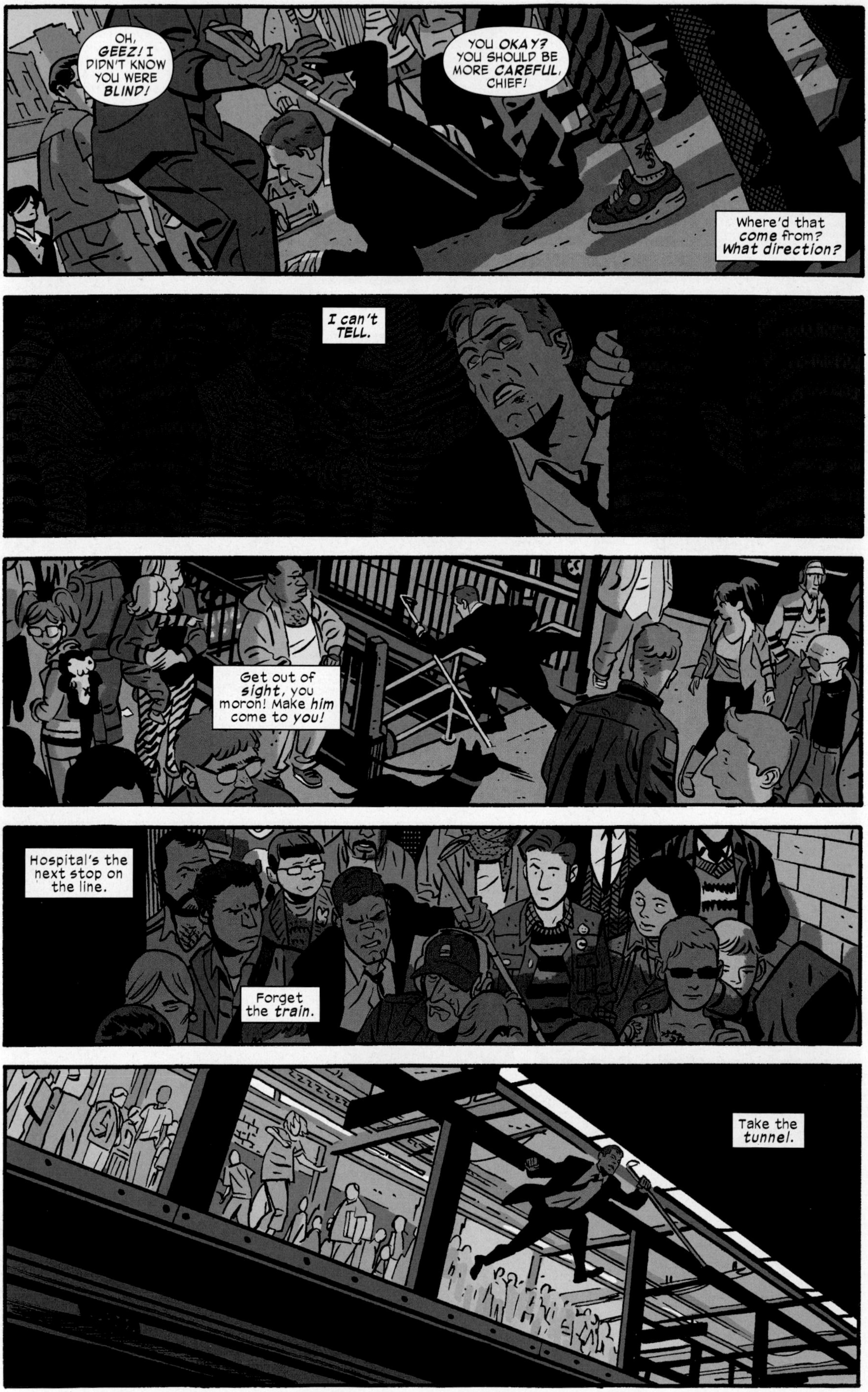
OH, GEEZ! I DIDN'T KNOW YOU WERE BLIND!
YOU OKAY? YOU SHOULD BE MORE CAREFUL, CHIEF!
Where'd that come from? What direction?
I can't TELL.
Get out of sight, you moron! Make him come to you!
Hospital's the next stop on the line.
Forget the train.
Take the tunnel.

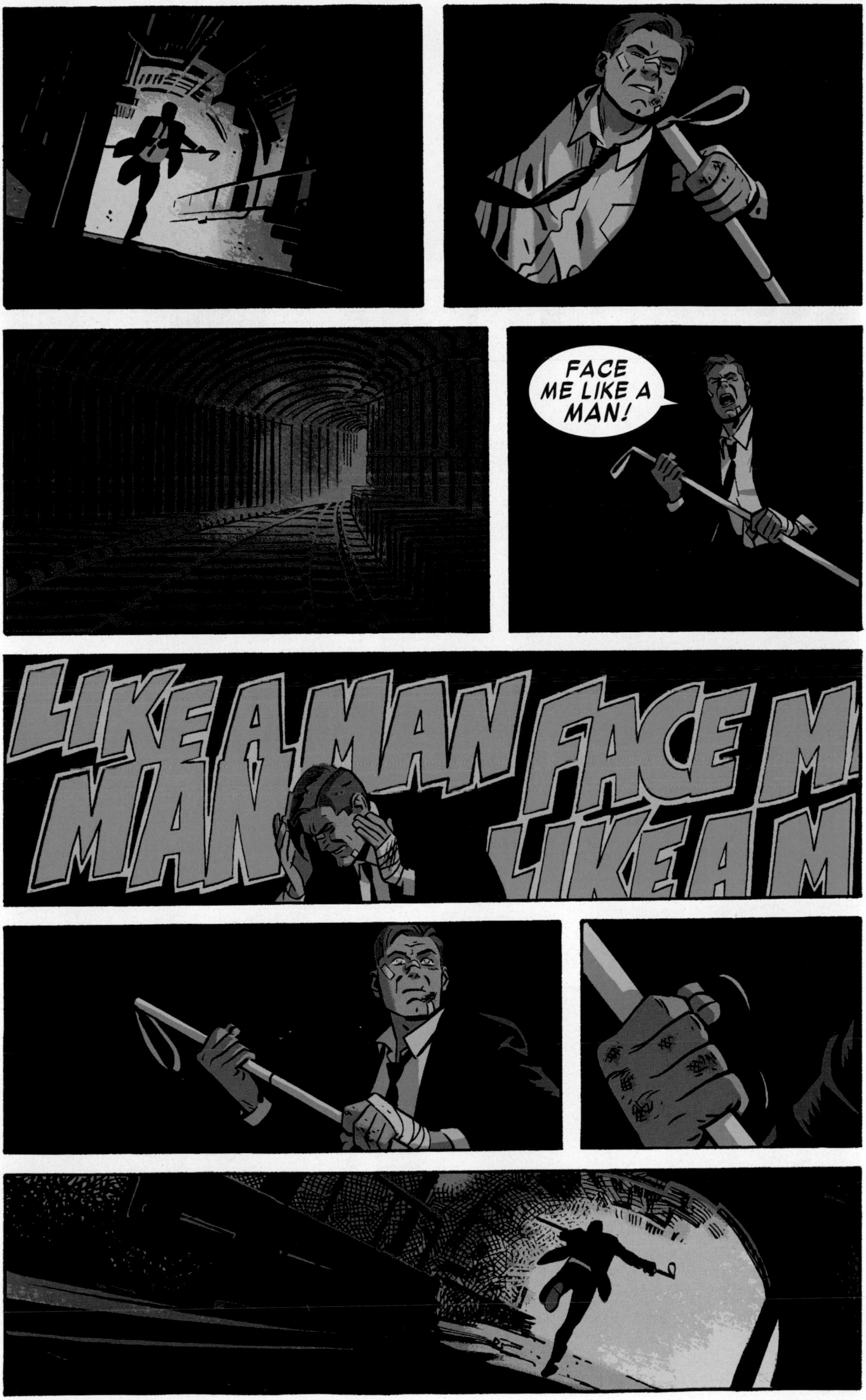
FACE ME LIKE A MAN!
LIKE A MAN FACE M
MAN
LIKE A M

Cancer ward. A hundred noises, a thousand smells. A chaotic jungle where I'm not the lion.

Foggy's room. They said the anti-nauseauls would take a half-hour and the potassium/magnesium drip another two, so that makes this the actual "*cocktail*," but--

--I don't remember--aren't they supposed to take him to a *ward* for this?

A syringe? Why not an I.V.? Is it *supposed* to smell like that? Like--

FOGGY, HAVE YOU EVER SEEN THIS NURSE BEFORE?

I...I DUNNO...

SIR, I'M GOING TO HAVE TO ASK YOU TO NOT UPSET MR. NELSON. YOU CAN WAIT OUTSIDE.

KRAKK!

YOU'D LIKE THAT, WOULDN'T YOU?

MATT, WHAT THE HELL--?

HE'S HERE TO KILL YOU, FOGGY!

WHAT ARE YOU *TALKING* ABOUT? HAVE YOU GONE *INSANE*?

OH, GOD. MAYBE. I DON'T *KNOW!* I'M *SORRY!* I--

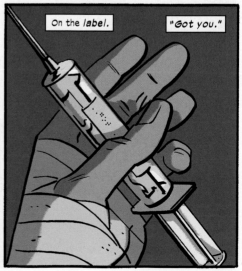

On the *label*.

"*Got you*."

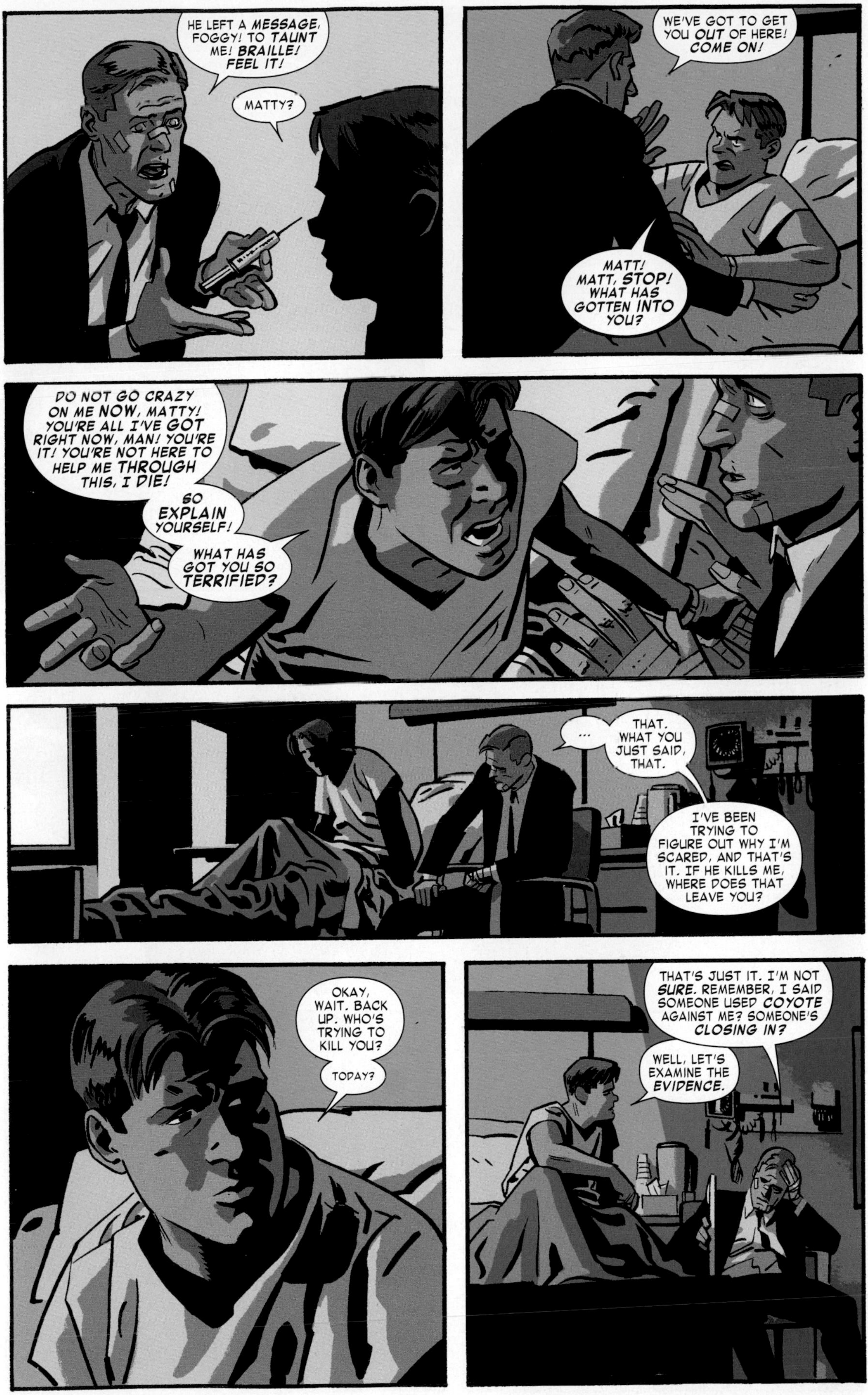
HE LEFT A MESSAGE, FOGGY! TO TAUNT ME! BRAILLE! FEEL IT!
MATTY?
WE'VE GOT TO GET YOU OUT OF HERE! COME ON!
MATT! MATT, STOP! WHAT HAS GOTTEN INTO YOU?
DO NOT GO CRAZY ON ME NOW, MATTY! YOU'RE ALL I'VE GOT RIGHT NOW, MAN! YOU'RE IT! YOU'RE NOT HERE TO HELP ME THROUGH THIS, I DIE!
SO EXPLAIN YOURSELF!
WHAT HAS GOT YOU SO TERRIFIED?
...
THAT. WHAT YOU JUST SAID, THAT.
I'VE BEEN TRYING TO FIGURE OUT WHY I'M SCARED, AND THAT'S IT. IF HE KILLS ME, WHERE DOES THAT LEAVE YOU?
OKAY, WAIT. BACK UP. WHO'S TRYING TO KILL YOU?
TODAY?
THAT'S JUST IT. I'M NOT SURE. REMEMBER, I SAID SOMEONE USED COYOTE AGAINST ME? SOMEONE'S CLOSING IN?
WELL, LET'S EXAMINE THE EVIDENCE.

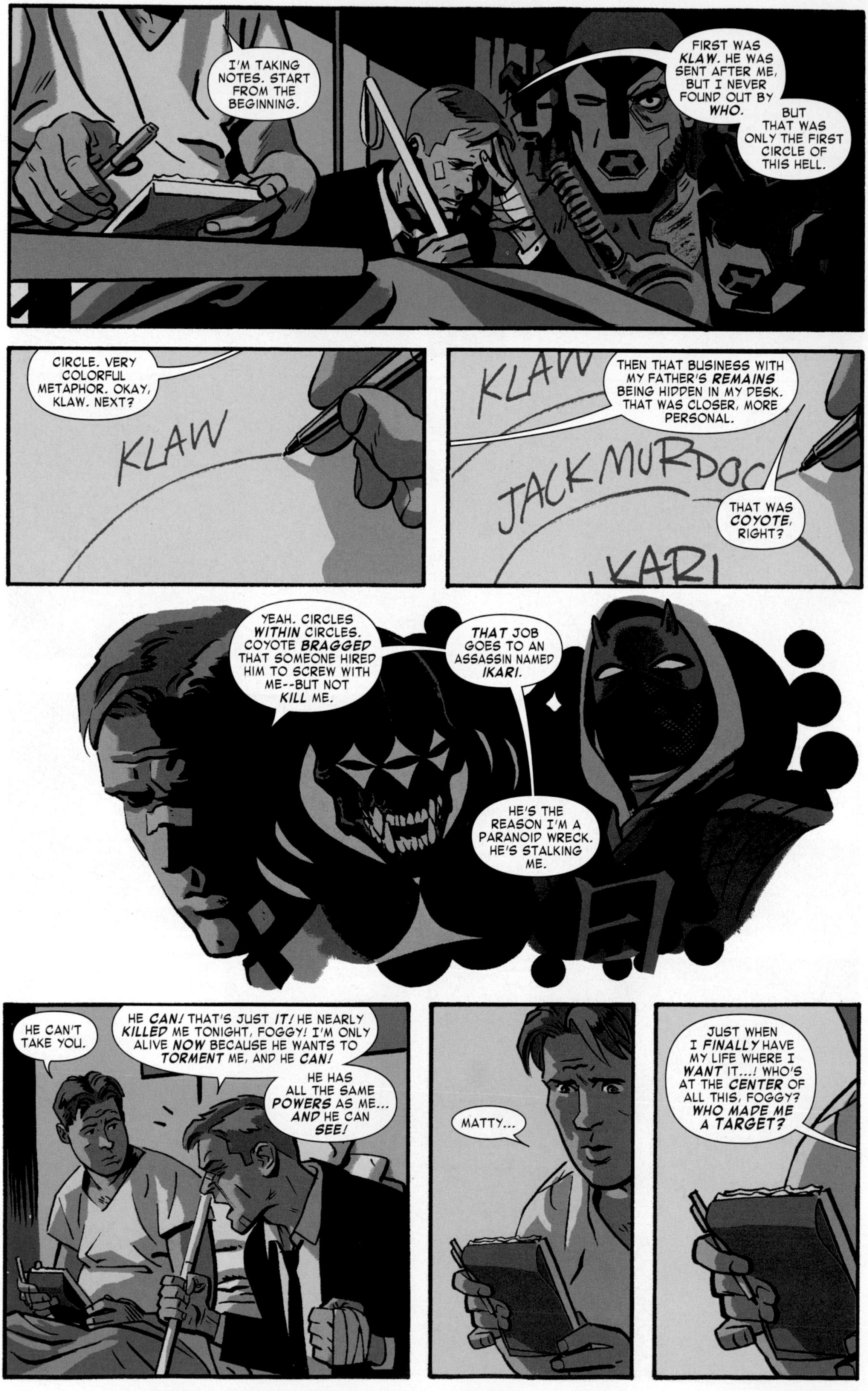
I'M TAKING NOTES. START FROM THE BEGINNING.
FIRST WAS KLAW. HE WAS SENT AFTER ME, BUT I NEVER FOUND OUT BY WHO.
BUT THAT WAS ONLY THE FIRST CIRCLE OF THIS HELL.
CIRCLE. VERY COLORFUL METAPHOR. OKAY, KLAW. NEXT?
KLAW
KLAW
THEN THAT BUSINESS WITH MY FATHER'S REMAINS BEING HIDDEN IN MY DESK. THAT WAS CLOSER, MORE PERSONAL.
JACK MURDOC
THAT WAS COYOTE, RIGHT?
YEAH. CIRCLES WITHIN CIRCLES. COYOTE BRAGGED THAT SOMEONE HIRED HIM TO SCREW WITH ME--BUT NOT KILL ME.
THAT JOB GOES TO AN ASSASSIN NAMED IKARI.
HE'S THE REASON I'M A PARANOID WRECK. HE'S STALKING ME.
HE CAN'T TAKE YOU.
HE CAN! THAT'S JUST IT! HE NEARLY KILLED ME TONIGHT, FOGGY! I'M ONLY ALIVE NOW BECAUSE HE WANTS TO TORMENT ME, AND HE CAN!
HE HAS ALL THE SAME POWERS AS ME... AND HE CAN SEE!
MATTY...
JUST WHEN I FINALLY HAVE MY LIFE WHERE I WANT IT...! WHO'S AT THE CENTER OF ALL THIS, FOGGY? WHO MADE ME A TARGET?

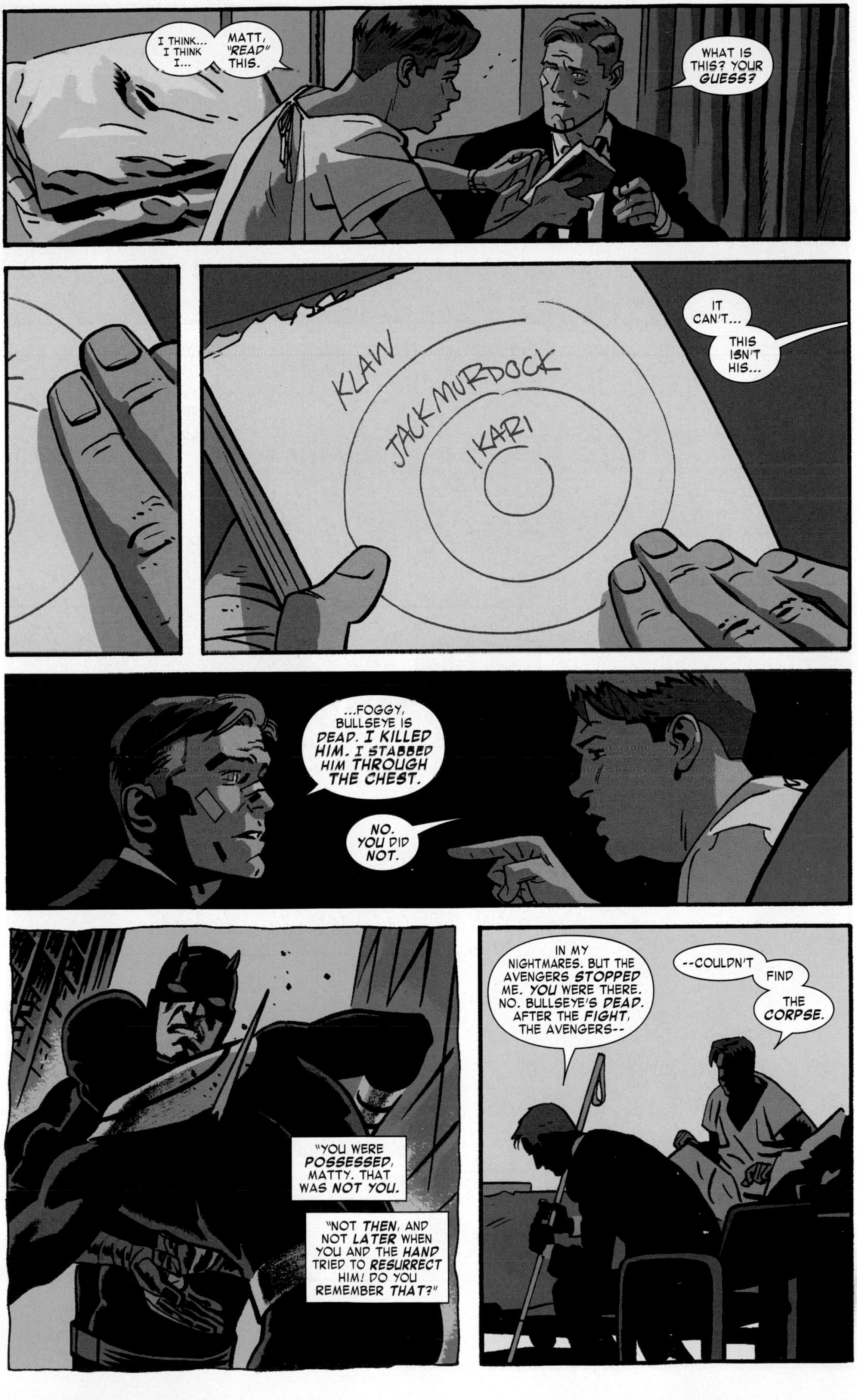
I THINK... I THINK I...
MATT, "READ" THIS.
WHAT IS THIS? YOUR GUESS?
KLAW
JACK MURDOCK
KARI
IT CAN'T...
THIS ISN'T HIS...
...FOGGY, BULLSEYE IS DEAD. I KILLED HIM. I STABBED HIM THROUGH THE CHEST.
NO. YOU DID NOT.
"YOU WERE POSSESSED, MATTY. THAT WAS NOT YOU.
"NOT THEN, AND NOT LATER WHEN YOU AND THE HAND TRIED TO RESURRECT HIM! DO YOU REMEMBER THAT?"
IN MY NIGHTMARES. BUT THE AVENGERS STOPPED ME. YOU WERE THERE. NO. BULLSEYE'S DEAD. AFTER THE FIGHT, THE AVENGERS--
--COULDN'T
FIND
THE CORPSE.

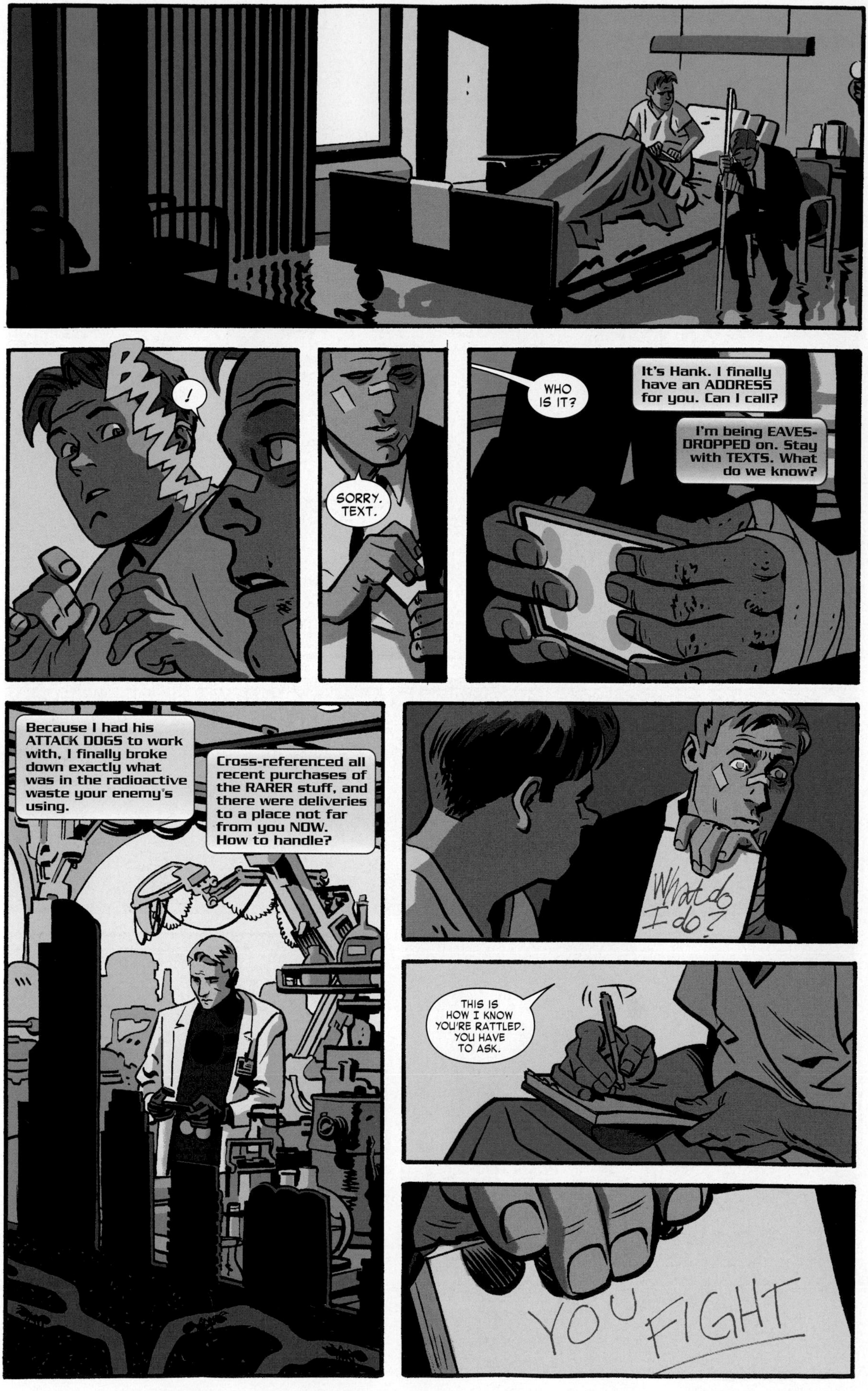

BWAMMM
!
SORRY. TEXT.
WHO IS IT?
It's Hank. I finally have an ADDRESS for you. Can I call?
I'm being EAVES-DROPPED on. Stay with TEXTS. What do we know?
Because I had his ATTACK DOGS to work with, I finally broke down exactly what was in the radioactive waste your enemy's using.
Cross-referenced all recent purchases of the RARER stuff, and there were deliveries to a place not far from you NOW. How to handle?
What do I do?
THIS IS HOW I KNOW YOU'RE RATTLED. YOU HAVE TO ASK.
YOU FIGHT

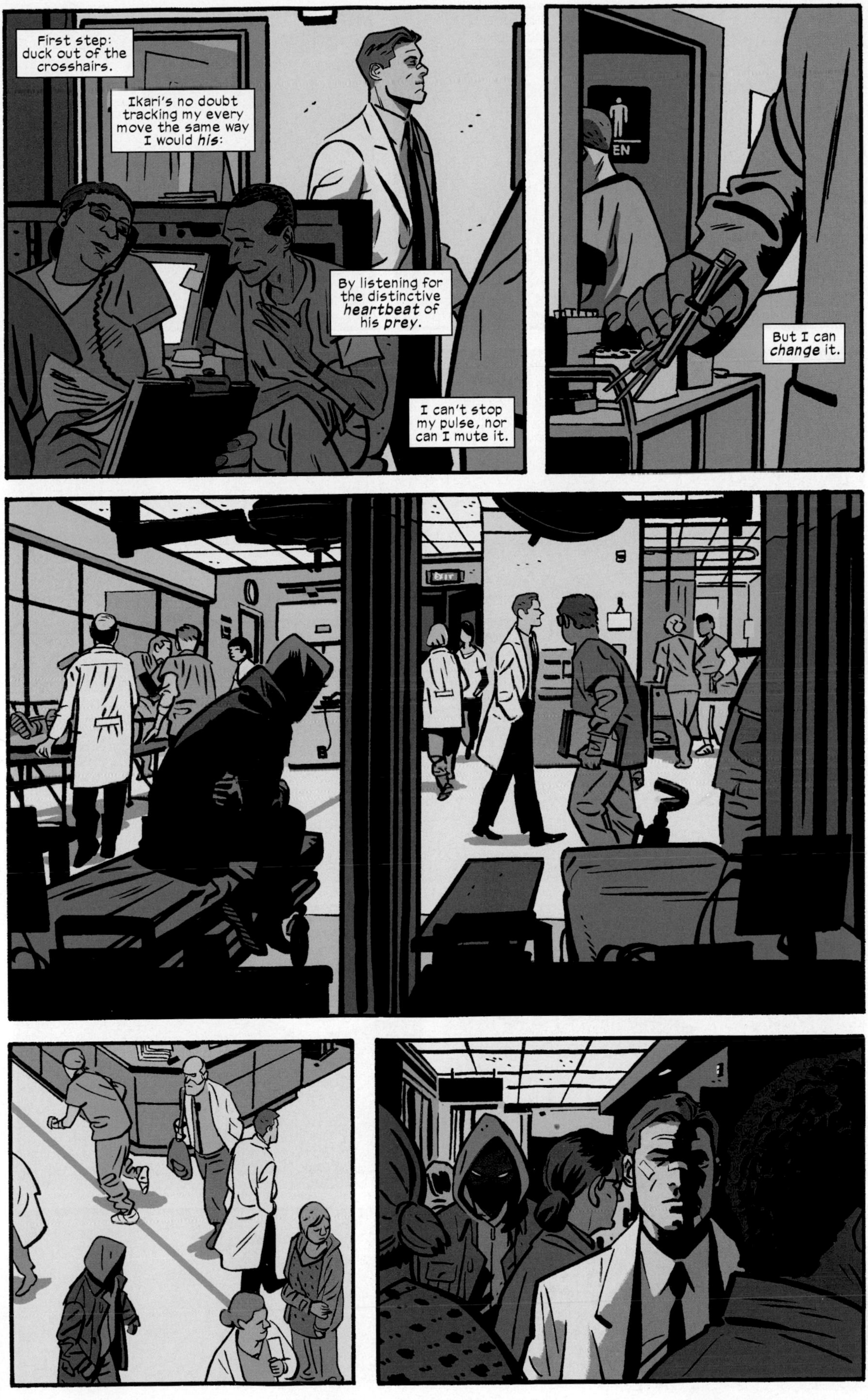
First step: duck out of the crosshairs.
Ikari's no doubt tracking my every move the same way I would *his*:
By listening for the distinctive *heartbeat* of his *prey*.
I can't stop my pulse, nor can I mute it.
But I can *change* it.

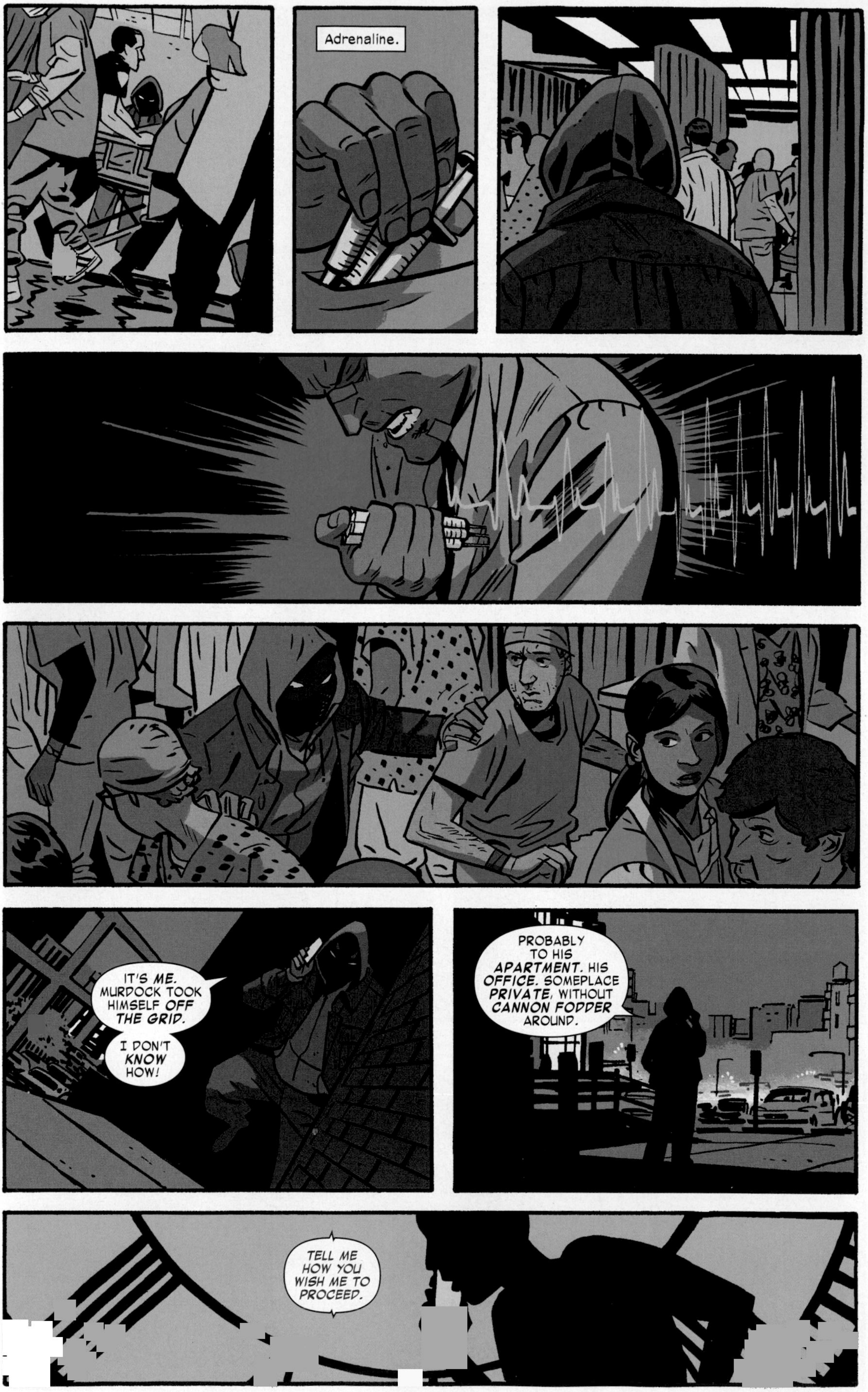

Adrenaline.
IT'S ME. MURDOCK TOOK HIMSELF OFF THE GRID.
I DON'T KNOW HOW!
PROBABLY TO HIS APARTMENT. HIS OFFICE. SOMEPLACE PRIVATE, WITHOUT CANNON FODDER AROUND.
TELL ME HOW YOU WISH ME TO PROCEED.

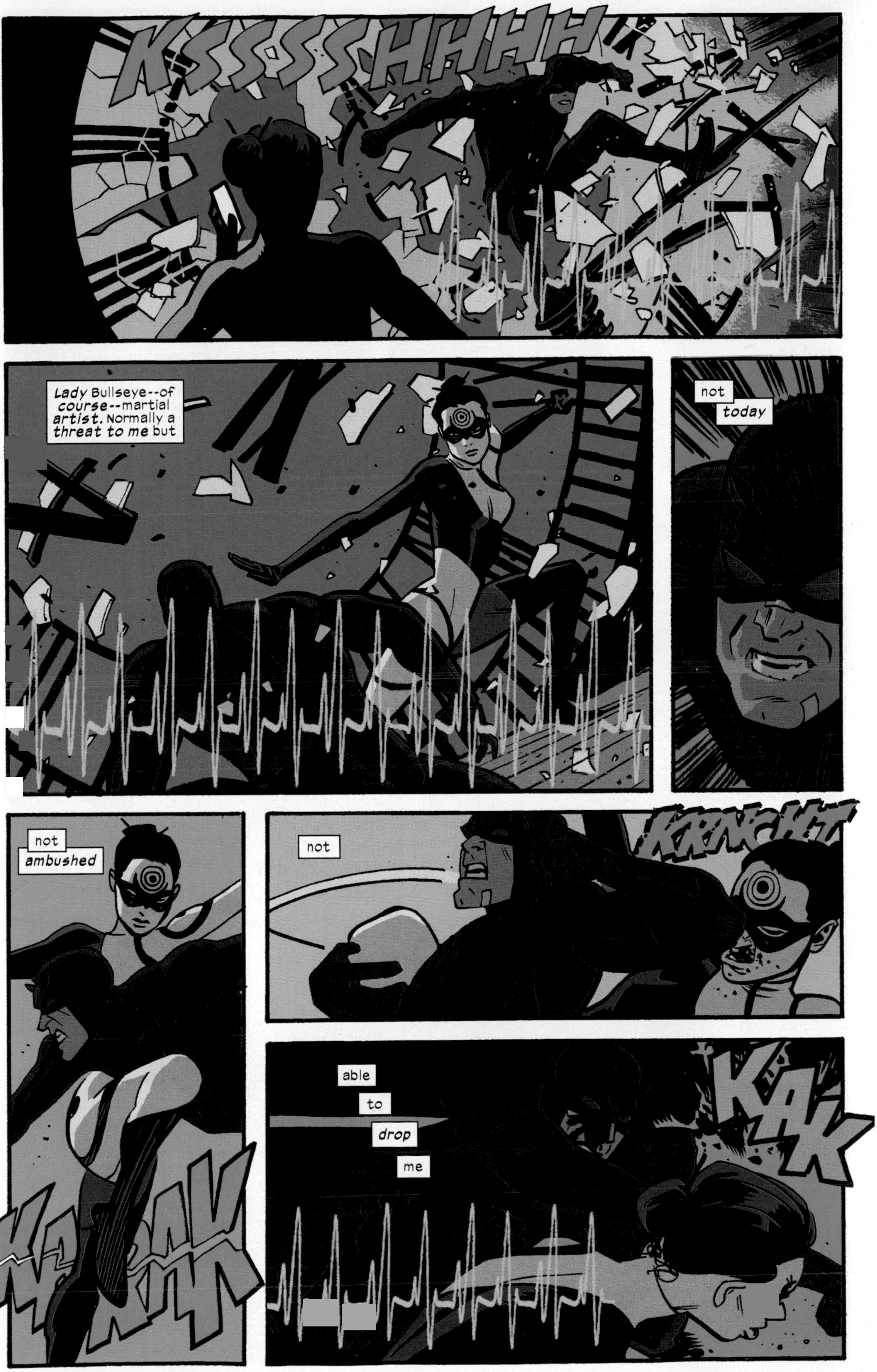
KSSSSHHHH
Lady Bullseye--of course--martial artist. Normally a threat to me but
not
today
not
ambushed
not
KRNCHT
able
to
drop
me
KAK

IT IS HIM, ISN'T IT?

WHERE IS HE? WHERE IS HE HIDING--?

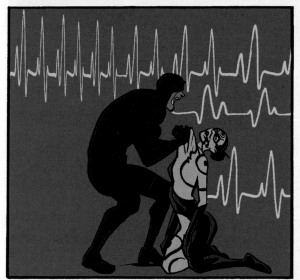

Wheeze of a respirator. Crackle of a voicebox and the smell of urine.

None of which disguises him.

SO THIS IS WHAT YOU'VE BECOME.

BULLSEYE, THE WORLD'S DEADLIEST MAN.

AN *INVALID* KEPT ALIVE BY *MACHINES.*

IF ALL THAT'S LEFT OF YOU IS YOUR SICK, TWISTED *MIND,* I CAN IMAGINE NO MORE FITTING *PUNISHMENT.*

I'D CALL THAT A *VICTORY.*

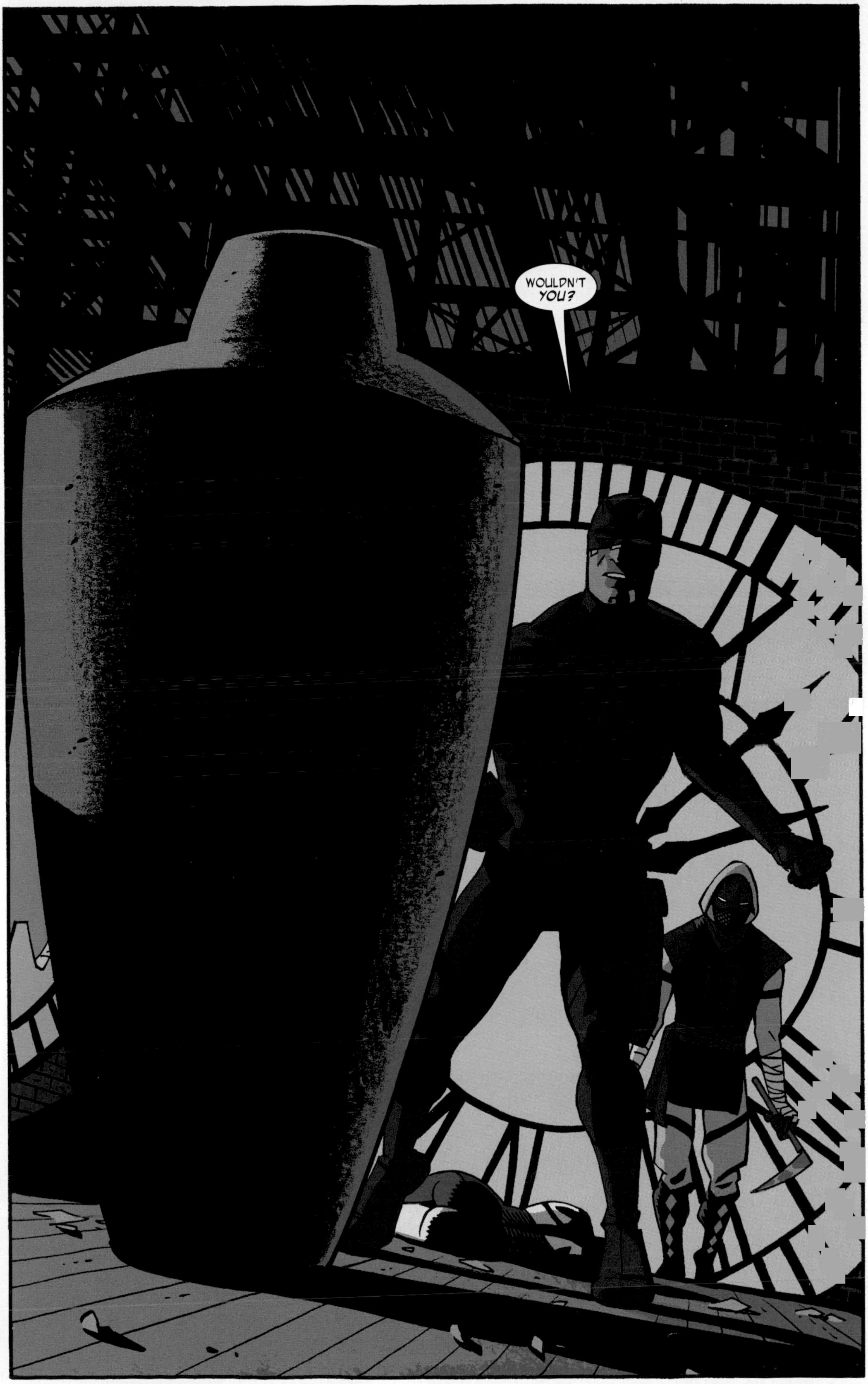
WOULDN'T YOU?

DD readers-

For this special extra-sized issue, I thought we'd take a couple pages to show some of the Behind the scenes work that Mark and Chris do to make Daredevil such a compelling read each month. Hope you like it!

-SW

MENS
GETTING UP TO FOLLOW
16

DAREDEVIL #26/Script/Ms. Page 1 MARK WAID

DAREDEVIL #26

SCRIPT FOR 20 PAGES/MARCH 11-25, 2013

PAGE SIXTEEN through SEVENTEEN

(However you think it paces out best, Chris!)

PANEL: A MINUTE LATER. MATT, IN A DOCTOR'S COAT, SNEAKS PAST SOME OTHERWISE-OCCUPIED NURSES AT THE NURSES' STATION--

DD CAPTION: First step: duck out of the crosshairs.

DD CAPTION: Ikari's no doubt tracking my every move the same way I would HIS:

DD CAPTION: By listening for the distinctive HEARTBEAT of his PREY.

PANEL: --AND STEALS SEVERAL SYRINGES MARKED "ADRENALINE."

DD CAPTION: I can't stop my pulse, nor can I mute it.

DD CAPTION: But I can CHANGE it.

PANELS: A MOMENT LATER, MATT'S WALKING SWIFTLY THROUGH THE EMERGENCY ROOM--LOTS AND LOTS OF HEARTBEATS ALL AROUND, INCLUDING HIS OWN HEARTLINE, CENTRAL--

--IKARI, IN A HOODIE, IS FOLLOWING HIM, TRACKING HIS HEARTBEAT--

--AND, UNNOTICED IN ALL THE CHAOS AND COMMOTION, MATT REMOVES THREE ADRENALINE SYRINGES FROM HIS DOCTOR'S COAT POCKET--

--AND JAMS THEM INTO HIS CHEST, SENDING HIS PULSERATE SOARING--

--BLENDING IN WITH ALL THE OTHER HEARTBEATS AS MATT DIVES THROUGH A THICK CROWD, IKARI IN PURSUIT--

--AND IKARI BREAKS THROUGH THE CROWD, A CACOPHONY OF OVERLAPPING HEARTLINES--AND NO SIGN OF MATT!

((more))

After all the inked art is in, Javier prepares "color flats" keeping in mind the setting and mood of the scene.. When this is done he creates the final, rendered color.

DAREDEVIL #26/Script/Ms. Page 2 MARK WAID

PAGES SIXTEEN through SEVENTEEN, continued

PANEL: BARKING INTO A CELLPHONE, IKARI TAKES OFF RUNNING INTO A NEARBY ALLEYWAY.

IKARI: It's ME. Murdock took himself OFF THE GRID.

IKARI: I don't KNOW how!

PANEL: FROM A LOW ROOFTOP, HE LOOKS DOWN HELPLESSLY, SEES NOTHING OF NOTE.

IKARI: Probably to his APARTMENT. His OFFICE. Someplace PRIVATE, without CANNON FODDER around.

PANEL: CUT TO LADY BULLSEYE IN THE CLOCK TOWER ON THE PHONE, AT THE OTHER END OF THE CALL.

PHONE/elec: Tell me how you wish me to proceed.

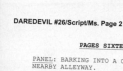

Mark and Chris work so closely together that the scripts can go from very detailed to very loose depending on the scene. Chris usually knows how to nail EXACTLY what Mark is looking for.

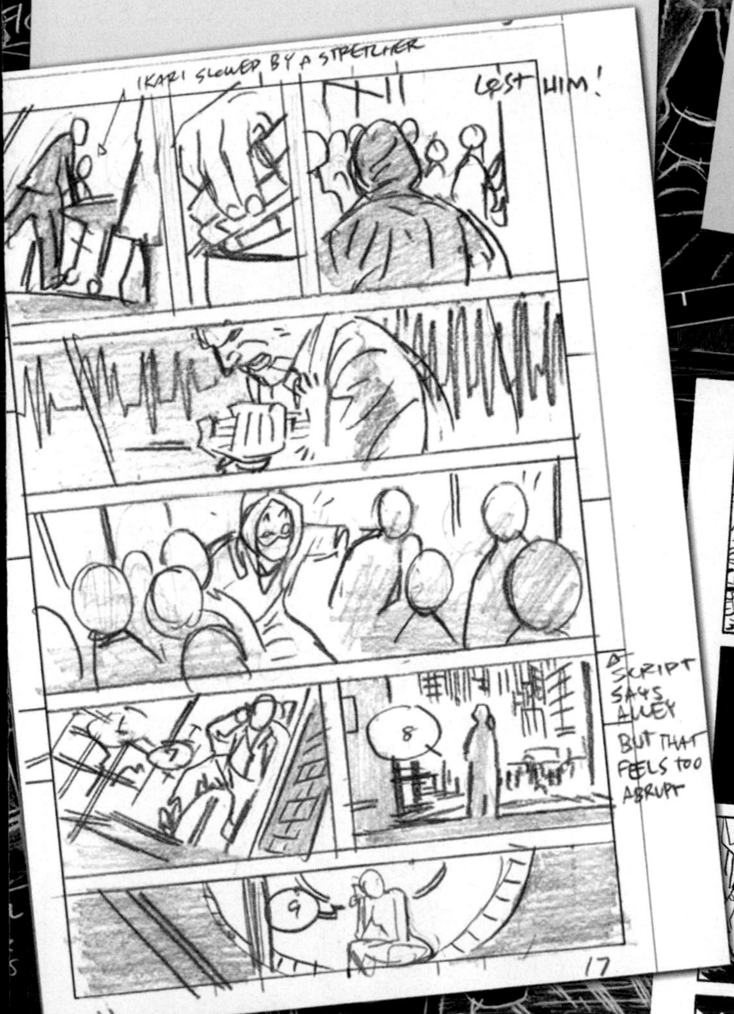

IKARI SLOWED BY A STRETCHER
LOST HIM!
SCRIPT SAYS ALLEY BUT THAT FEELS TOO ABRUPT
17

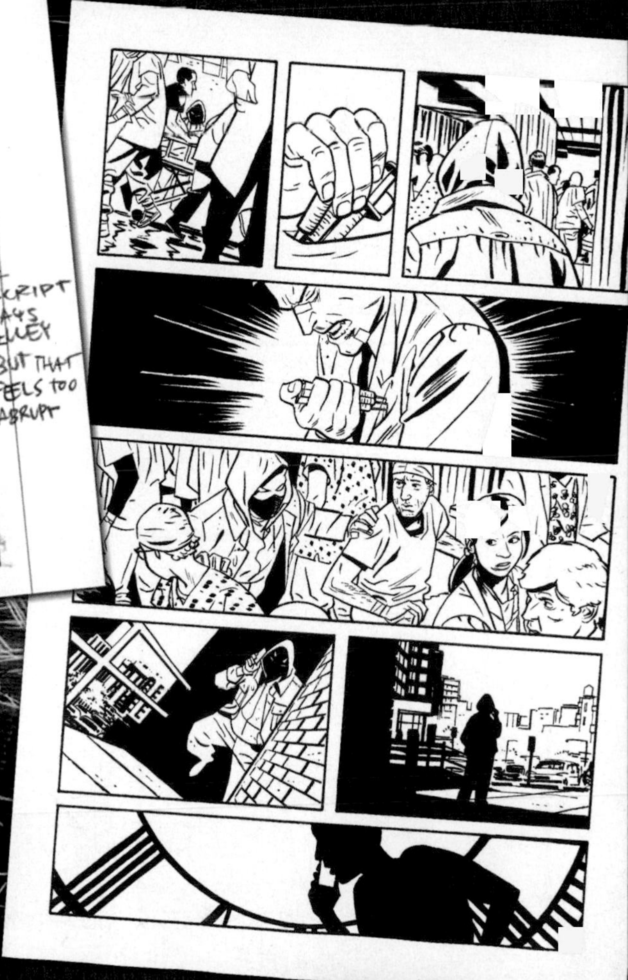

Production: irene y. lee

MY NAME IS FRANKLIN NELSON. DAREDEVIL'S BEST FRIEND. I'M IN THE HOSPITAL FOR CANCER.

MY LIFE SUCKS.

PUNCHING CANCER

THEY'RE WAITING FOR YOU, MR. NELSON.

≈SIGH≈

IT'LL BE GOOD FOR YOU AND THEM.

I'M NOT THE GUY FOR THIS, DR. FINE.

I WOULDN'T BE SO SURE. I'M NOT TERRIFIC WITH CHILDREN.

THE LAST TIME I BABYSAT, I LEARNED THE HARD WAY EXACTLY HOW MANY FIRE TRUCKS THERE ARE IN QUEENS.

YOU'RE NOT BABYSITTING. YOU'RE SPEAKING TO A GROUP.

SURELY A TRIAL LITIGATOR CAN DO THAT WITH EASE. BESIDES, YOU PROMISED. AND IT GETS YOU OUT OF BED.

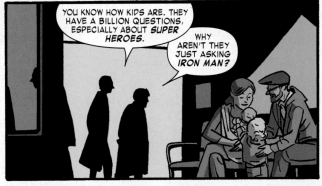

YOU KNOW HOW KIDS ARE. THEY HAVE A BILLION QUESTIONS, ESPECIALLY ABOUT SUPER HEROES.

WHY AREN'T THEY JUST ASKING IRON MAN?

BECAUSE HE'S NOT YET ARRIVED, AND THEY KNOW THAT YOU'VE MET THE FANTASTIC FOUR AND SUB-MARINER AND GOD KNOWS WHO ELSE.

CELEBRITY BY ASSOCIATION.

I'VE BEEN THEIR LAWYER. WE DON'T HANG OUT.

RUMOR HAS IT YOU KNOW DAREDEVIL QUITE WELL.

THEY'LL WANT TO HEAR ABOUT HIM, TOO.

TRUST ME, YOU'LL DO FINE. IT'S NOT A BIG DEAL.

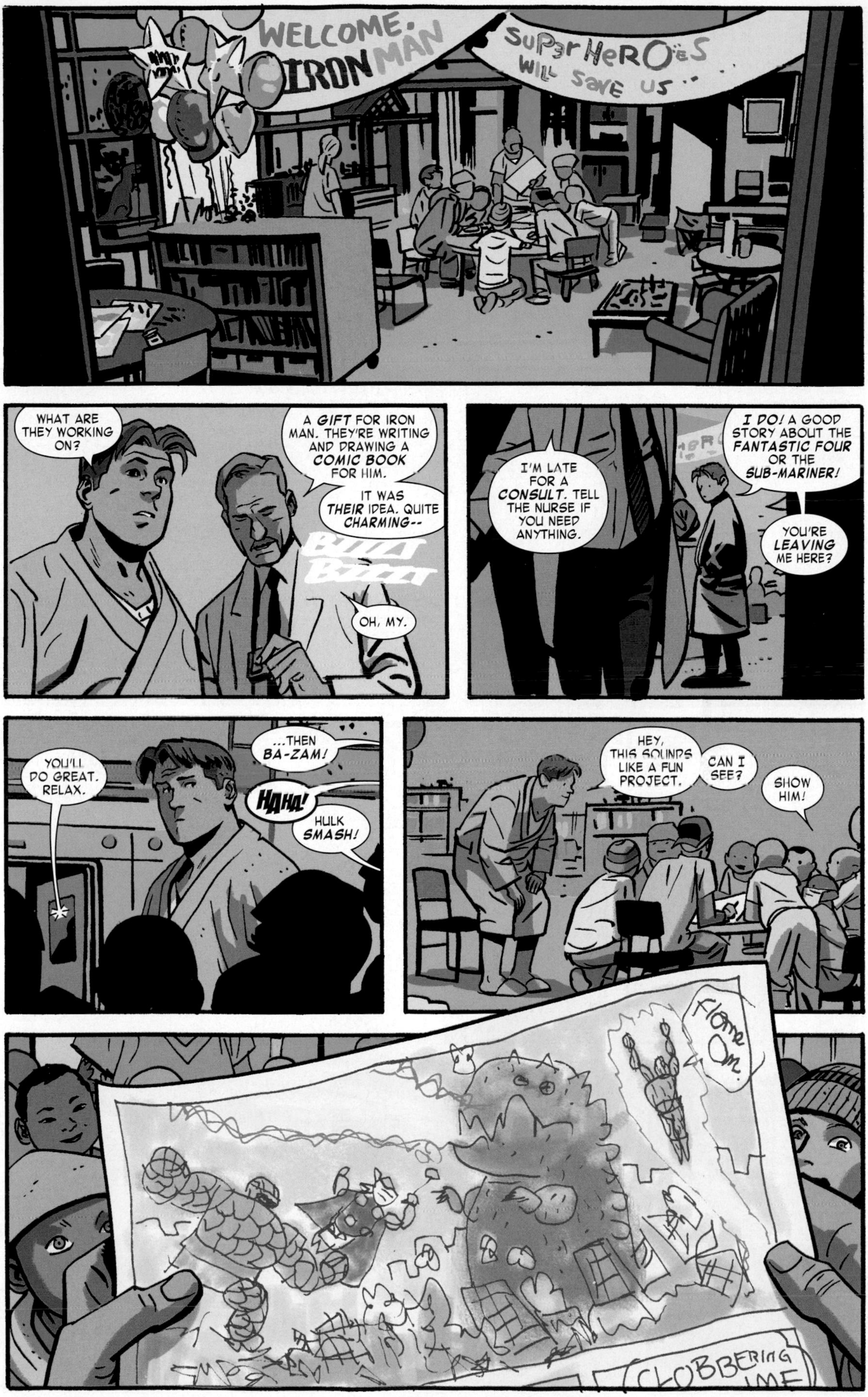
WELCOME, IRON MAN
SUPERHEROES WILL SAVE US...
WHAT ARE THEY WORKING ON?
A GIFT FOR IRON MAN. THEY'RE WRITING AND DRAWING A COMIC BOOK FOR HIM.
IT WAS THEIR IDEA. QUITE CHARMING--
BZZZT BZZZT
OH, MY.
I'M LATE FOR A CONSULT. TELL THE NURSE IF YOU NEED ANYTHING.
I DO! A GOOD STORY ABOUT THE FANTASTIC FOUR OR THE SUB-MARINER!
YOU'RE LEAVING ME HERE?
YOU'LL DO GREAT. RELAX.
...THEN BA-ZAM!
HAHA!
HULK SMASH!
HEY, THIS SOUNDS LIKE A FUN PROJECT.
CAN I SEE?
SHOW HIM!
Flame On.
CLOBBERING TIME

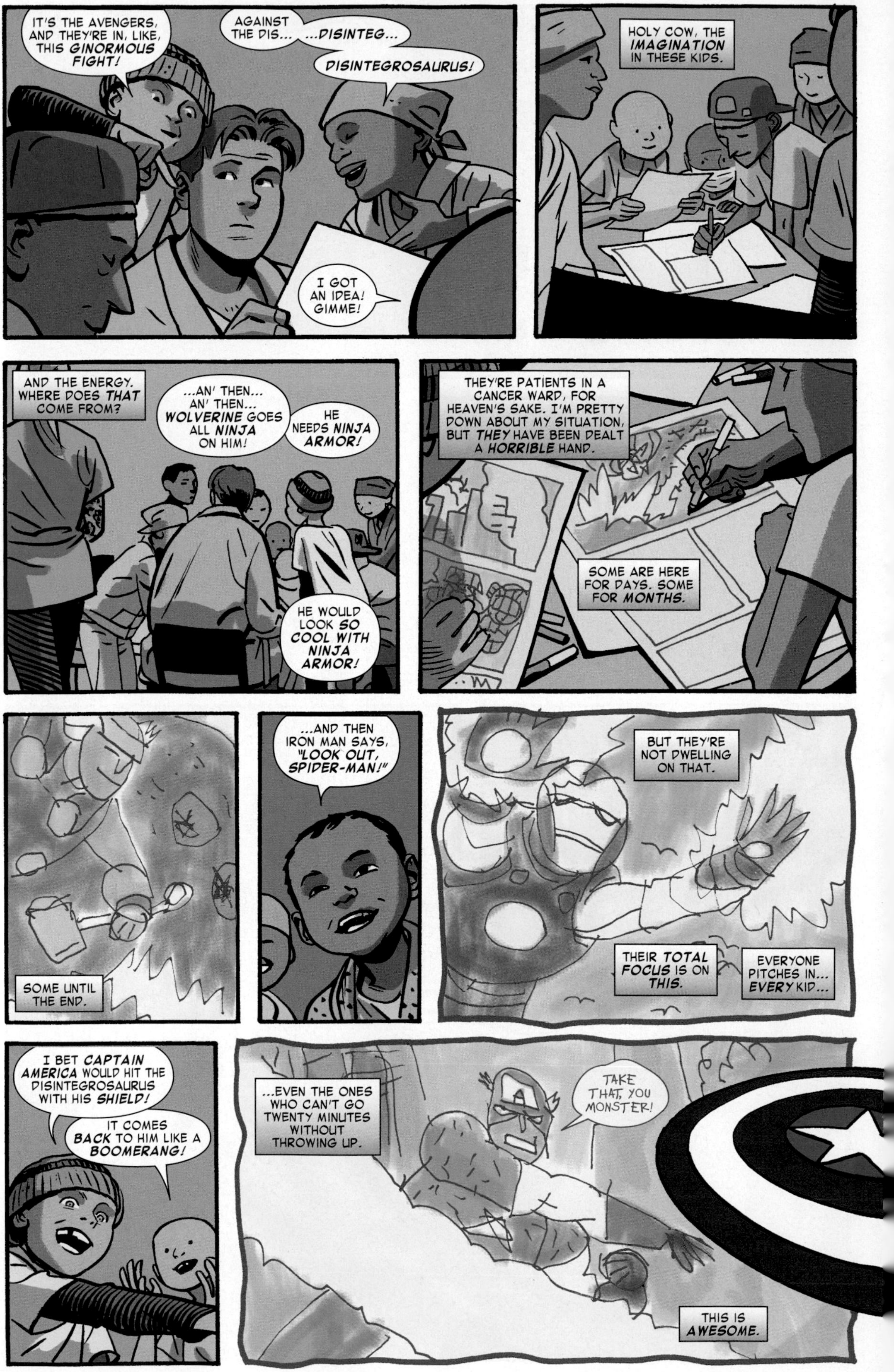
IT'S THE AVENGERS, AND THEY'RE IN, LIKE, THIS GINORMOUS FIGHT!
AGAINST THE DIS...
...DISINTEG...
DISINTEGROSAURUS!
I GOT AN IDEA! GIMME!
HOLY COW, THE IMAGINATION IN THESE KIDS.
AND THE ENERGY. WHERE DOES THAT COME FROM?
...AN' THEN... AN' THEN... WOLVERINE GOES ALL NINJA ON HIM!
HE NEEDS NINJA ARMOR!
HE WOULD LOOK SO COOL WITH NINJA ARMOR!
THEY'RE PATIENTS IN A CANCER WARD, FOR HEAVEN'S SAKE. I'M PRETTY DOWN ABOUT MY SITUATION, BUT THEY HAVE BEEN DEALT A HORRIBLE HAND.
SOME ARE HERE FOR DAYS. SOME FOR MONTHS.
SOME UNTIL THE END.
...AND THEN IRON MAN SAYS, "LOOK OUT, SPIDER-MAN!"
BUT THEY'RE NOT DWELLING ON THAT.
THEIR TOTAL FOCUS IS ON THIS.
EVERYONE PITCHES IN... EVERY KID...
I BET CAPTAIN AMERICA WOULD HIT THE DISINTEGROSAURUS WITH HIS SHIELD!
IT COMES BACK TO HIM LIKE A BOOMERANG!
...EVEN THE ONES WHO CAN'T GO TWENTY MINUTES WITHOUT THROWING UP.
TAKE THAT, YOU MONSTER!
THIS IS AWESOME.

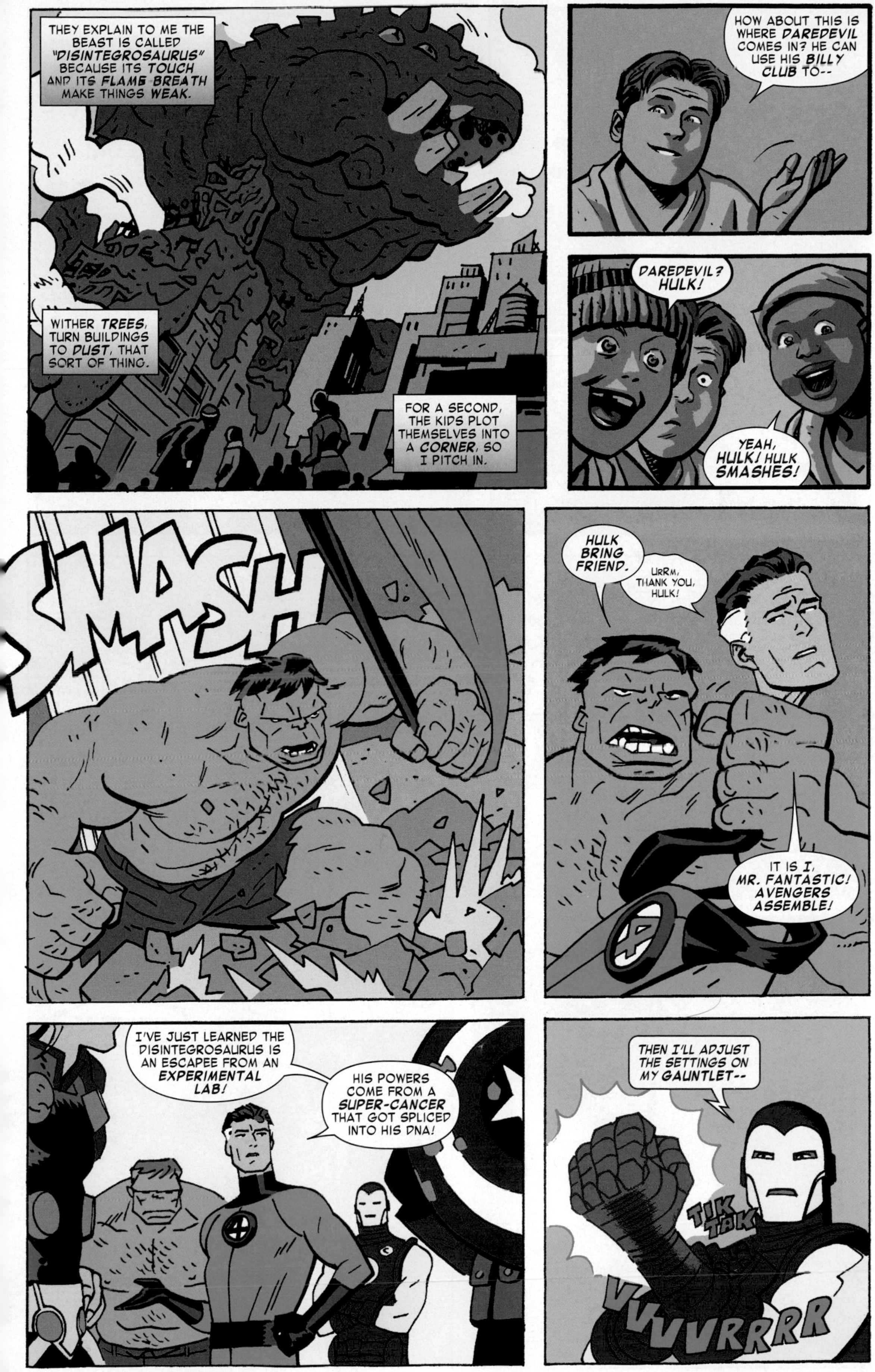
THEY EXPLAIN TO ME THE BEAST IS CALLED "DISINTEGROSAURUS" BECAUSE ITS TOUCH AND ITS FLAME BREATH MAKE THINGS WEAK.
WITHER TREES, TURN BUILDINGS TO DUST, THAT SORT OF THING.
FOR A SECOND, THE KIDS PLOT THEMSELVES INTO A CORNER, SO I PITCH IN.
HOW ABOUT THIS IS WHERE DAREDEVIL COMES IN? HE CAN USE HIS BILLY CLUB TO--
DAREDEVIL? HULK!
YEAH, HULK! HULK SMASHES!
SMASH
HULK BRING FRIEND.
URRM, THANK YOU, HULK!
IT IS I, MR. FANTASTIC! AVENGERS ASSEMBLE!
I'VE JUST LEARNED THE DISINTEGROSAURUS IS AN ESCAPEE FROM AN EXPERIMENTAL LAB!
HIS POWERS COME FROM A SUPER-CANCER THAT GOT SPLICED INTO HIS DNA!
THEN I'LL ADJUST THE SETTINGS ON MY GAUNTLET--
TIK TAK
VVVVRRRRR

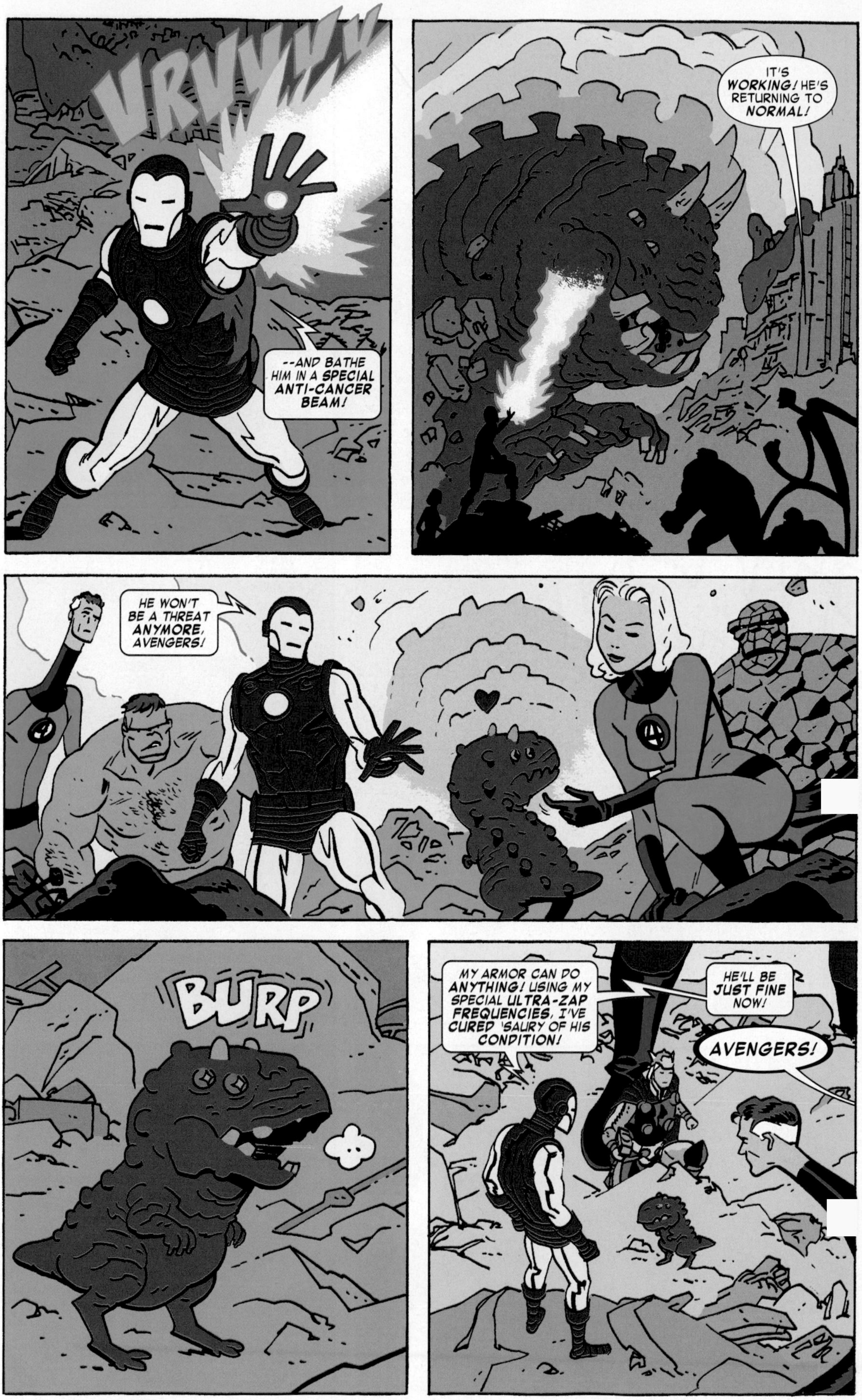
VRVVVV
--AND BATHE HIM IN A SPECIAL ANTI-CANCER BEAM!
IT'S WORKING! HE'S RETURNING TO NORMAL!
HE WON'T BE A THREAT ANYMORE, AVENGERS!
BURP
MY ARMOR CAN DO ANYTHING! USING MY SPECIAL ULTRA-ZAP FREQUENCIES, I'VE CURED 'SAURY OF HIS CONDITION!
HE'LL BE JUST FINE NOW!
AVENGERS!

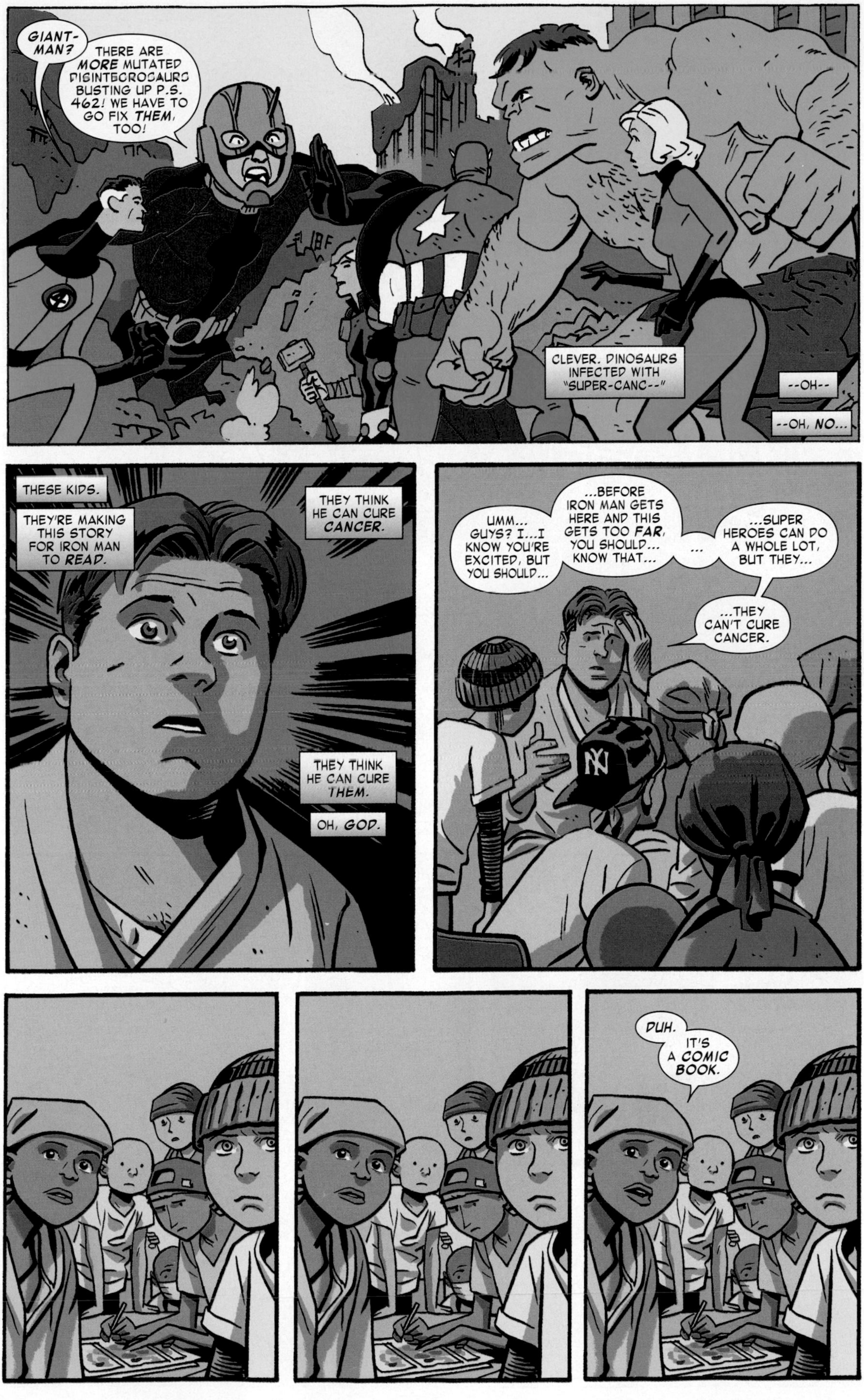
GIANT-MAN?
THERE ARE MORE MUTATED DISINTEGROSAURS BUSTING UP P.S. 462! WE HAVE TO GO FIX THEM, TOO!
CLEVER. DINOSAURS INFECTED WITH "SUPER-CANC--"
--OH--
--OH, NO...
THESE KIDS.
THEY'RE MAKING THIS STORY FOR IRON MAN TO READ.
THEY THINK HE CAN CURE CANCER.
THEY THINK HE CAN CURE THEM.
OH, GOD.
UMM... GUYS? I...I KNOW YOU'RE EXCITED, BUT YOU SHOULD...
...BEFORE IRON MAN GETS HERE AND THIS GETS TOO FAR, YOU SHOULD... KNOW THAT...
...
...SUPER HEROES CAN DO A WHOLE LOT, BUT THEY...
...THEY CAN'T CURE CANCER.
DUH.
IT'S A COMIC BOOK.

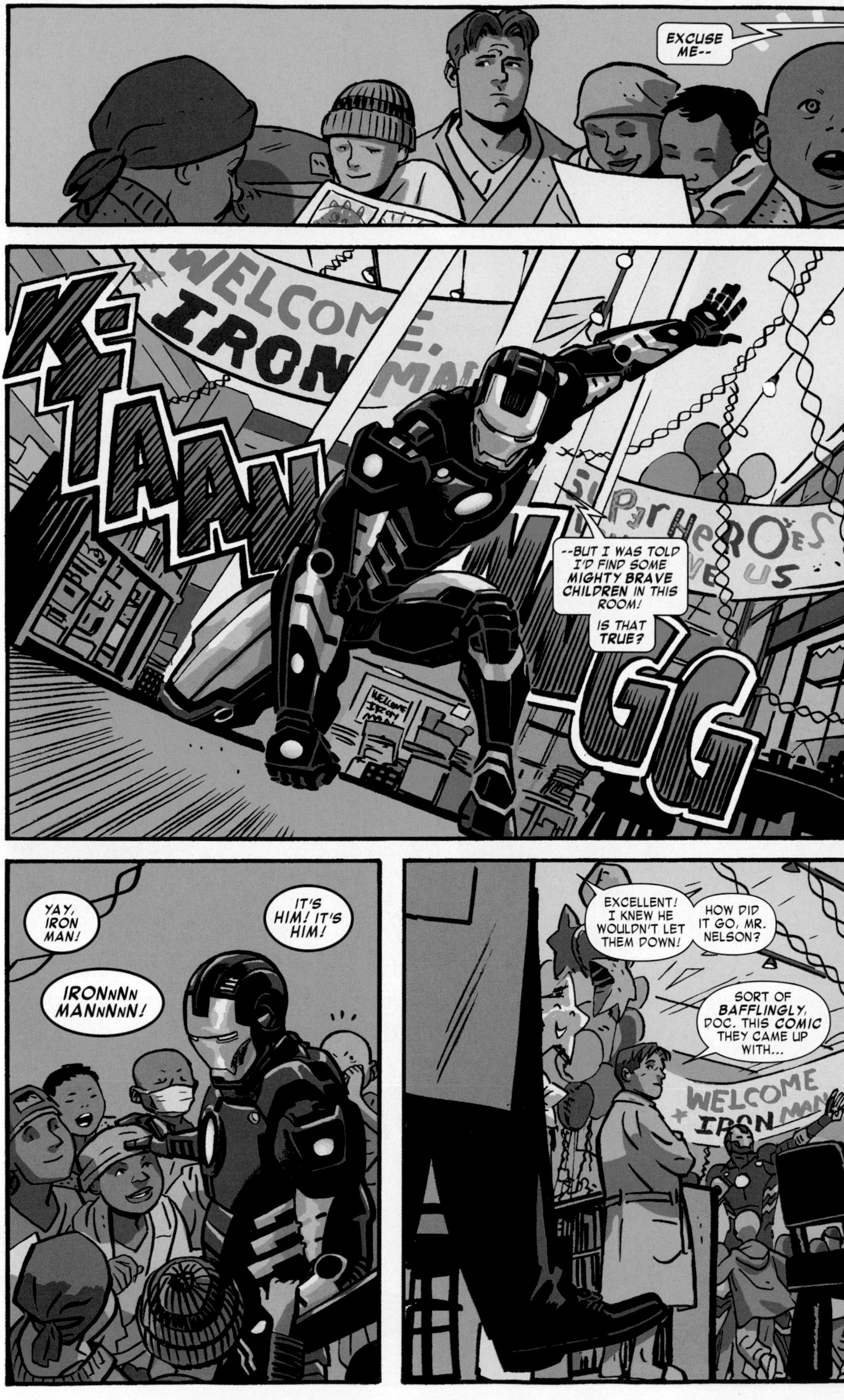
EXCUSE ME--
WELCOME, IRON MAN
K-TAAWNGG
--BUT I WAS TOLD I'D FIND SOME MIGHTY BRAVE CHILDREN IN THIS ROOM!
IS THAT TRUE?
YAY, IRON MAN!
IT'S HIM! IT'S HIM!
IRONNNN MANNNNN!
EXCELLENT! I KNEW HE WOULDN'T LET THEM DOWN!
HOW DID IT GO, MR. NELSON?
SORT OF BAFFLINGLY, DOC. THIS COMIC THEY CAME UP WITH...
WELCOME IRON MAN

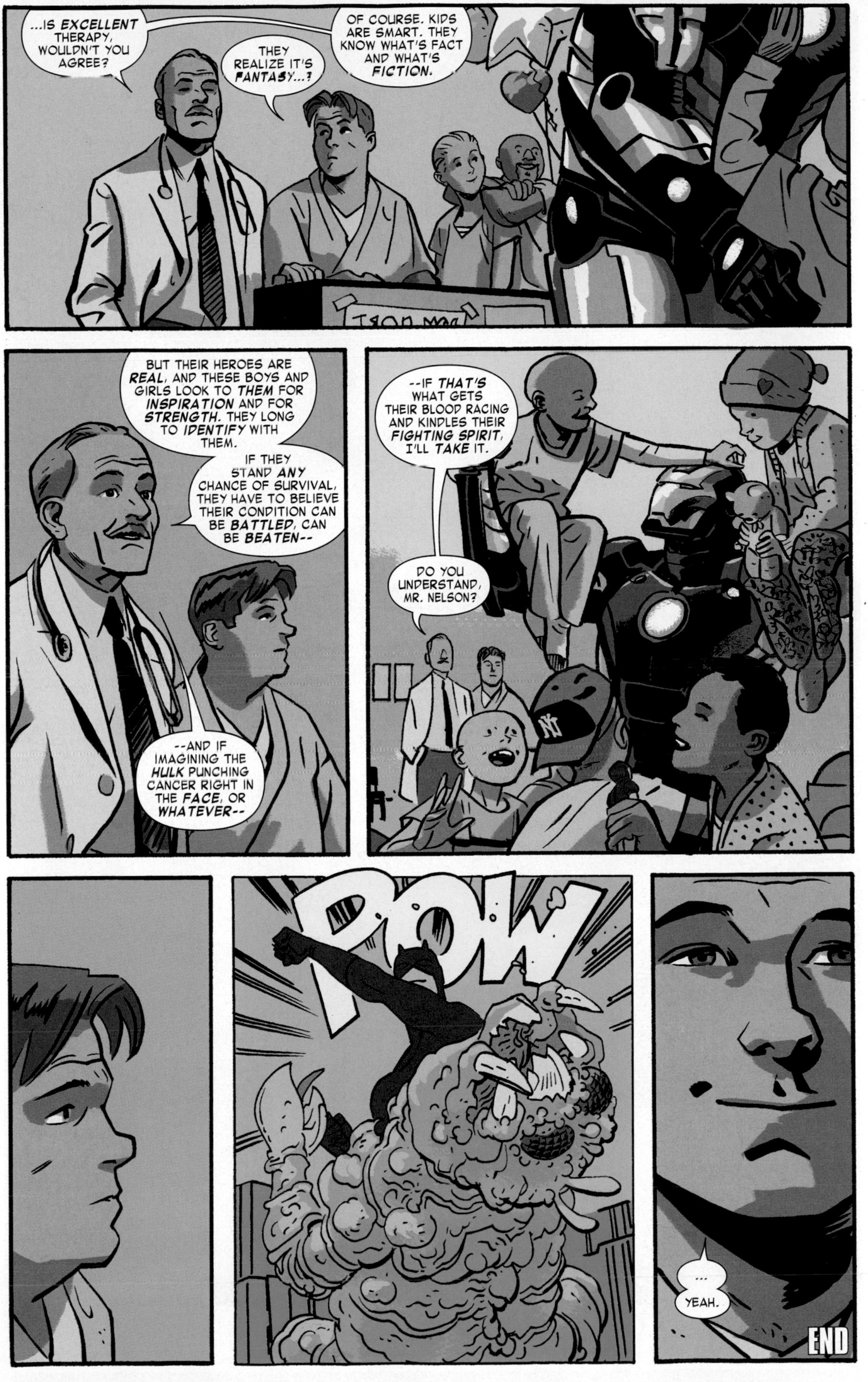
...IS EXCELLENT THERAPY, WOULDN'T YOU AGREE?
THEY REALIZE IT'S FANTASY...?
OF COURSE. KIDS ARE SMART. THEY KNOW WHAT'S FACT AND WHAT'S FICTION.
BUT THEIR HEROES ARE REAL, AND THESE BOYS AND GIRLS LOOK TO THEM FOR INSPIRATION AND FOR STRENGTH. THEY LONG TO IDENTIFY WITH THEM.
IF THEY STAND ANY CHANCE OF SURVIVAL, THEY HAVE TO BELIEVE THEIR CONDITION CAN BE BATTLED, CAN BE BEATEN--
--AND IF IMAGINING THE HULK PUNCHING CANCER RIGHT IN THE FACE, OR WHATEVER--
--IF THAT'S WHAT GETS THEIR BLOOD RACING AND KINDLES THEIR FIGHTING SPIRIT, I'LL TAKE IT.
DO YOU UNDERSTAND, MR. NELSON?
POW
...
YEAH.
END

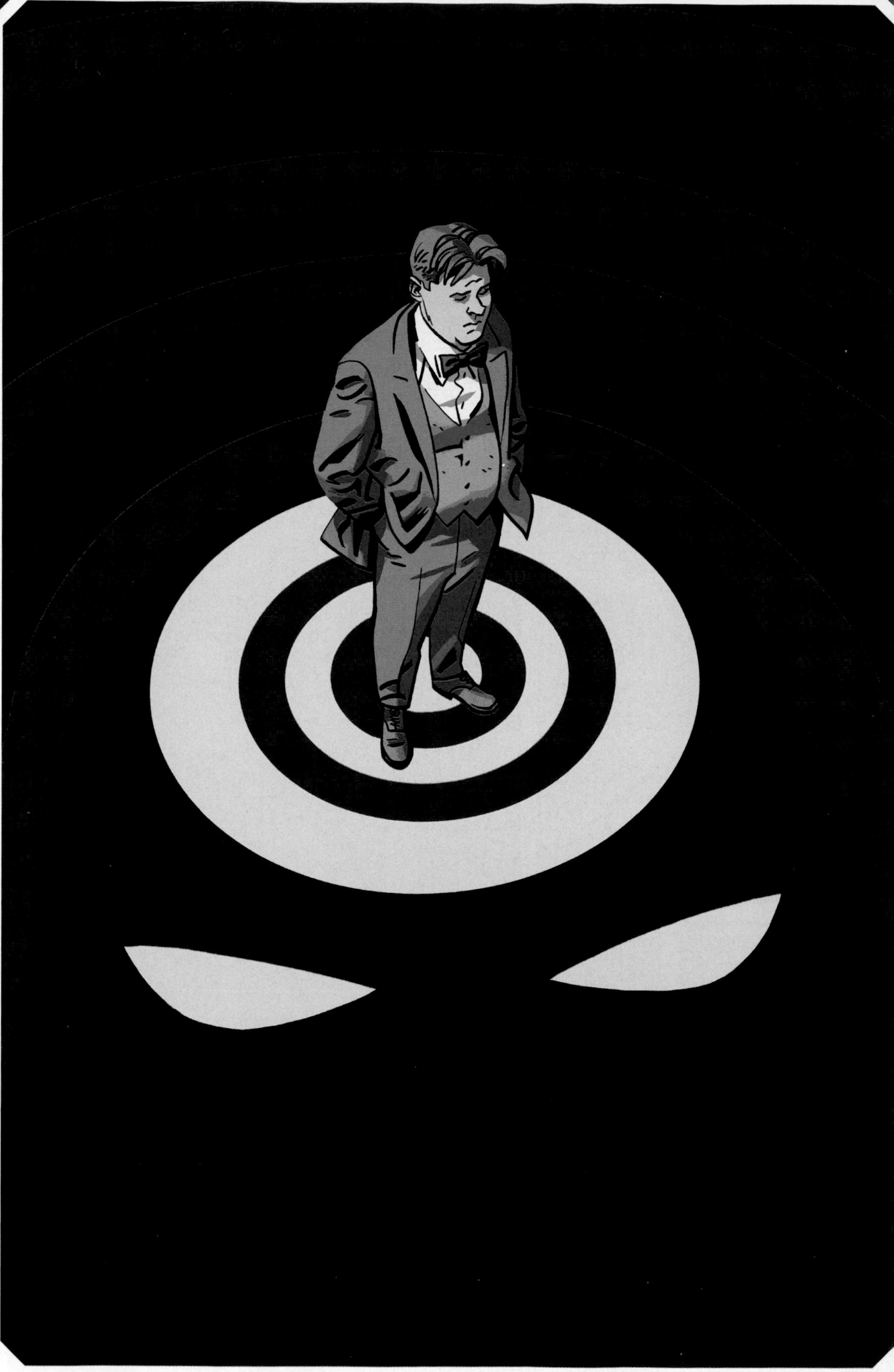

TWENTY-SEVEN

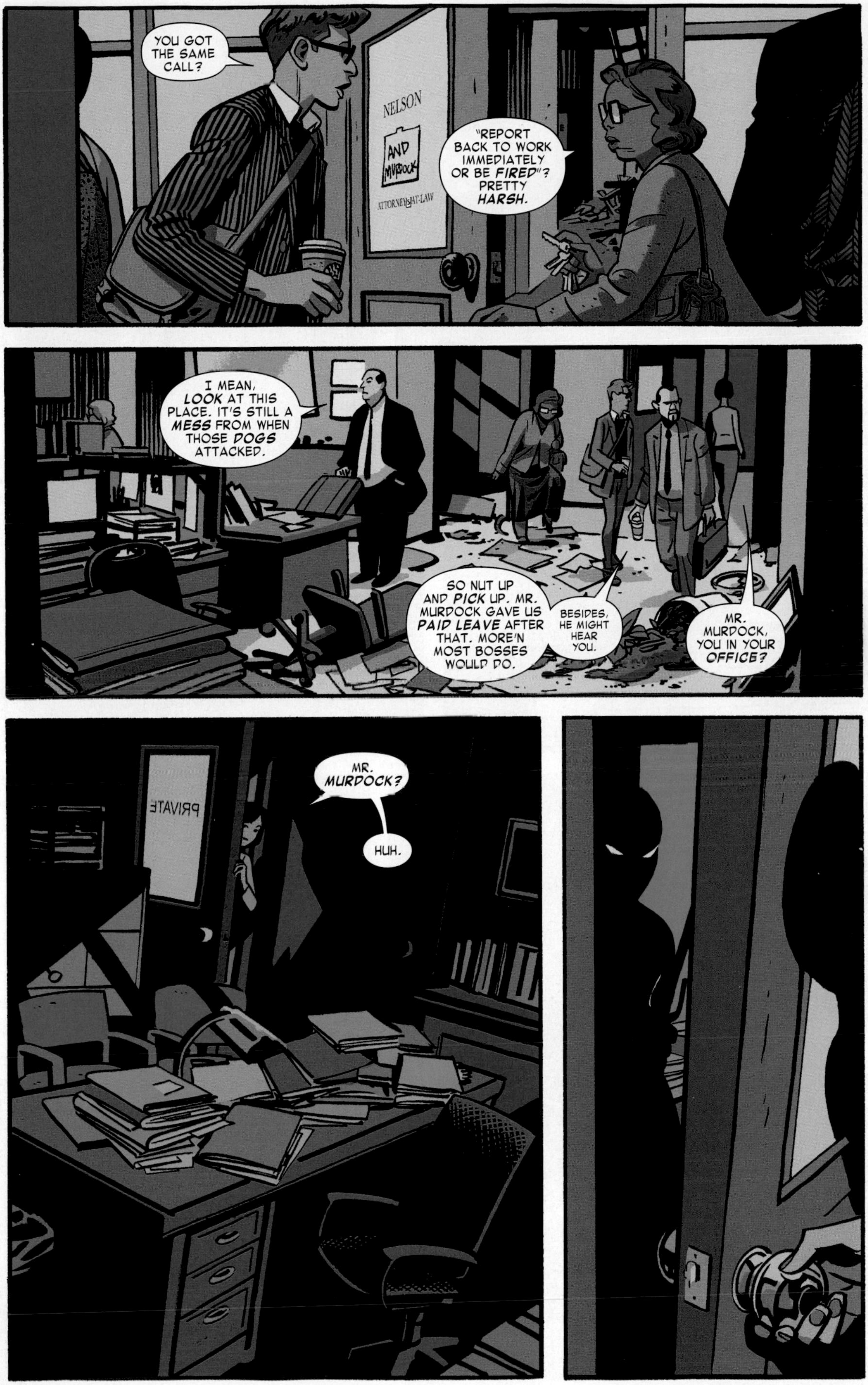
YOU GOT THE SAME CALL?
NELSON
AND MURDOCK
ATTORNEYS-AT-LAW
"REPORT BACK TO WORK IMMEDIATELY OR BE FIRED"? PRETTY HARSH.
I MEAN, LOOK AT THIS PLACE. IT'S STILL A MESS FROM WHEN THOSE DOGS ATTACKED.
SO NUT UP AND PICK UP. MR. MURDOCK GAVE US PAID LEAVE AFTER THAT. MORE'N MOST BOSSES WOULD DO.
BESIDES, HE MIGHT HEAR YOU.
MR. MURDOCK, YOU IN YOUR OFFICE?
PRIVATE
MR. MURDOCK?
HUH.

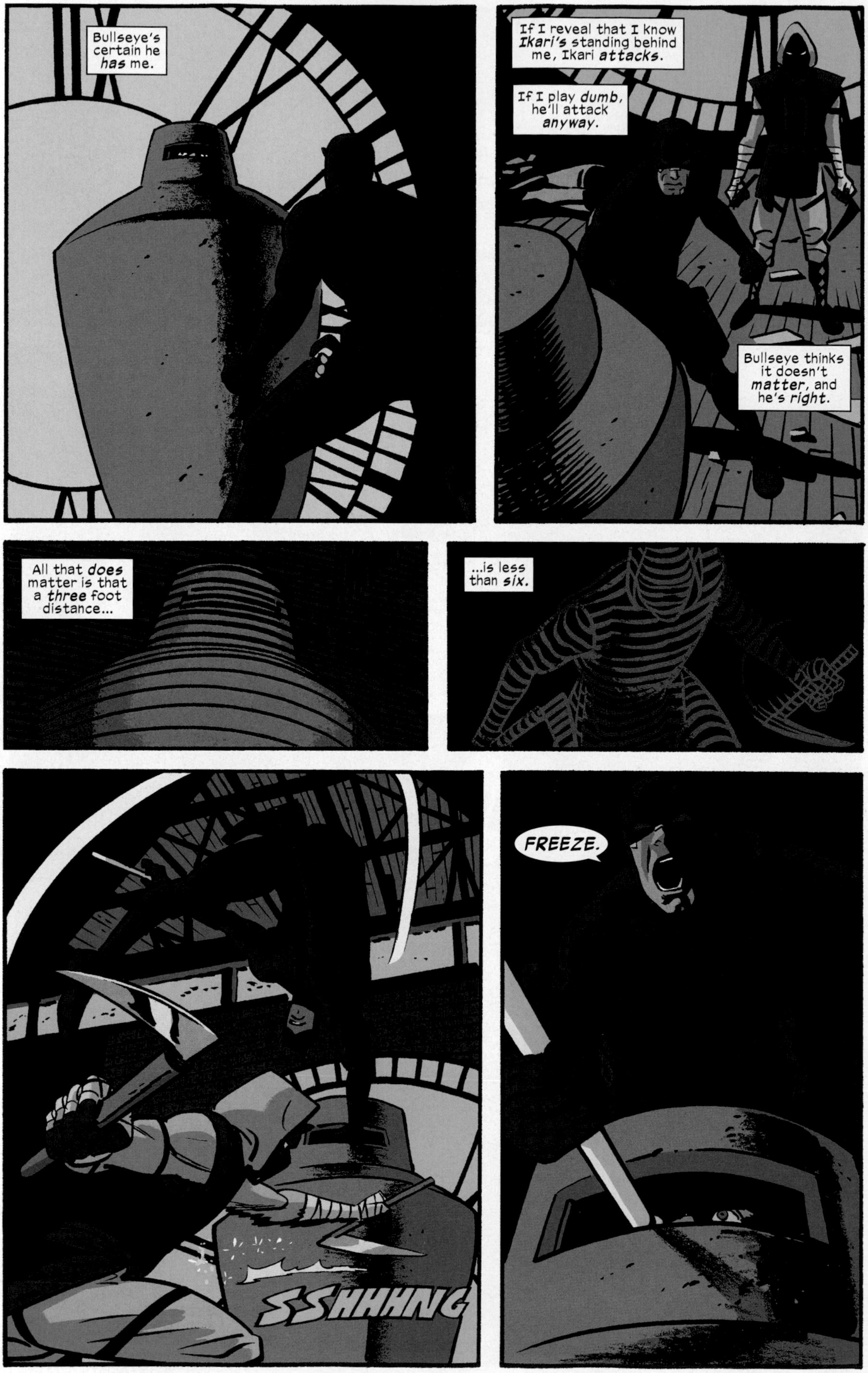

Bullseye's certain he has me.
If I reveal that I know Ikari's standing behind me, Ikari attacks.
If I play dumb, he'll attack anyway.
Bullseye thinks it doesn't matter, and he's right.
All that does matter is that a three foot distance...
...is less than six.
SSHHHNG
FREEZE.

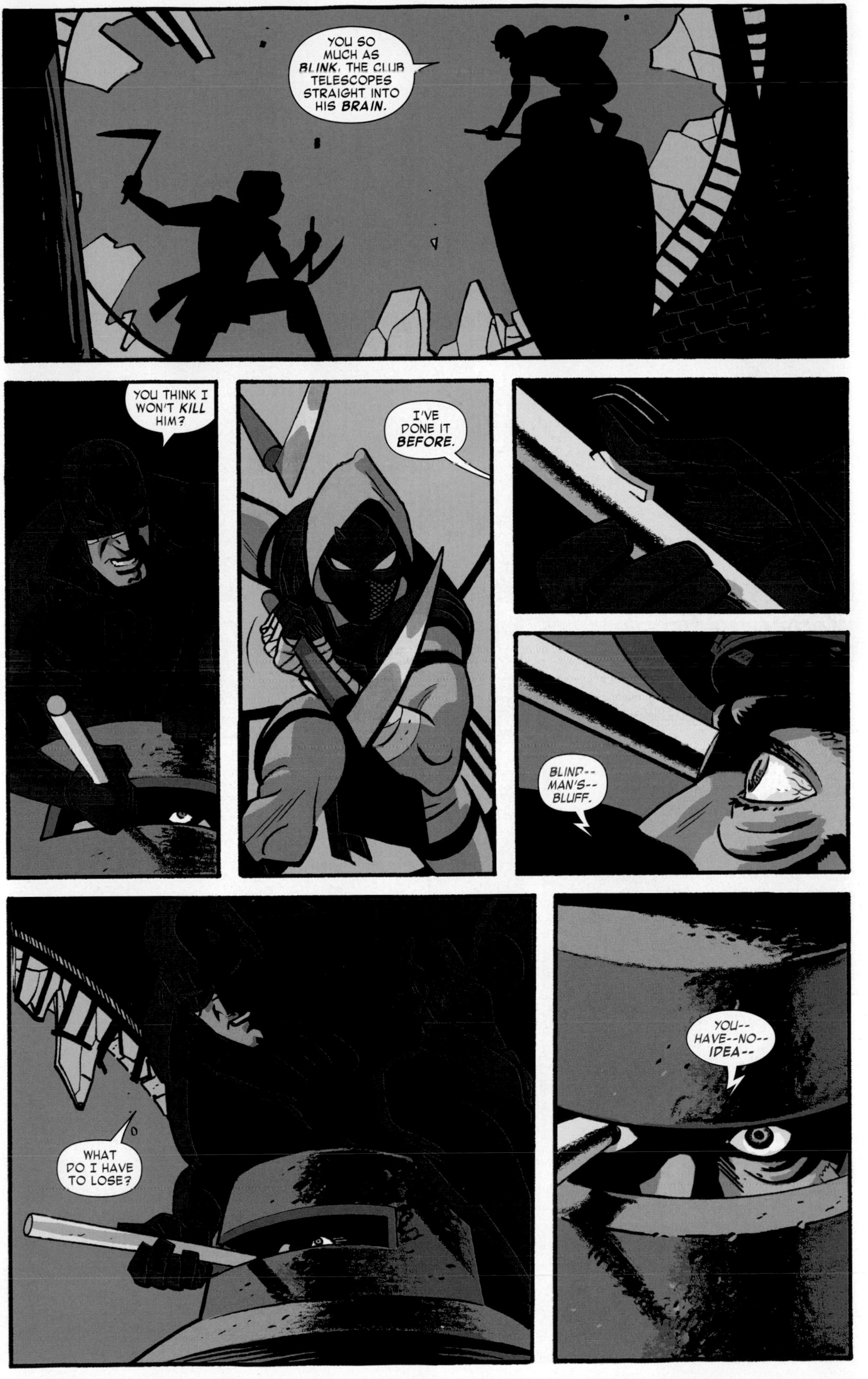
YOU SO MUCH AS BLINK, THE CLUB TELESCOPES STRAIGHT INTO HIS BRAIN.
YOU THINK I WON'T KILL HIM?
I'VE DONE IT BEFORE.
BLIND-- MAN'S-- BLUFF.
WHAT DO I HAVE TO LOSE?
YOU-- HAVE--NO-- IDEA--

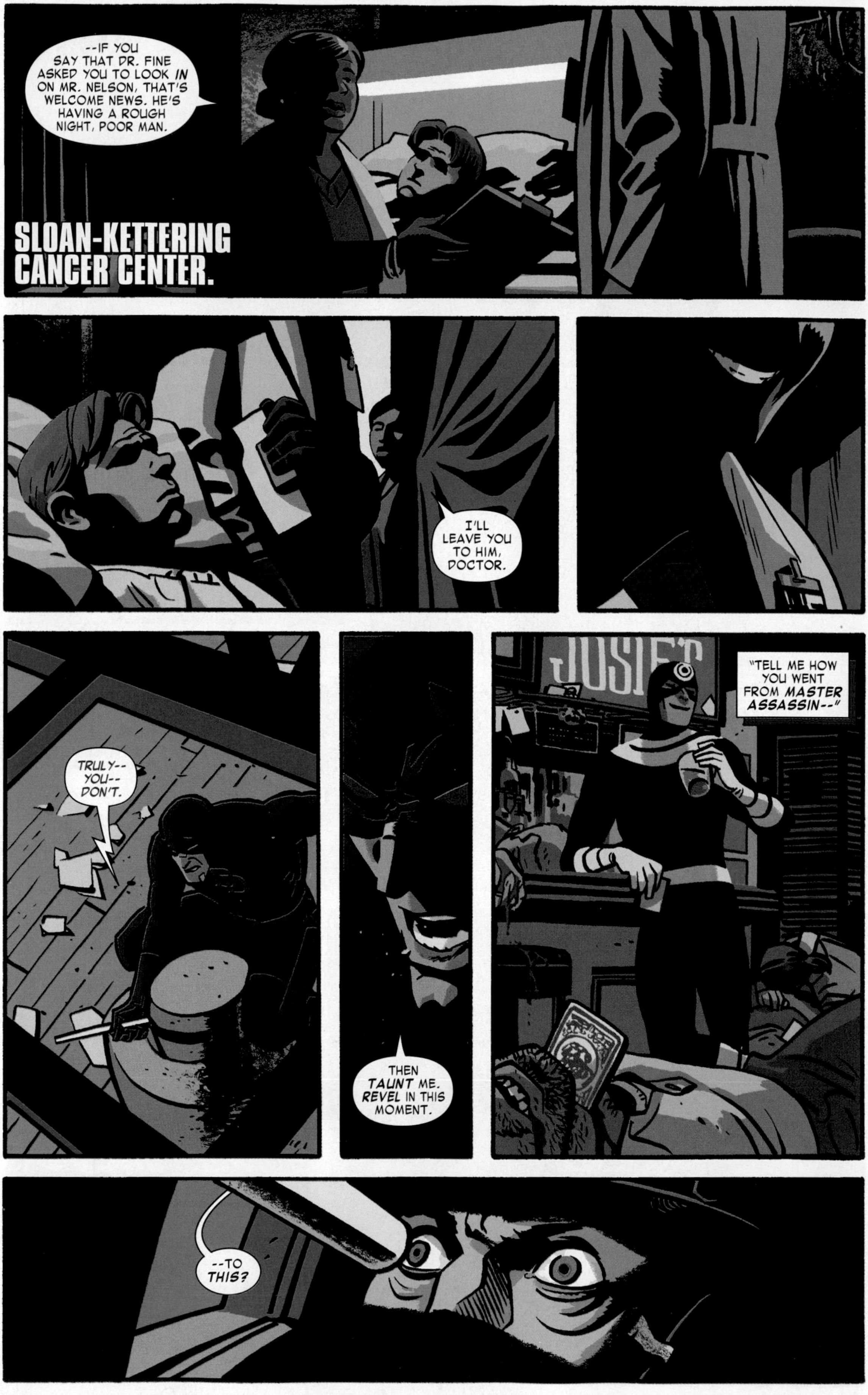
--IF YOU SAY THAT DR. FINE ASKED YOU TO LOOK IN ON MR. NELSON, THAT'S WELCOME NEWS. HE'S HAVING A ROUGH NIGHT, POOR MAN.
SLOAN-KETTERING CANCER CENTER.
I'LL LEAVE YOU TO HIM, DOCTOR.
TRULY-- YOU-- DON'T.
THEN TAUNT ME. REVEL IN THIS MOMENT.
JOSIE'S
"TELL ME HOW YOU WENT FROM MASTER ASSASSIN--"
--TO THIS?

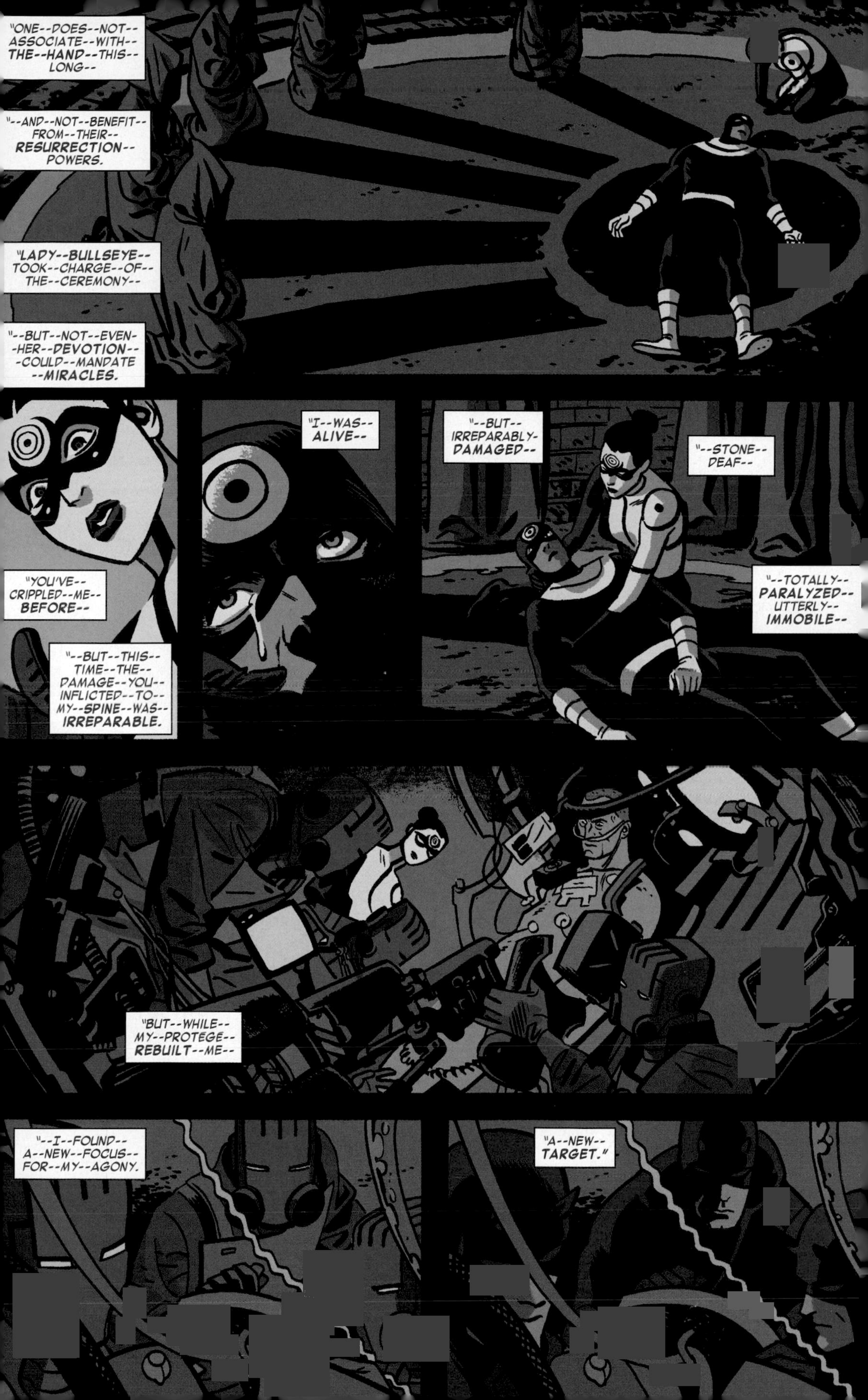
"ONE--DOES--NOT--ASSOCIATE--WITH--THE--HAND--THIS--LONG--
"--AND--NOT--BENEFIT--FROM--THEIR--RESURRECTION--POWERS.
"LADY--BULLSEYE--TOOK--CHARGE--OF--THE--CEREMONY--
"--BUT--NOT--EVEN--HER--DEVOTION--COULD--MANDATE--MIRACLES.
"YOU'VE--CRIPPLED--ME--BEFORE--
"--BUT--THIS--TIME--THE--DAMAGE--YOU--INFLICTED--TO--MY--SPINE--WAS--IRREPARABLE.
"I--WAS--ALIVE--
"--BUT--IRREPARABLY--DAMAGED--
"--STONE--DEAF--
"--TOTALLY--PARALYZED--UTTERLY--IMMOBILE--
"BUT--WHILE--MY--PROTEGE--REBUILT--ME--
"--I--FOUND--A--NEW--FOCUS--FOR--MY--AGONY.
"A--NEW--TARGET."

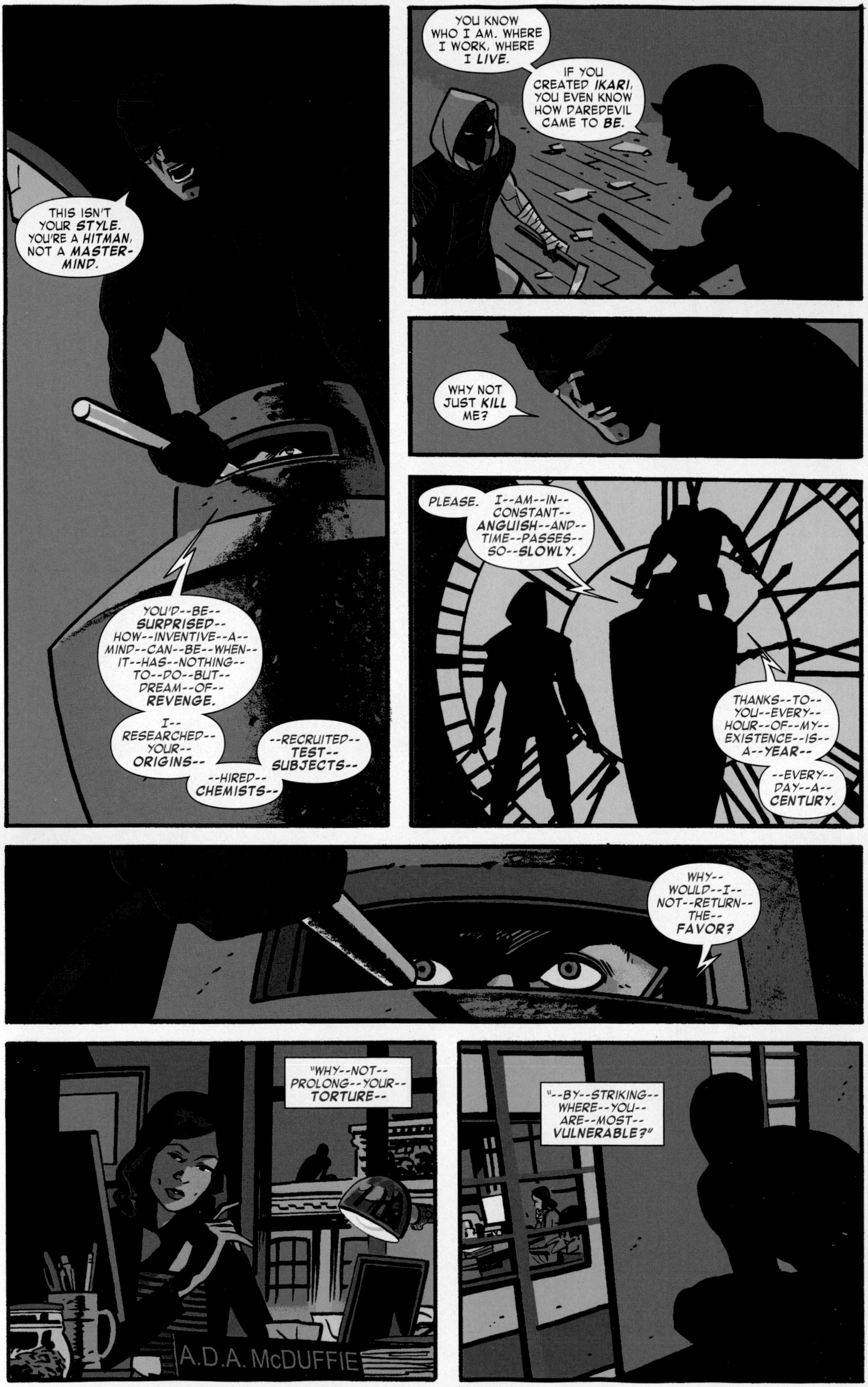
THIS ISN'T YOUR STYLE. YOU'RE A HITMAN, NOT A MASTER-MIND.
YOU'D--BE--SURPRISED--HOW--INVENTIVE--A--MIND--CAN--BE--WHEN--IT--HAS--NOTHING--TO--DO--BUT--DREAM--OF--REVENGE.
I--RESEARCHED--YOUR--ORIGINS--
--HIRED--CHEMISTS--
--RECRUITED--TEST--SUBJECTS--
YOU KNOW WHO I AM. WHERE I WORK, WHERE I LIVE.
IF YOU CREATED IKARI, YOU EVEN KNOW HOW DAREDEVIL CAME TO BE.
WHY NOT JUST KILL ME?
PLEASE.
I--AM--IN--CONSTANT--ANGUISH--AND--TIME--PASSES--SO--SLOWLY.
THANKS--TO--YOU--EVERY--HOUR--OF--MY--EXISTENCE--IS--A--YEAR--
--EVERY--DAY--A--CENTURY.
WHY--WOULD--I--NOT--RETURN--THE--FAVOR?
"WHY--NOT--PROLONG--YOUR--TORTURE--
A.D.A. McDUFFIE
"--BY--STRIKING--WHERE--YOU--ARE--MOST--VULNERABLE?"

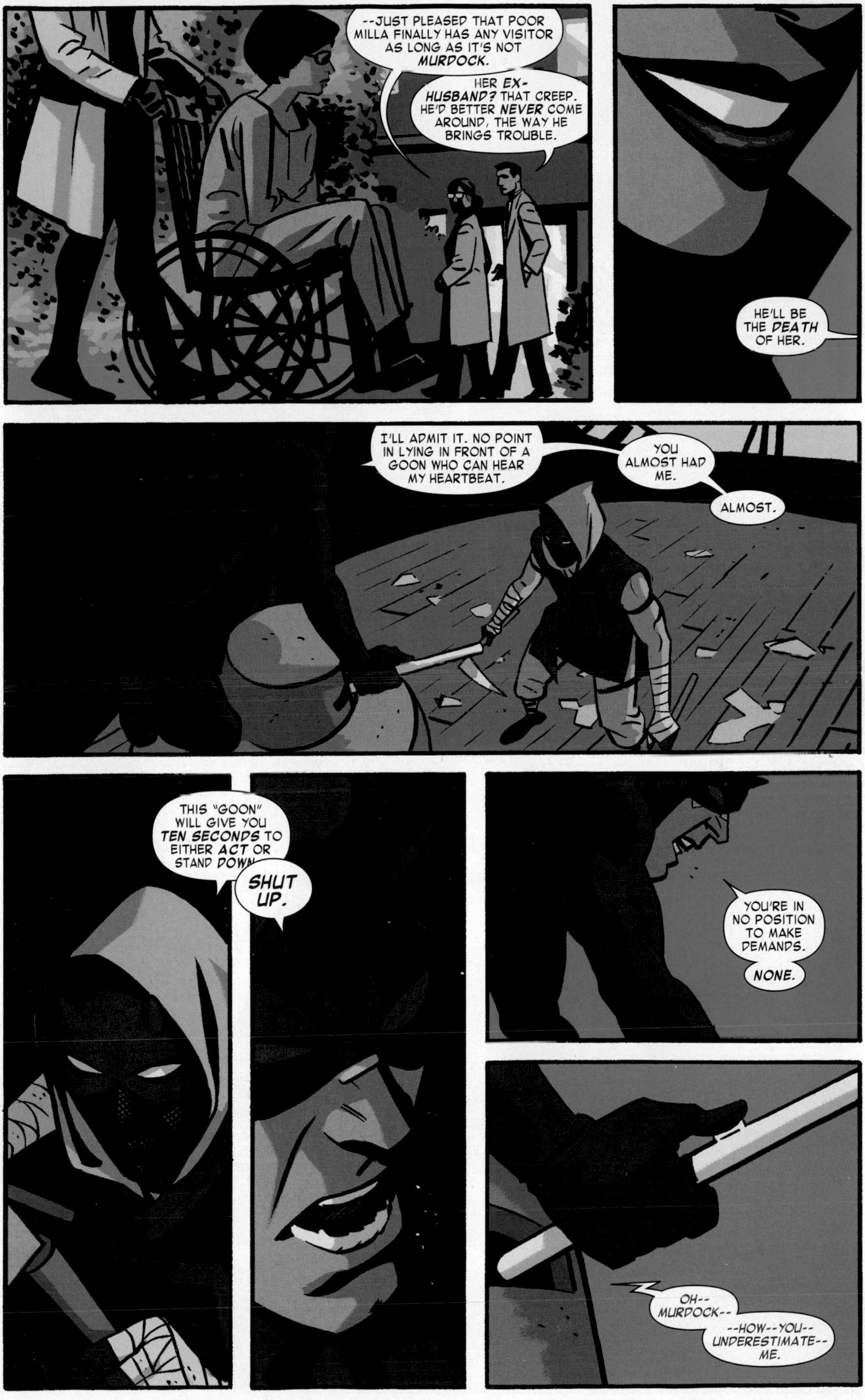
--JUST PLEASED THAT POOR MILLA FINALLY HAS ANY VISITOR AS LONG AS IT'S NOT MURDOCK.
HER EX-HUSBAND? THAT CREEP. HE'D BETTER NEVER COME AROUND, THE WAY HE BRINGS TROUBLE.
HE'LL BE THE DEATH OF HER.
I'LL ADMIT IT. NO POINT IN LYING IN FRONT OF A GOON WHO CAN HEAR MY HEARTBEAT.
YOU ALMOST HAD ME.
ALMOST.
THIS "GOON" WILL GIVE YOU TEN SECONDS TO EITHER ACT OR STAND DOWN--
SHUT UP.
YOU'RE IN NO POSITION TO MAKE DEMANDS.
NONE.
OH-- MURDOCK--
--HOW--YOU-- UNDERESTIMATE-- ME.

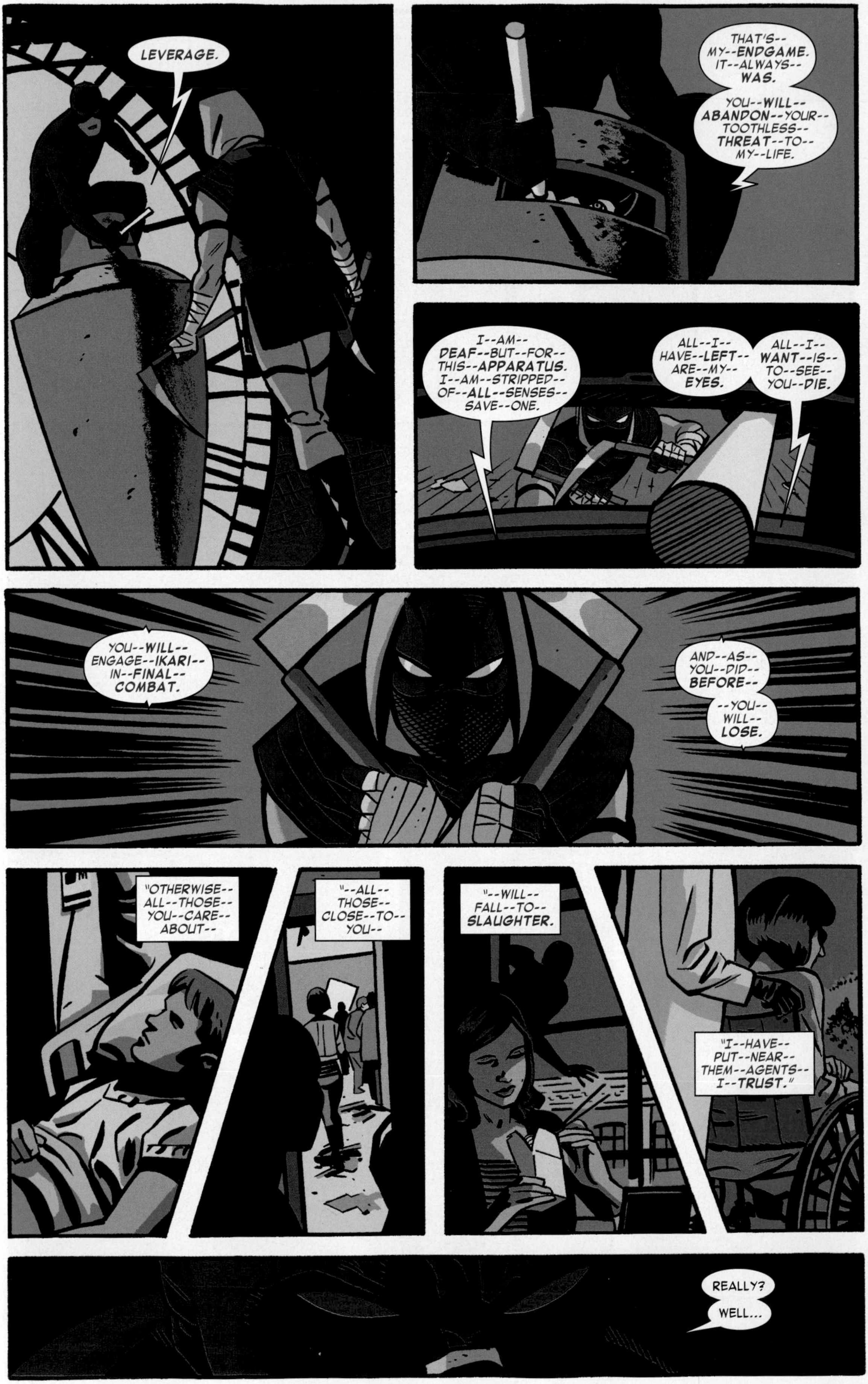
LEVERAGE.
THAT'S--MY--ENDGAME. IT--ALWAYS--WAS.
YOU--WILL--ABANDON--YOUR--TOOTHLESS--THREAT--TO--MY--LIFE.
I--AM--DEAF--BUT--FOR--THIS--APPARATUS. I--AM--STRIPPED--OF--ALL--SENSES--SAVE--ONE.
ALL--I--HAVE--LEFT--ARE--MY--EYES.
ALL--I--WANT--IS--TO--SEE--YOU--DIE.
YOU--WILL--ENGAGE--IKARI--IN--FINAL--COMBAT.
AND--AS--YOU--DID--BEFORE--
--YOU--WILL--LOSE.
"OTHERWISE--ALL--THOSE--YOU--CARE--ABOUT--
"--ALL--THOSE--CLOSE--TO--YOU--
"--WILL--FALL--TO--SLAUGHTER.
"I--HAVE--PUT--NEAR--THEM--AGENTS--I--TRUST."
REALLY?
WELL...

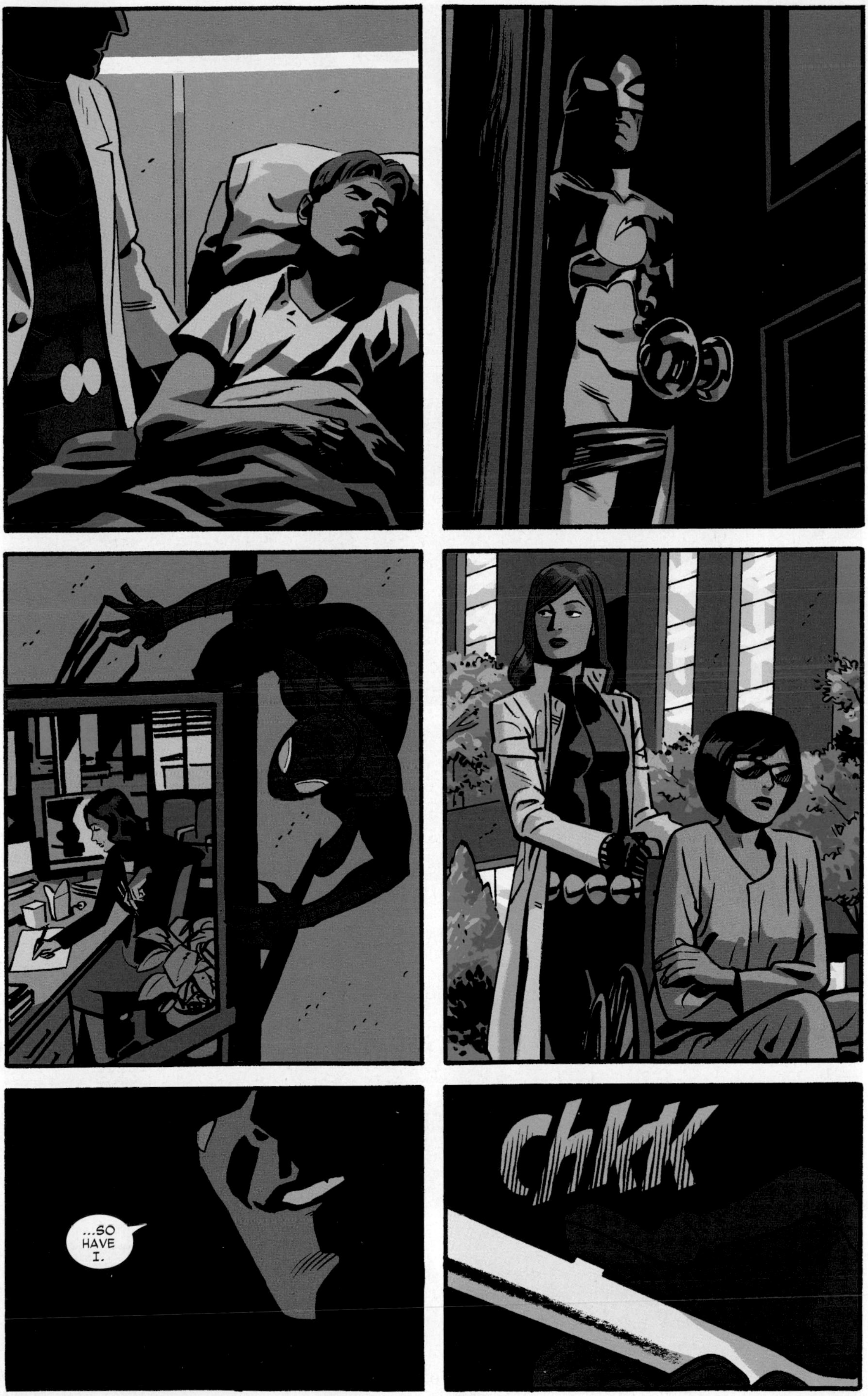
...SO HAVE I.
CHKK

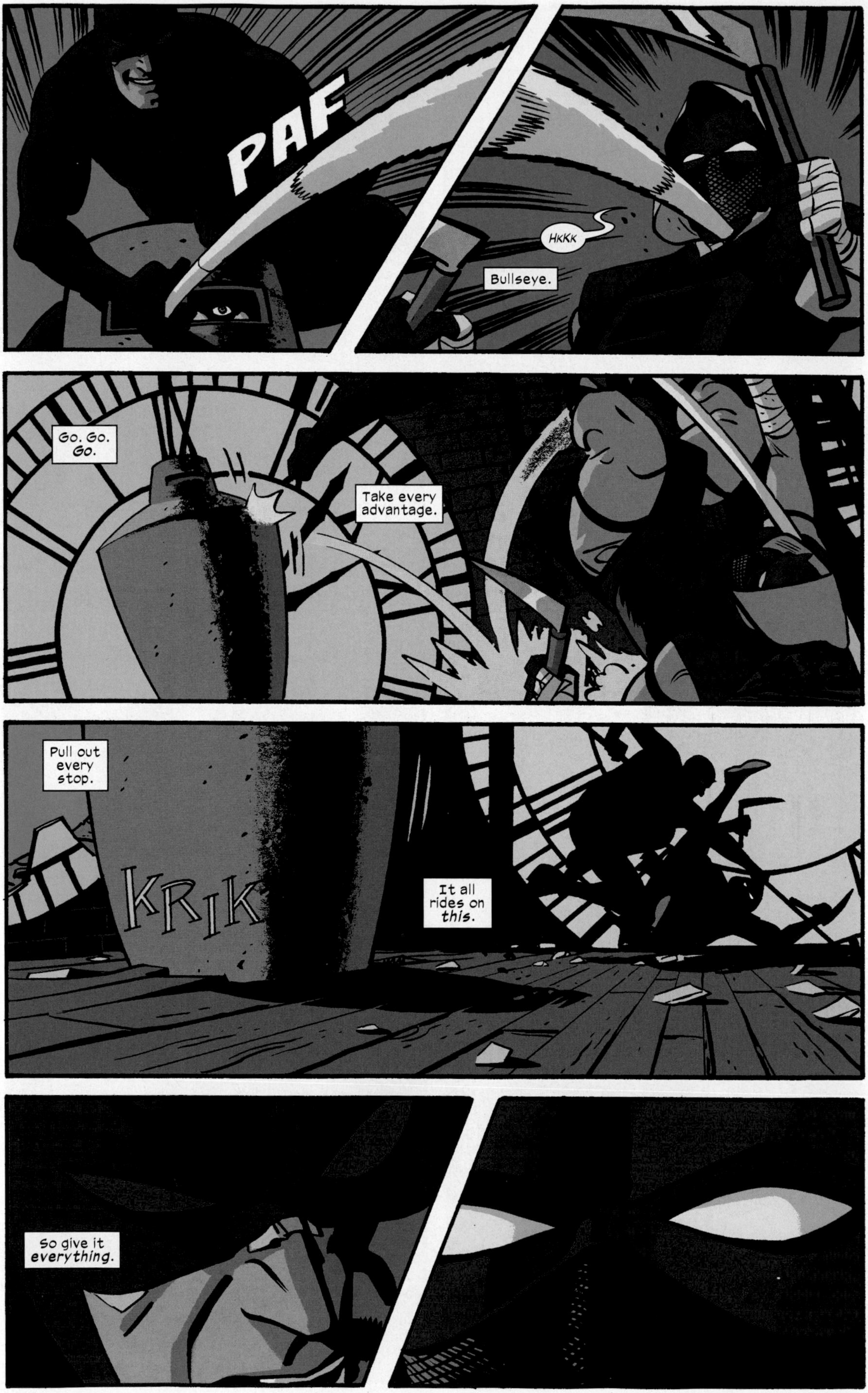
PAF
HKKK
Bullseye.
Go. Go. Go.
Take every advantage.
Pull out every stop.
KRIK
It all rides on *this*.
So give it *everything*.

Now that I've used up all my *sleight of hand,* though, I realize it's not *enough.*

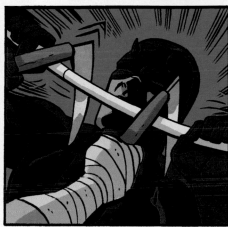

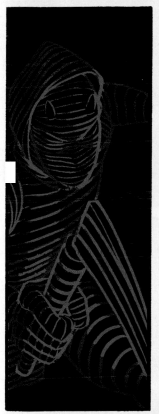

Unlike *Ikari,* I'm *ragged*--running on *empty.*

I'm going to die after all.

And then it hits me.

A familiar *stench* from beneath the floorboards.

Snf

PAF

zzzip

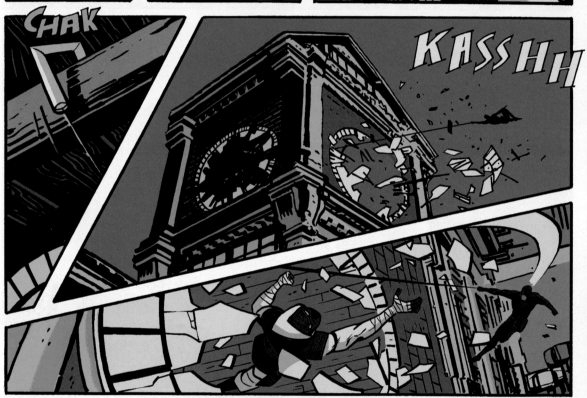

CHAK

KASSHH

The smell of one last *Hail Mary.*

KRRSSH

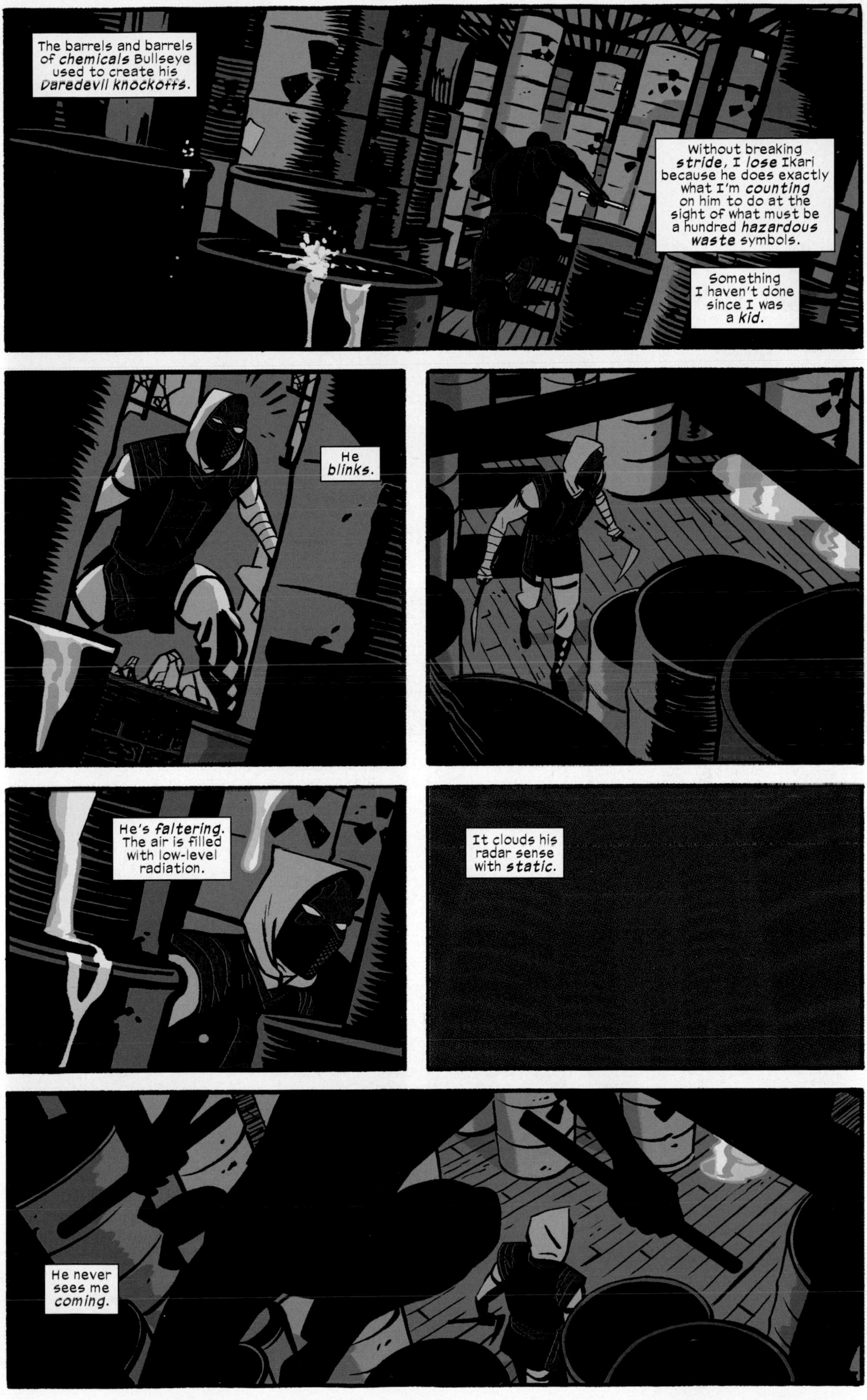
The barrels and barrels of chemicals Bullseye used to create his Daredevil knockoffs.
Without breaking stride, I lose Ikari because he does exactly what I'm counting on him to do at the sight of what must be a hundred hazardous waste symbols.
Something I haven't done since I was a kid.
He blinks.
He's faltering. The air is filled with low-level radiation.
It clouds his radar sense with static.
He never sees me coming.

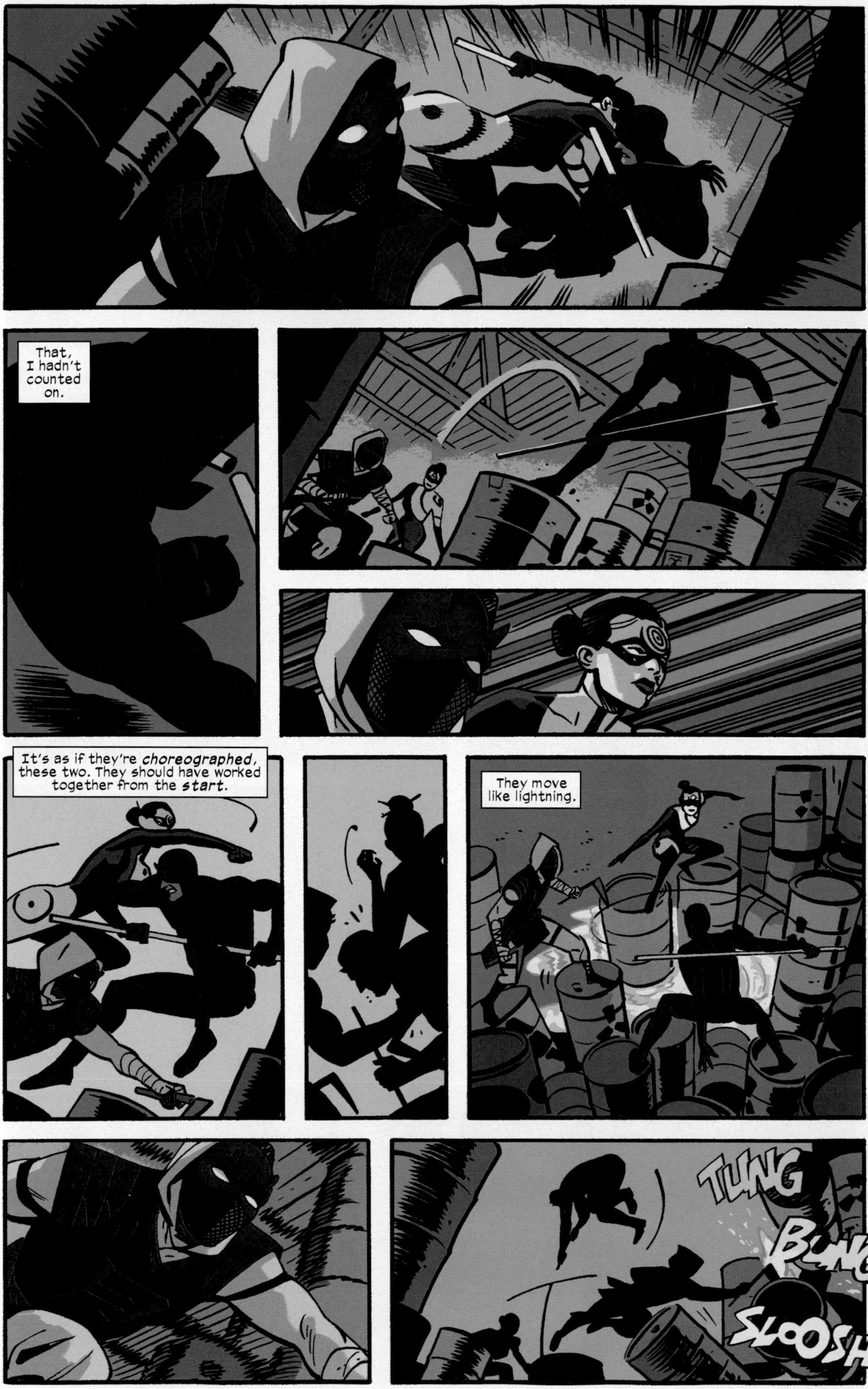
That, I hadn't counted on.
It's as if they're *choreographed*, these two. They should have worked together from the *start*.
They move like lightning.
TUNG
BUNG
SLOOSH

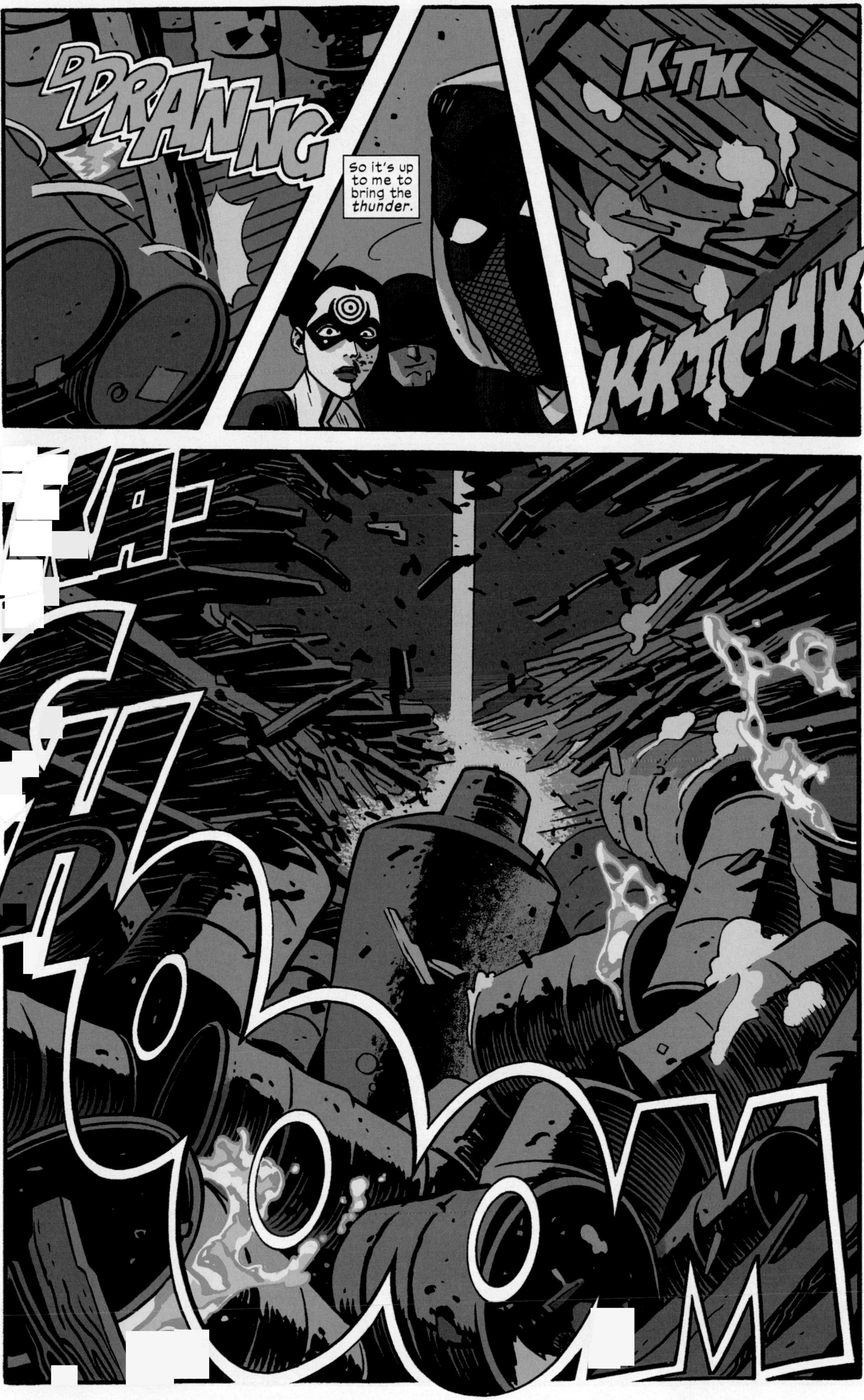
DDRANNG
So it's up to me to bring the *thunder*.
KTK
KKTCHK

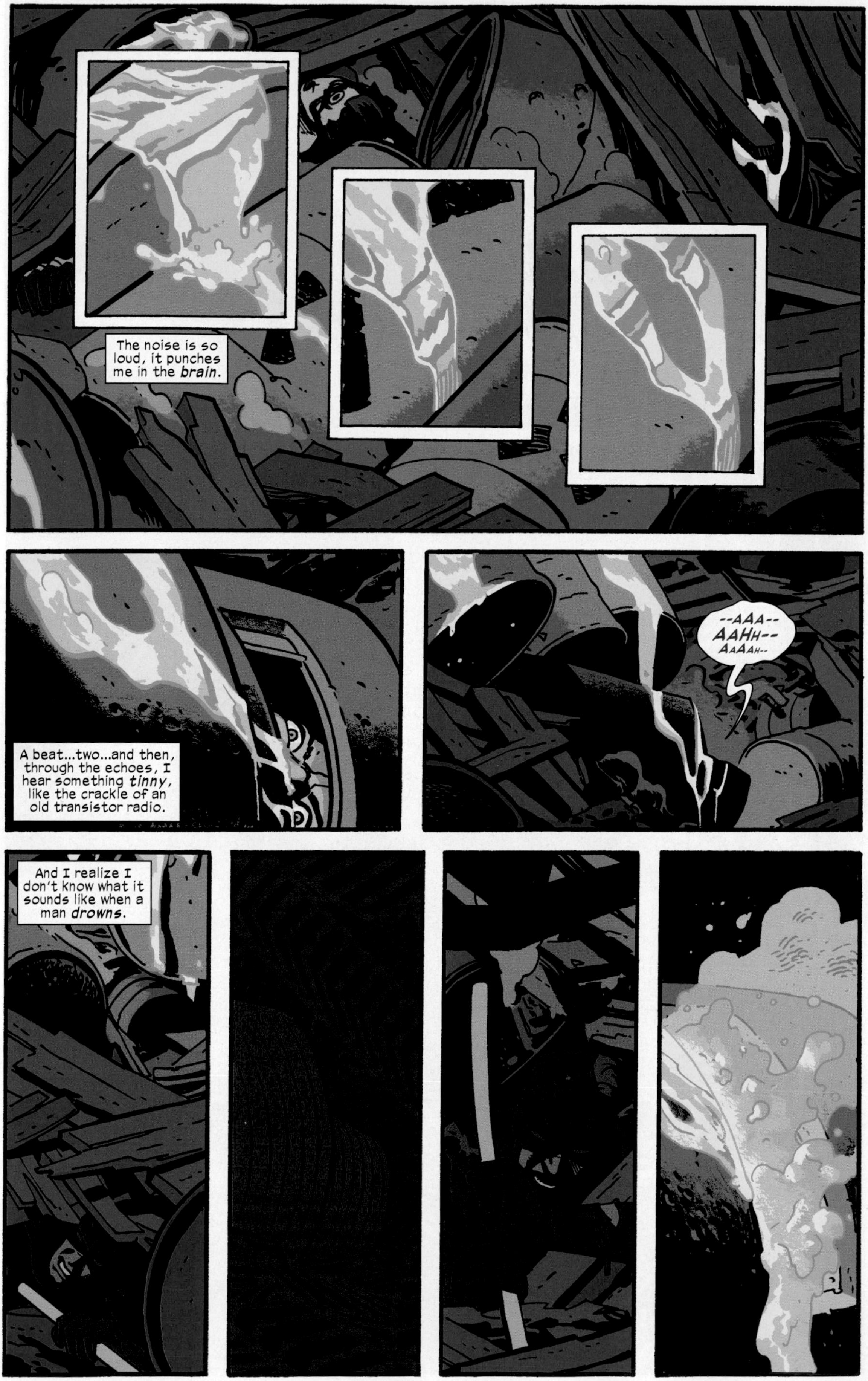

The noise is so loud, it punches me in the *brain*.
A beat...two...and then, through the echoes, I hear something *tinny*, like the crackle of an old transistor radio.
--AAA--
AAHH--
AAAAH--
And I realize I don't know what it sounds like when a man *drowns*.

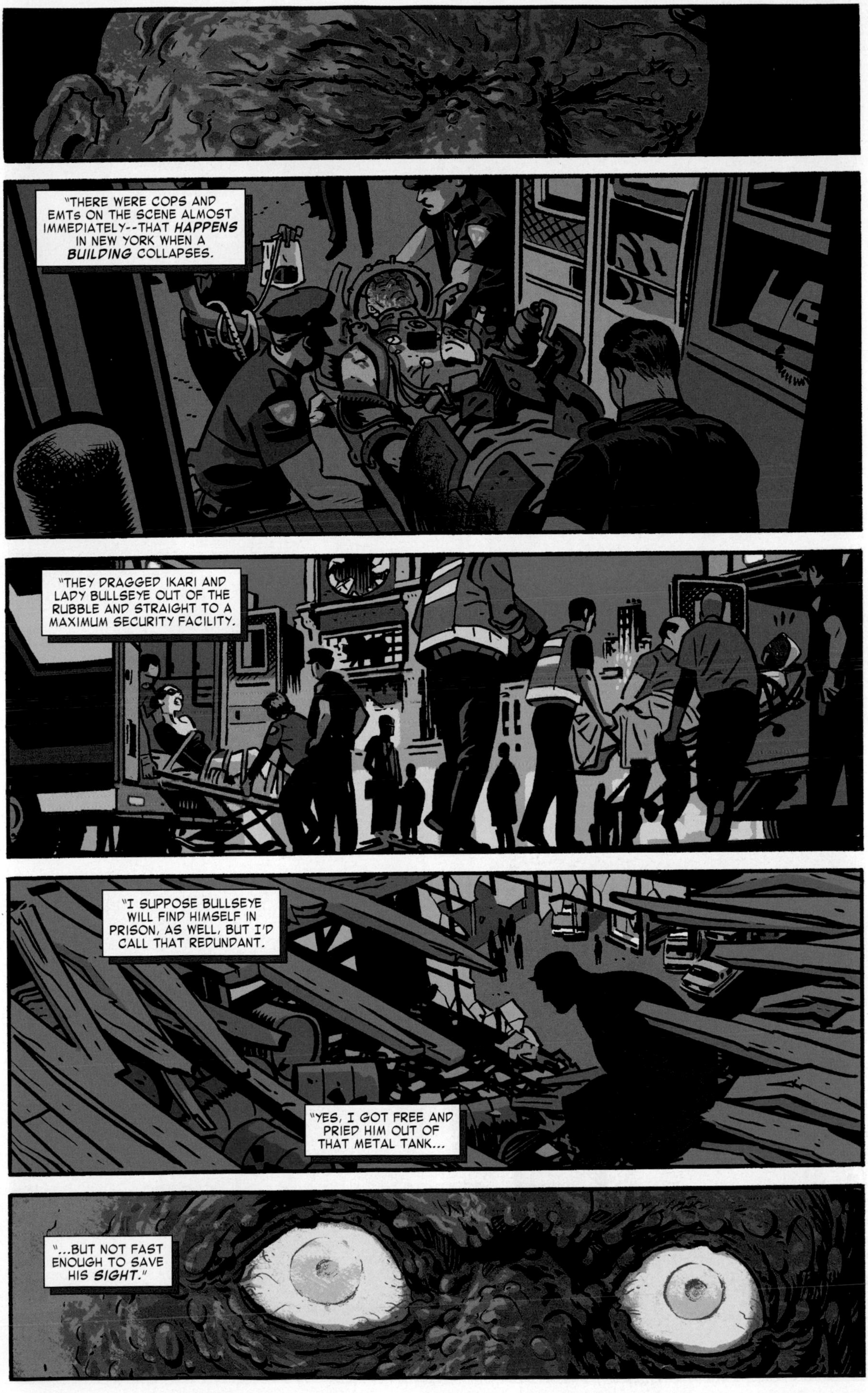
"THERE WERE COPS AND EMTS ON THE SCENE ALMOST IMMEDIATELY--THAT HAPPENS IN NEW YORK WHEN A BUILDING COLLAPSES.
"THEY DRAGGED IKARI AND LADY BULLSEYE OUT OF THE RUBBLE AND STRAIGHT TO A MAXIMUM SECURITY FACILITY.
"I SUPPOSE BULLSEYE WILL FIND HIMSELF IN PRISON, AS WELL, BUT I'D CALL THAT REDUNDANT.
"YES, I GOT FREE AND PRIED HIM OUT OF THAT METAL TANK...
"...BUT NOT FAST ENOUGH TO SAVE HIS SIGHT."

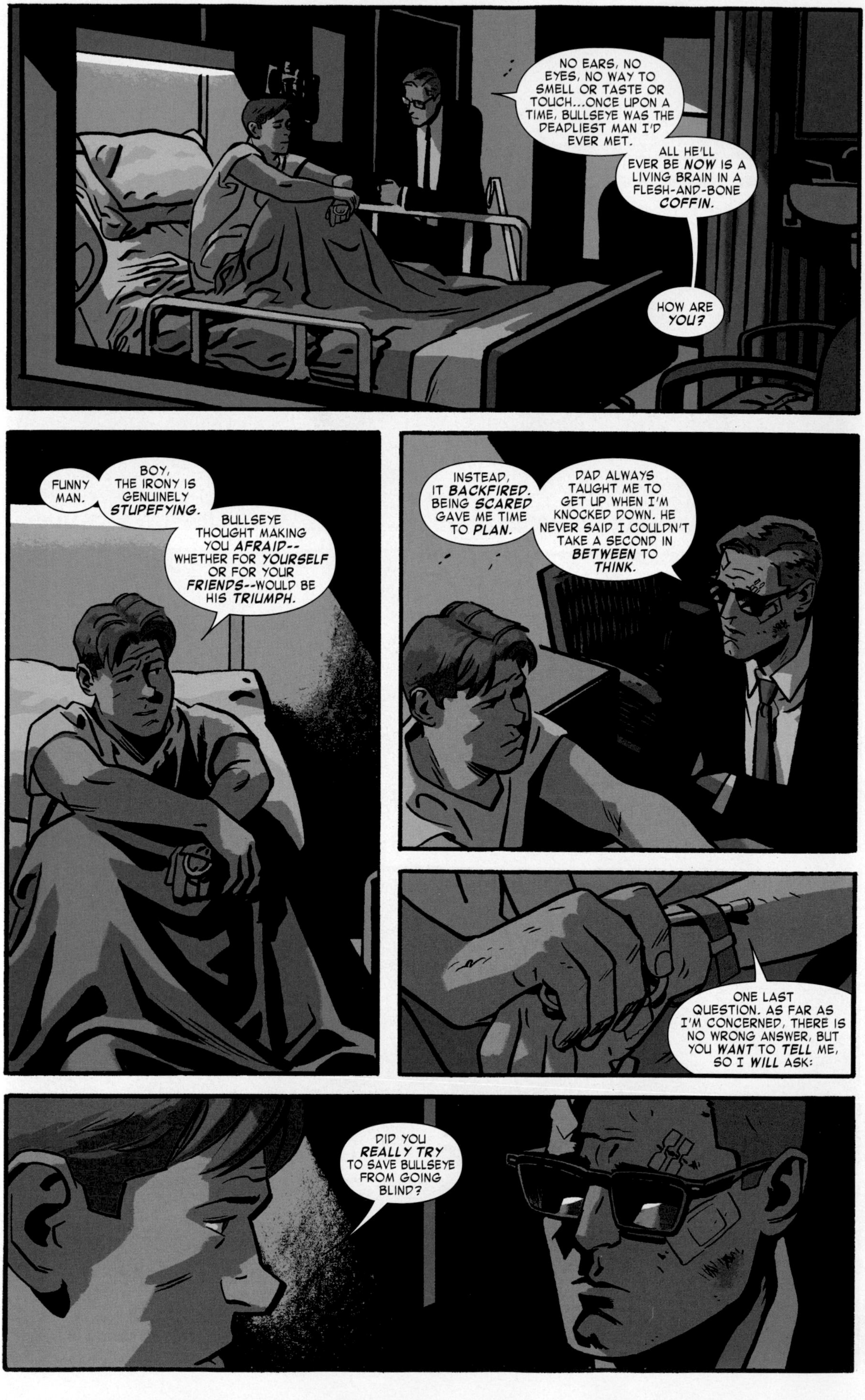
NO EARS, NO EYES, NO WAY TO SMELL OR TASTE OR TOUCH...ONCE UPON A TIME, BULLSEYE WAS THE DEADLIEST MAN I'D EVER MET.
ALL HE'LL EVER BE NOW IS A LIVING BRAIN IN A FLESH-AND-BONE COFFIN.
HOW ARE YOU?
FUNNY MAN.
BOY, THE IRONY IS GENUINELY STUPEFYING.
BULLSEYE THOUGHT MAKING YOU AFRAID-- WHETHER FOR YOURSELF OR FOR YOUR FRIENDS--WOULD BE HIS TRIUMPH.
INSTEAD, IT BACKFIRED. BEING SCARED GAVE ME TIME TO PLAN.
DAD ALWAYS TAUGHT ME TO GET UP WHEN I'M KNOCKED DOWN. HE NEVER SAID I COULDN'T TAKE A SECOND IN BETWEEN TO THINK.
ONE LAST QUESTION. AS FAR AS I'M CONCERNED, THERE IS NO WRONG ANSWER, BUT YOU WANT TO TELL ME, SO I WILL ASK:
DID YOU REALLY TRY TO SAVE BULLSEYE FROM GOING BLIND?

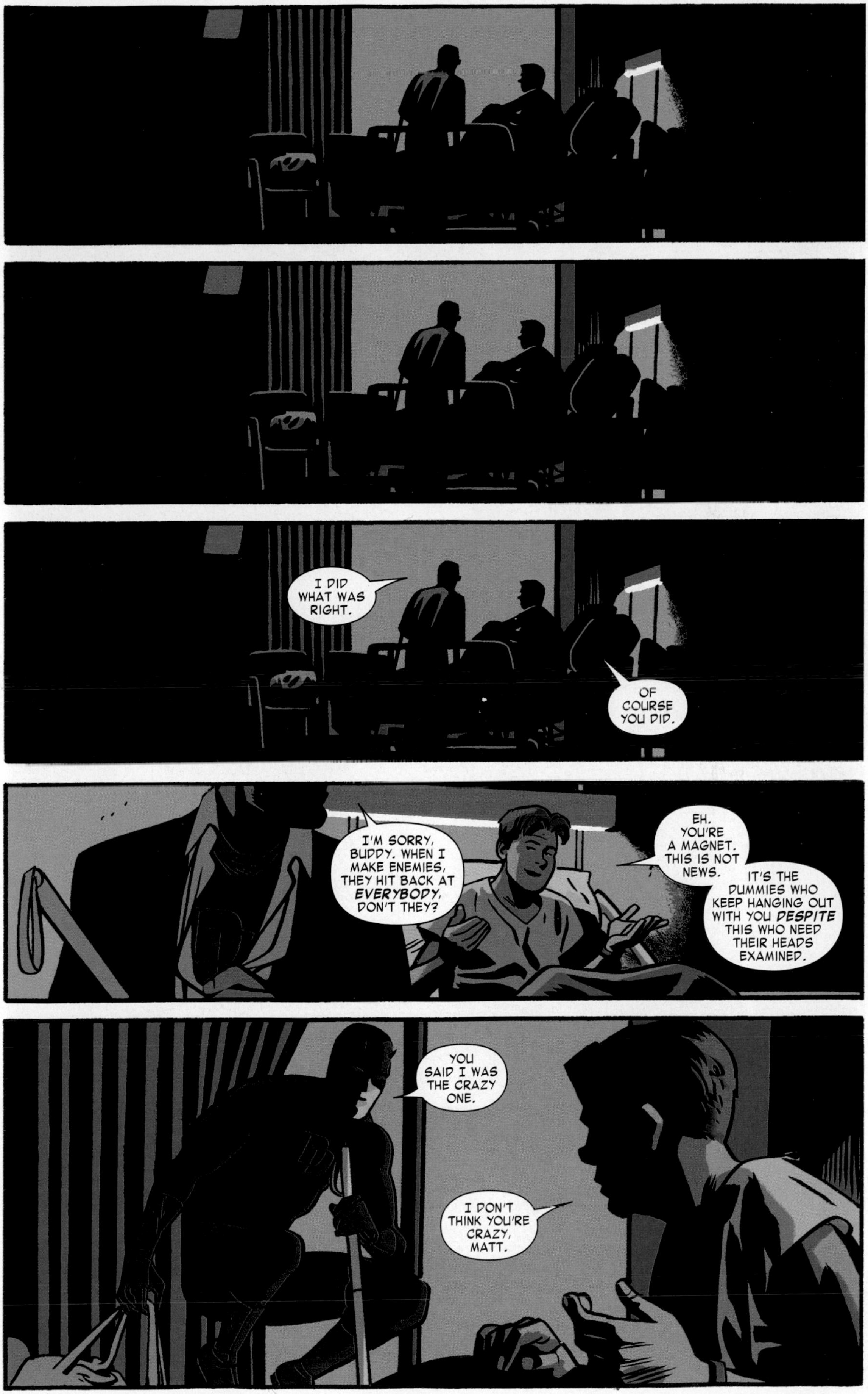
I DID WHAT WAS RIGHT.
OF COURSE YOU DID.
...
I'M SORRY, BUDDY. WHEN I MAKE ENEMIES, THEY HIT BACK AT *EVERYBODY*, DON'T THEY?
EH. YOU'RE A MAGNET. THIS IS NOT NEWS.
IT'S THE DUMMIES WHO KEEP HANGING OUT WITH YOU *DESPITE* THIS WHO NEED THEIR HEADS EXAMINED.
YOU SAID I WAS THE CRAZY ONE.
I DON'T THINK YOU'RE CRAZY, MATT.

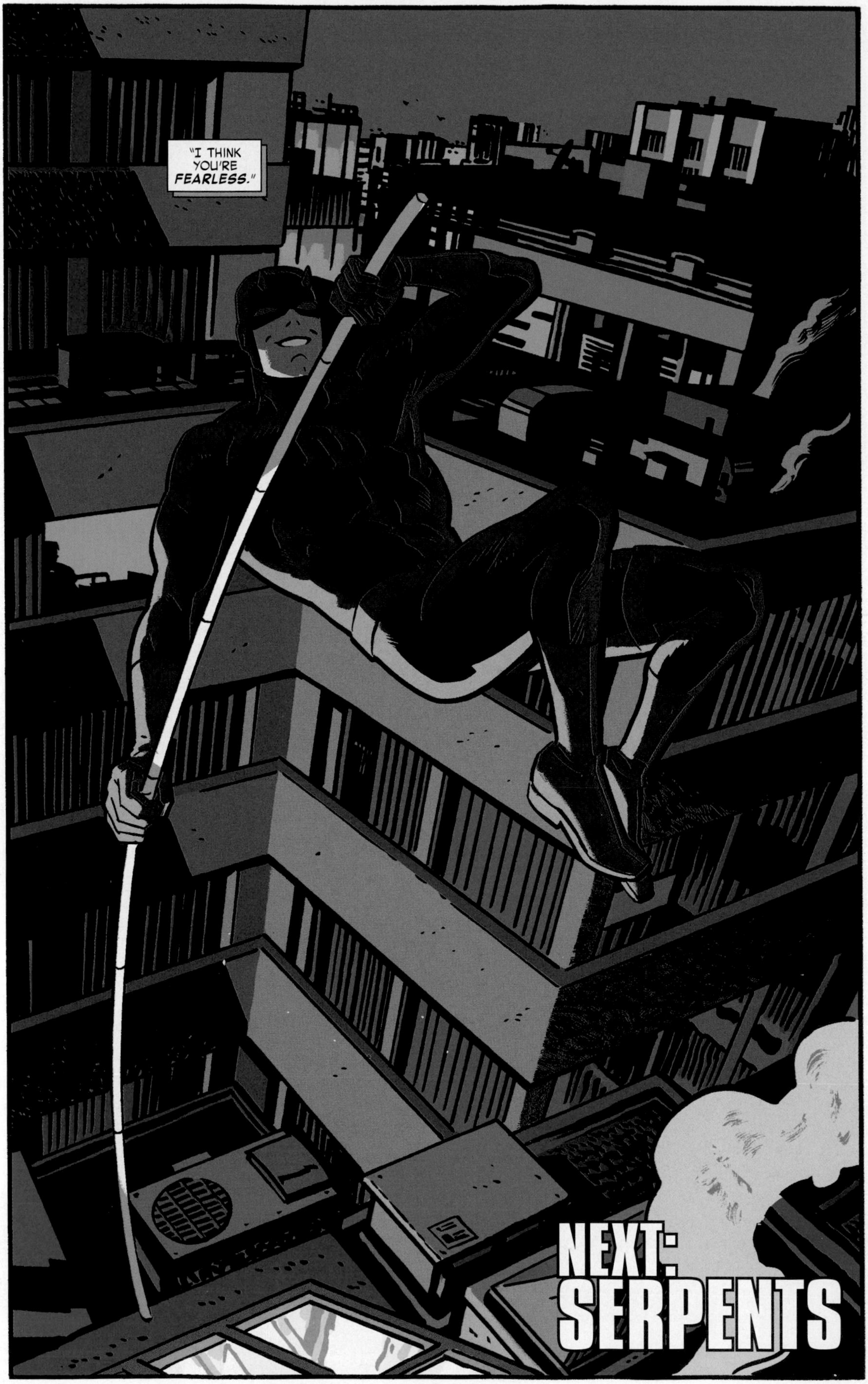
"I THINK YOU'RE FEARLESS."
NEXT: SERPENTS

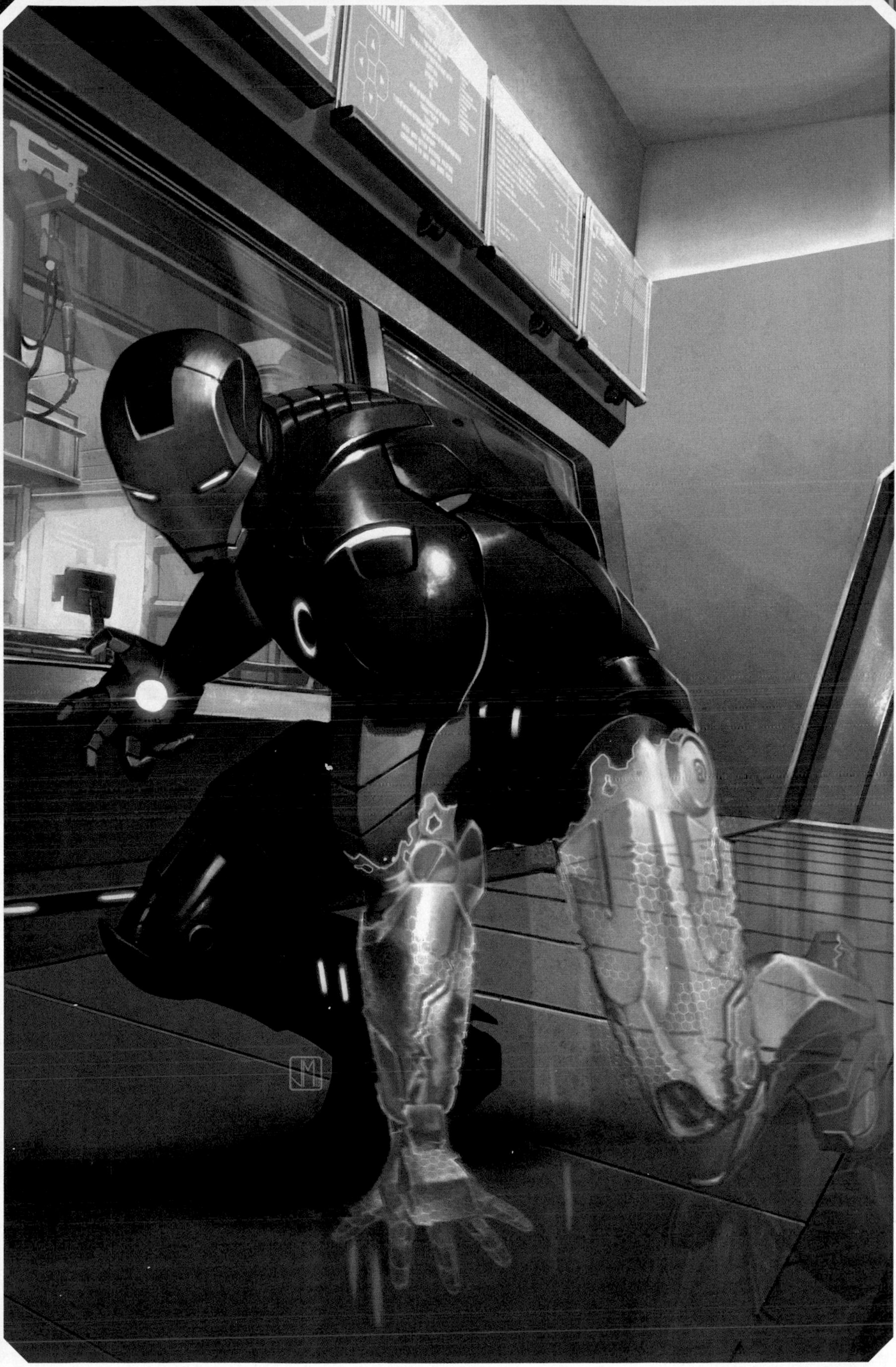

TWENTY-FIVE *MANY ARMORS OF IRON MAN VARIANT BY JORGE MOLINA*

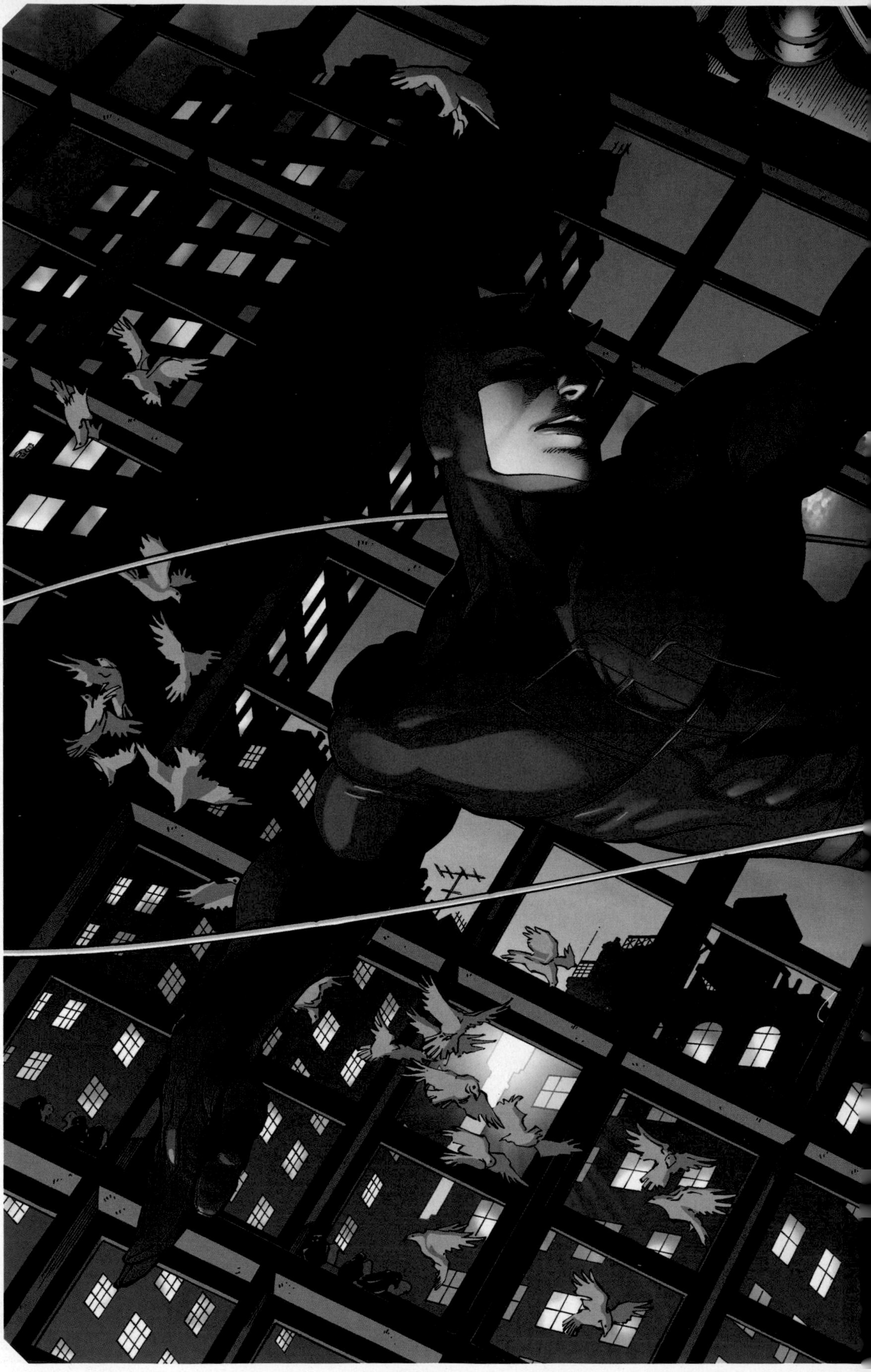

TWENTY-FIVE

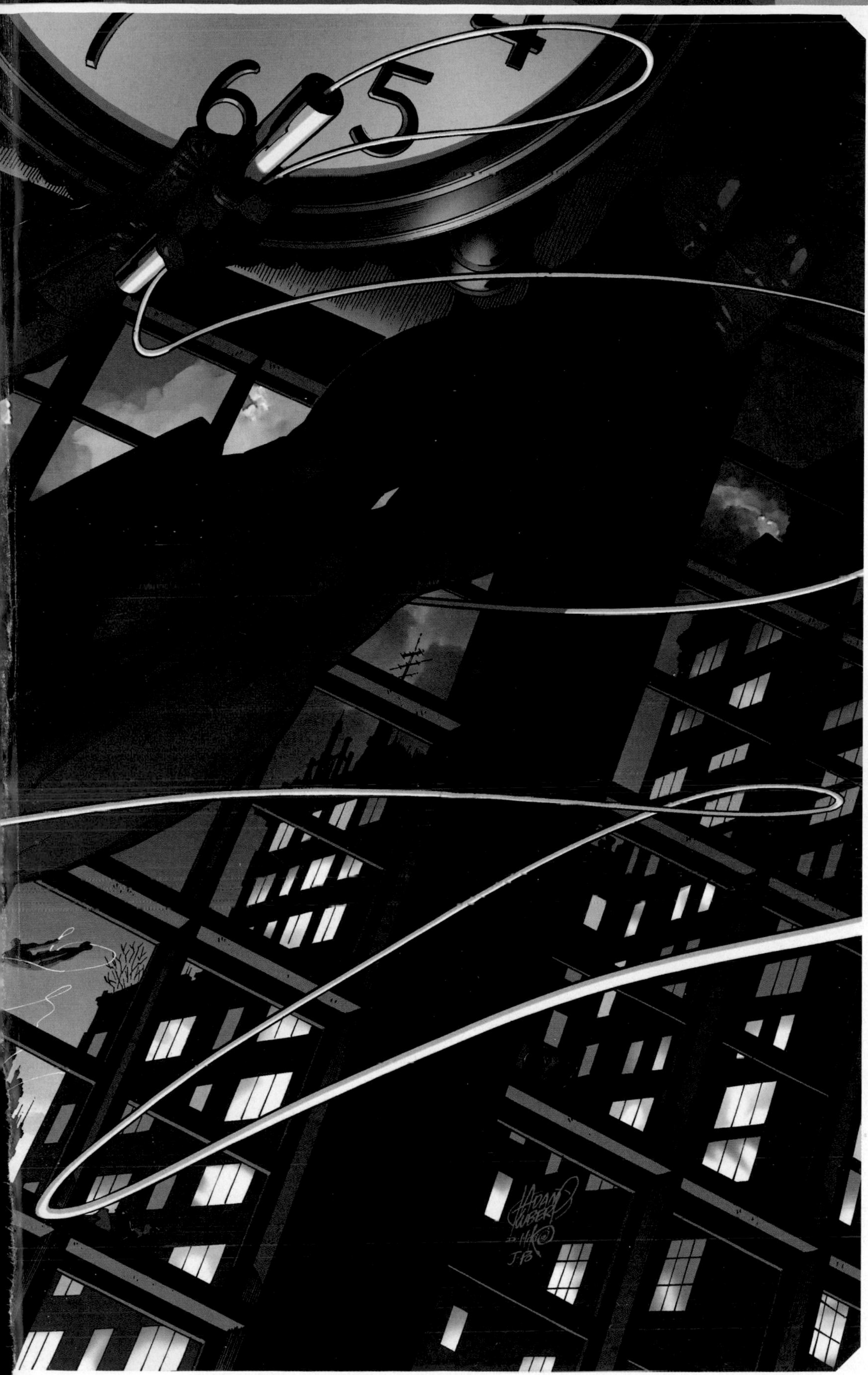
4
5
6

VARIANT BY ADAM KUBERT, DANNY MIKI & JUSTIN PONSOR

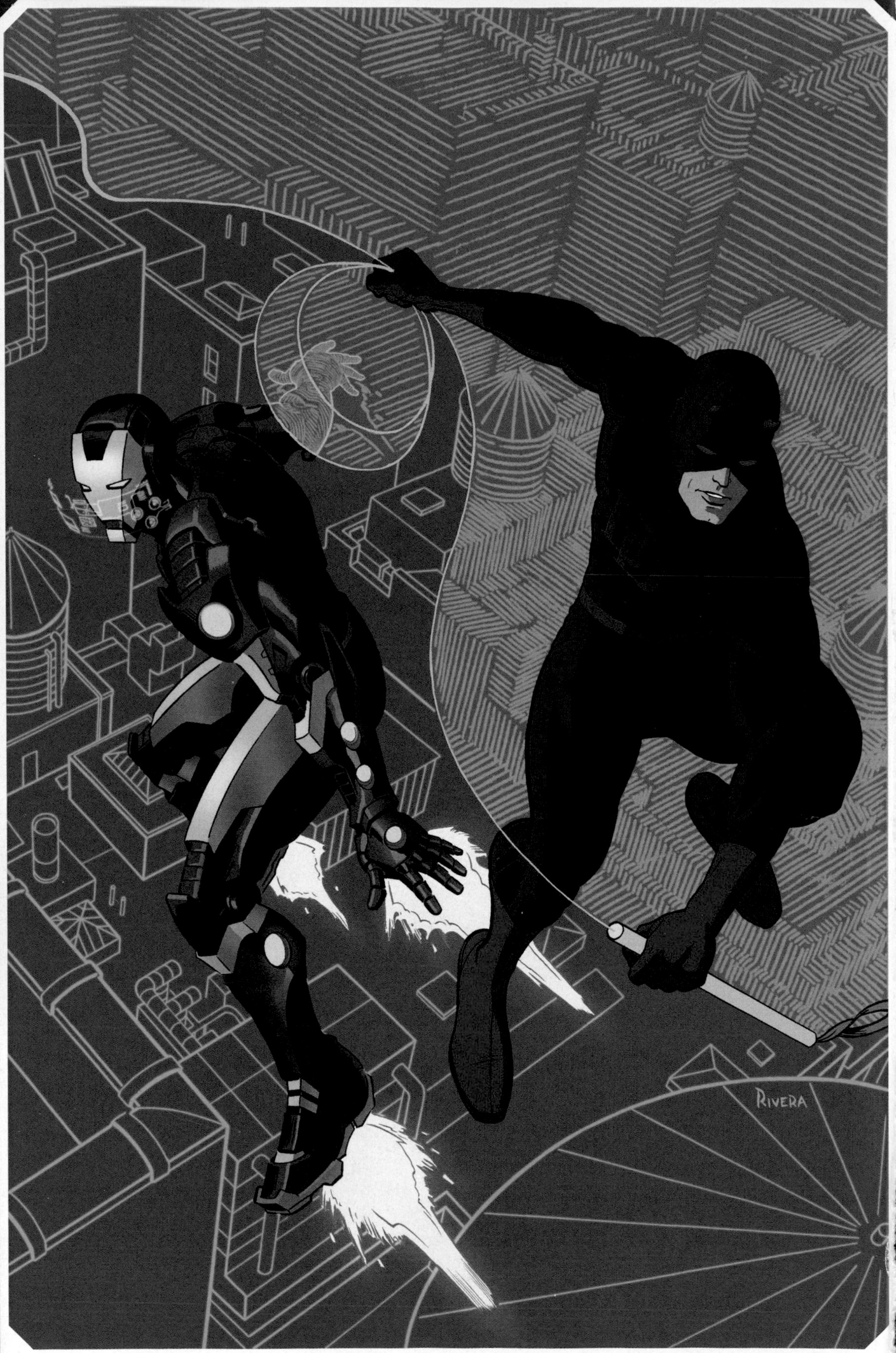
RIVERA

TWENTY-SIX *VARIANT BY PAOLO RIVERA*